Lewis & Clark

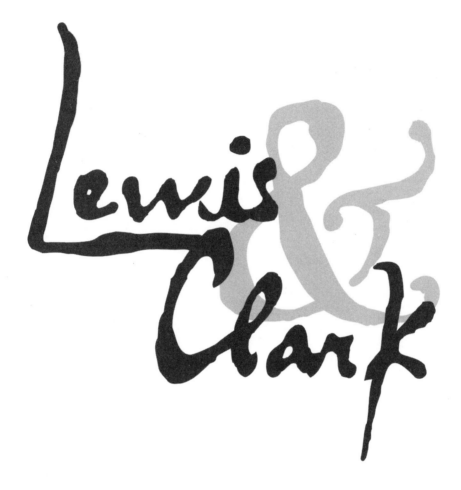

For Edward & Judith

Thanks to Kim Chaloner, Chris and Katie Sinderson, The Bertozzi Family,
Mickey Duzyj, Bob Mecoy, Mark Siegel, Jessica Abel and Matt Madden,
Calista Brill, Ken Burns, Mike Cavallaro, Ted Chaloner and Lydia Walshin,
Amelia Coulter, Michel Fiffe, Simon Fraser, Gina Gagliano, Tom Hart,
Dean Haspiel, Joe Infurnari, John Kuramoto, Jason Little, David Mazzucchelli,
Christine Norrie, Paul Pope, Leland Purvis, Zak Schiller, Brian Selznick,
James Sturm, Colleen Venable, and Boaz Yakin.

First Second
New York & London

Text and Illustrations Copyright © 2011 by Nicholas Bertozzi

Published by First Second
First Second is an imprint of Roaring Brook Press,
a division of Holtzbrinck Publishing Holdings Limited Partnership,
175 Fifth Avenue, New York, NY 10010

Distributed in Canada by H. B. Fenn and Company Ltd.
distributed in the United Kingdom by Macmillan Children's Books,
a division of Pan Macmillan.

Library of Congress Cataloging-in-Publication Data

Bertozzi, Nick.
  Lewis & Clark / Nick Bertozzi.—1st ed.
    p. cm.
  Summary: Presents, in graphic novel format, the adventures of explorers
Lewis and Clark during their journey from St. Louis to the Pacific Ocean.
  ISBN 978-1-59643-450-9
  1. Lewis, Meriwether, 1774–1809—Juvenile fiction. 2. Clark, William,
1770–1838—Juvenile fiction. 3. Lewis and Clark Expedition
(1804–1806)—Juvenile fiction. 4. Graphic novels. [1. Graphic novels. 2.
Lewis, Meriwether, 1774–1809—Fiction. 3. Clark, William,
1770–1838—Fiction. 4. Lewis and Clark Expedition (1804–1806)—Fiction. 5.
Explorers—Fiction.] I. Title. II. Title: Lewis and Clark.
  PZ7.7.B47Lew 2011
  917.804'20922—dc22

                                        2010036255

First Second books are available for special promotions and premiums.
For details, contact: Director of Special Markets, Holtzbrinck Publishers.

Book design by Colleen AF Venable and Danica Novgorodoff

First Edition 2011
Printed in the United States of America

10 9 8 7 6 5 4 3 2 1

C.4

Nick Bertozzi

First Second

New York & London

This version of Lewis and Clark's Voyage of Discovery is in no way intended to be a replacement for the many scholarly recountings of the journey. But it is my hope that something else of equal value is communicated here: the *experience* of that remarkable expedition.

—Nick Bertozzi

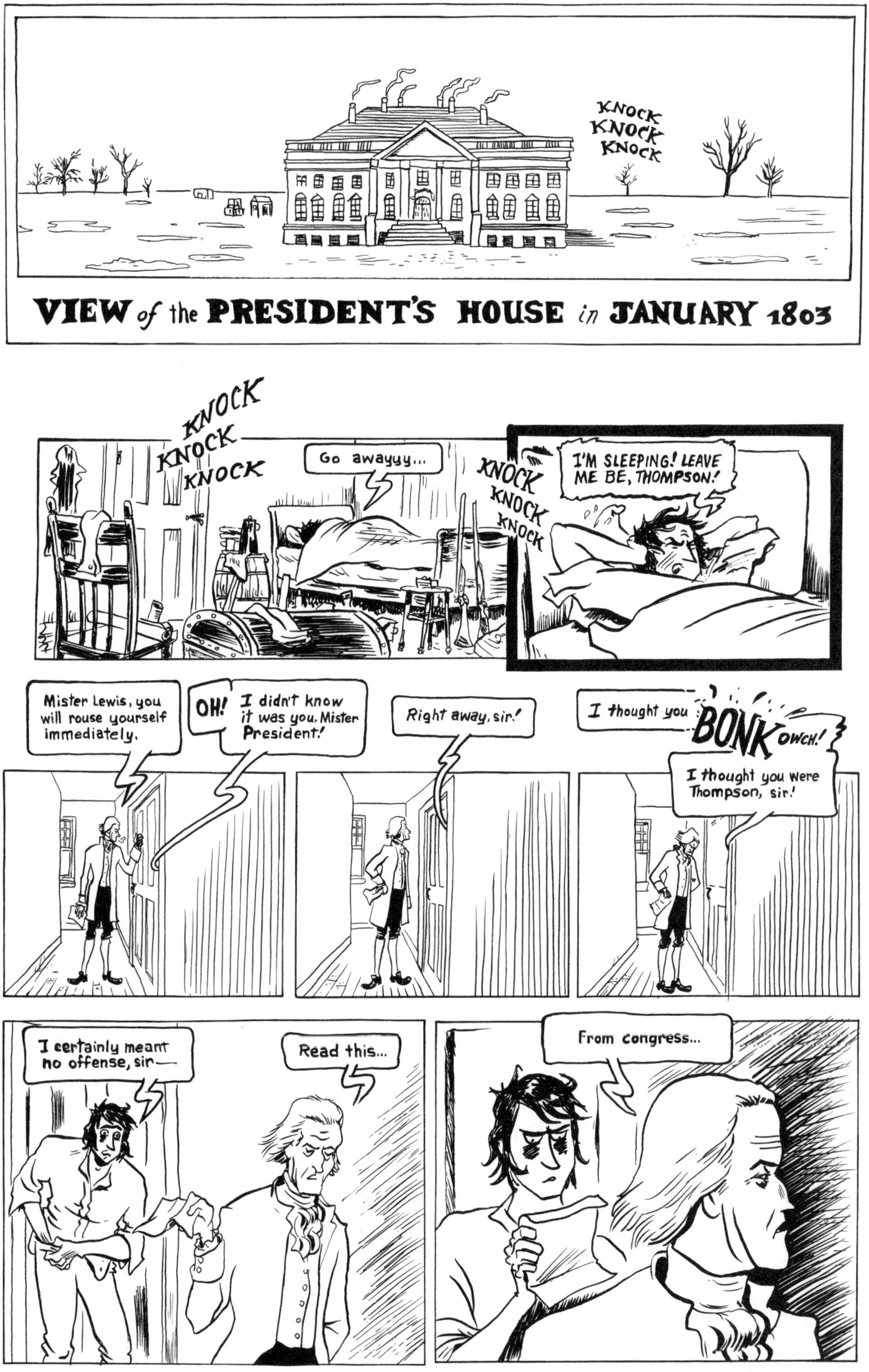
KNOCK
KNOCK
KNOCK
VIEW of the PRESIDENT'S HOUSE in JANUARY 1803
KNOCK
KNOCK
KNOCK
Go awayyy...
KNOCK
KNOCK
KNOCK
I'M SLEEPING! LEAVE ME BE, THOMPSON!
Mister Lewis, you will rouse yourself immediately.
OH!
I didn't know it was you, Mister President!
Right away, sir!
I thought you
BONK
OWCH!
I thought you were Thompson, sir!
I certainly meant no offense, sir—
Read this...
From congress...

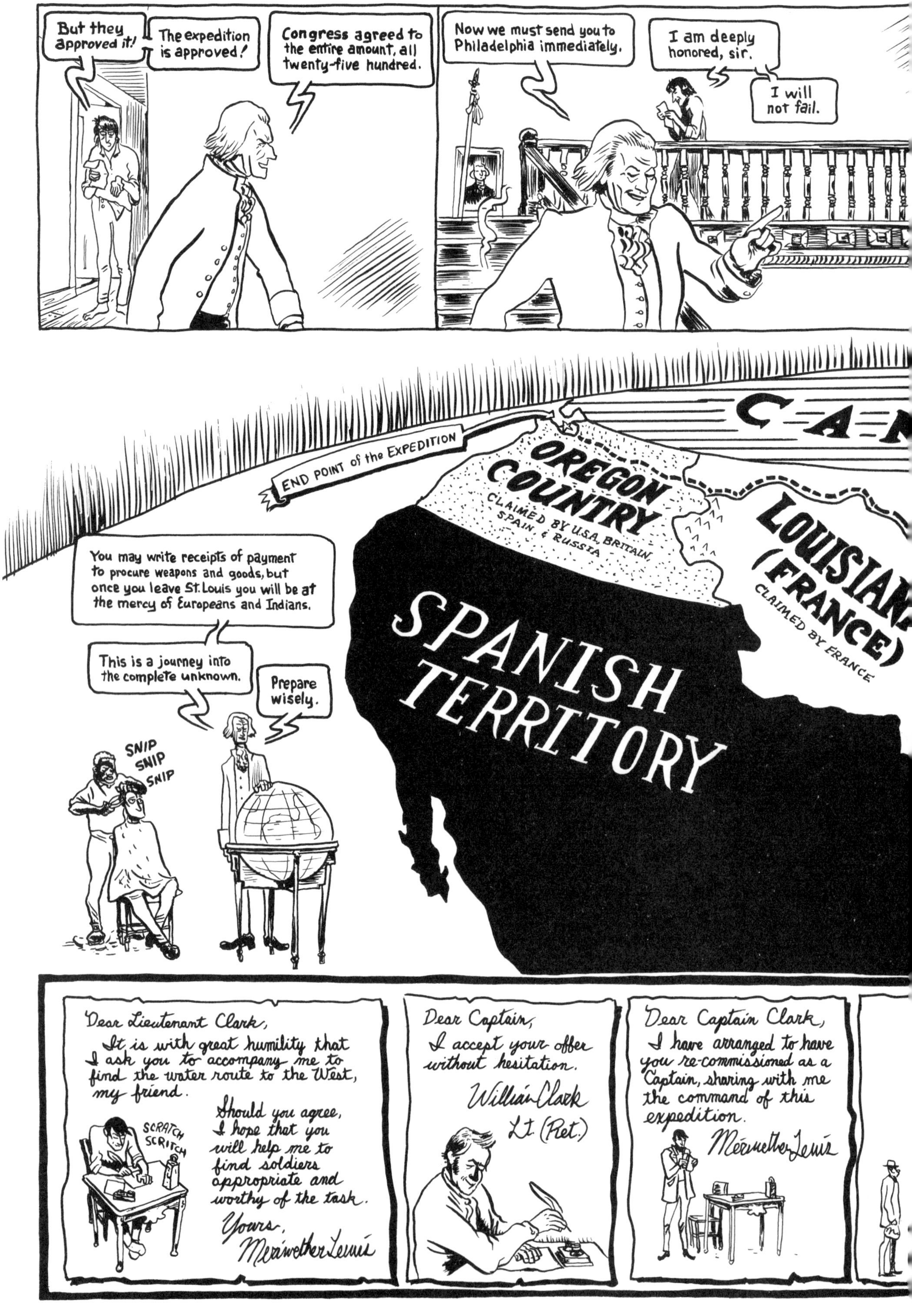
But they approved it!
The expedition is approved!
Congress agreed to the entire amount, all twenty-five hundred.
Now we must send you to Philadelphia immediately.
I am deeply honored, sir.
I will not fail.
END POINT of the EXPEDITION
OREGON COUNTRY
CLAIMED BY U.S.A, BRITAIN, SPAIN, & RUSSIA
LOUISIAN
(FRANCE)
CLAIMED BY FRANCE
SPANISH TERRITORY
CA
You may write receipts of payment to procure weapons and goods, but once you leave St. Louis you will be at the mercy of Europeans and Indians.
This is a journey into the complete unknown.
Prepare wisely.
SNIP SNIP SNIP
Dear Lieutenant Clark,
It is with great humility that I ask you to accompany me to find the water route to the West, my friend.
Should you agree, I hope that you will help me to find soldiers appropriate and worthy of the task.
Yours,
Meriwether Lewis
SCRATCH SCRATCH
Dear Captain,
I accept your offer without hesitation.
William Clark
Lt. (Ret.)
Dear Captain Clark,
I have arranged to have you re-commissioned as a Captain, sharing with me the command of this expedition.
Meriwether Lewis

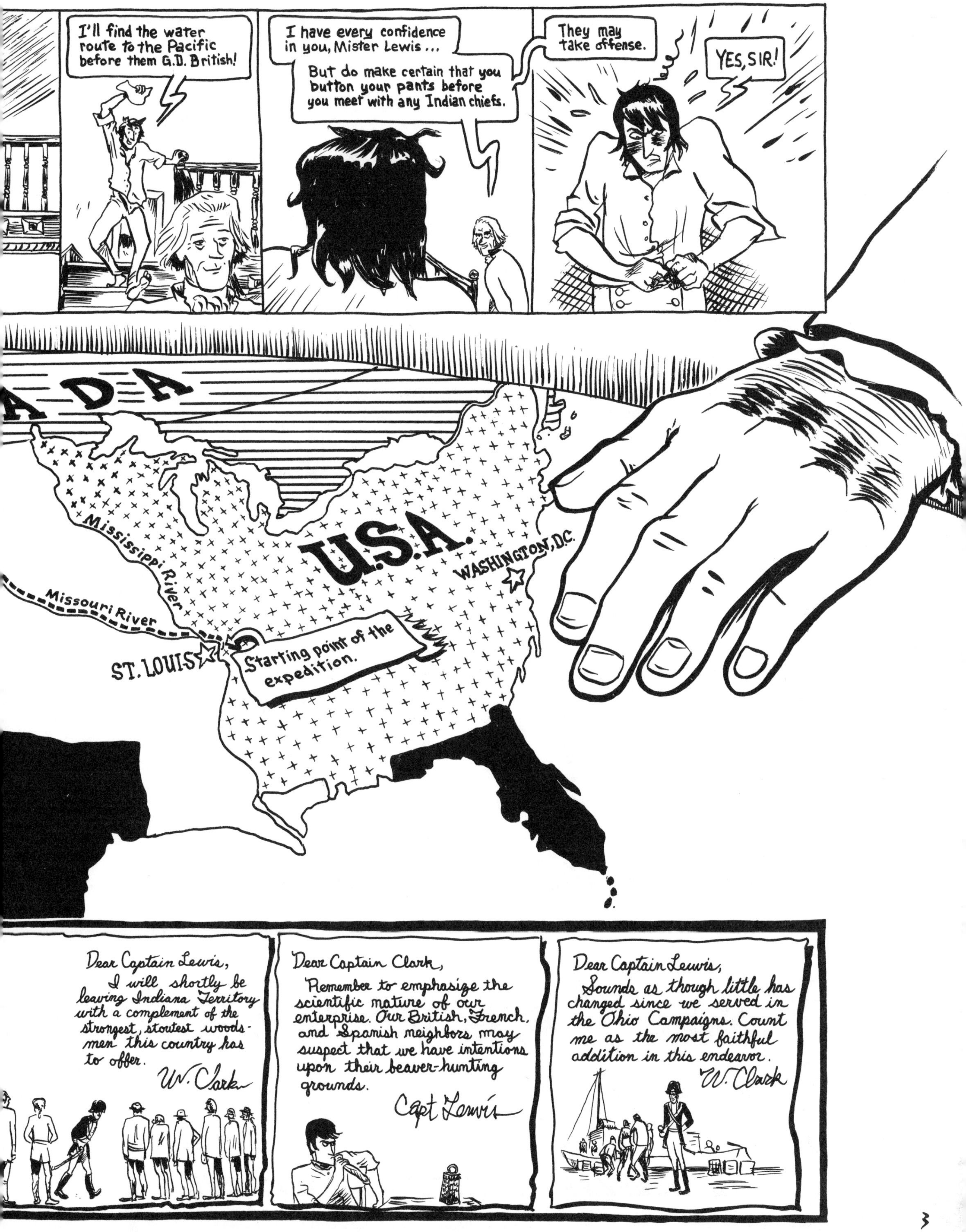

I'll find the water route to the Pacific before them G.D. British!
I have every confidence in you, Mister Lewis...
But do make certain that you button your pants before you meet with any Indian chiefs.
They may take offense.
YES, SIR!
ADA
U.S.A.
Mississippi River
Missouri River
WASHINGTON, DC.
ST. LOUIS
Starting point of the expedition.
Dear Captain Lewis,
I will shortly be leaving Indiana Territory with a complement of the strongest, stoutest woodsmen this country has to offer.
W. Clark
Dear Captain Clark,
Remember to emphasize the scientific nature of our enterprise. Our British, French, and Spanish neighbors may suspect that we have intentions upon their beaver-hunting grounds.
Capt Lewis
Dear Captain Lewis,
Sounds as though little has changed since we served in the Ohio Campaigns. Count me as the most faithful addition in this endeavor.
W. Clark

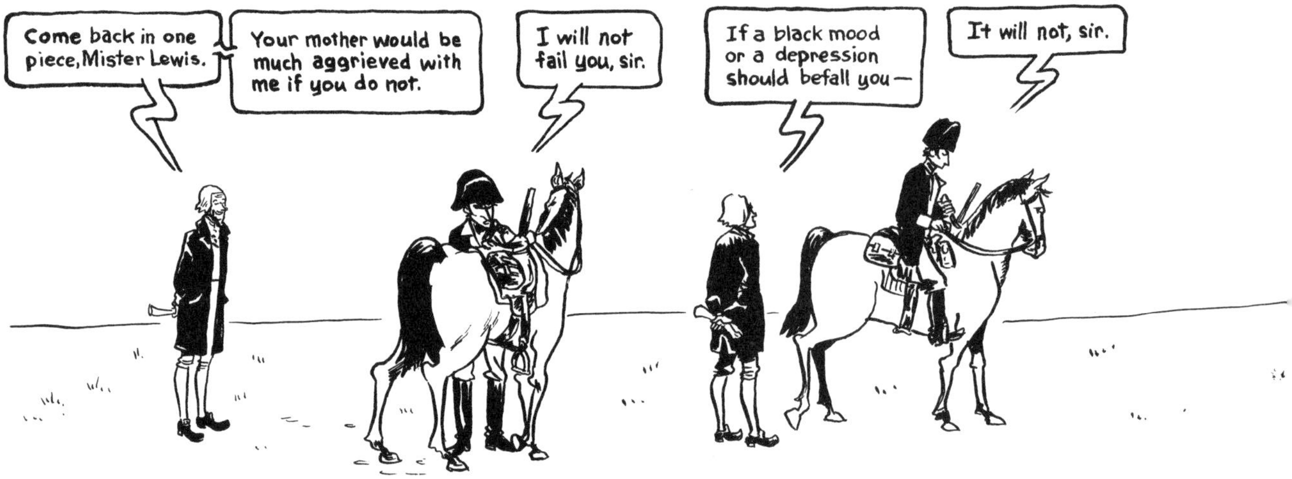

Come back in one piece, Mister Lewis.
Your mother would be much aggrieved with me if you do not.
I will not fail you, sir.
If a black mood or a depression should befall you—
It will not, sir.

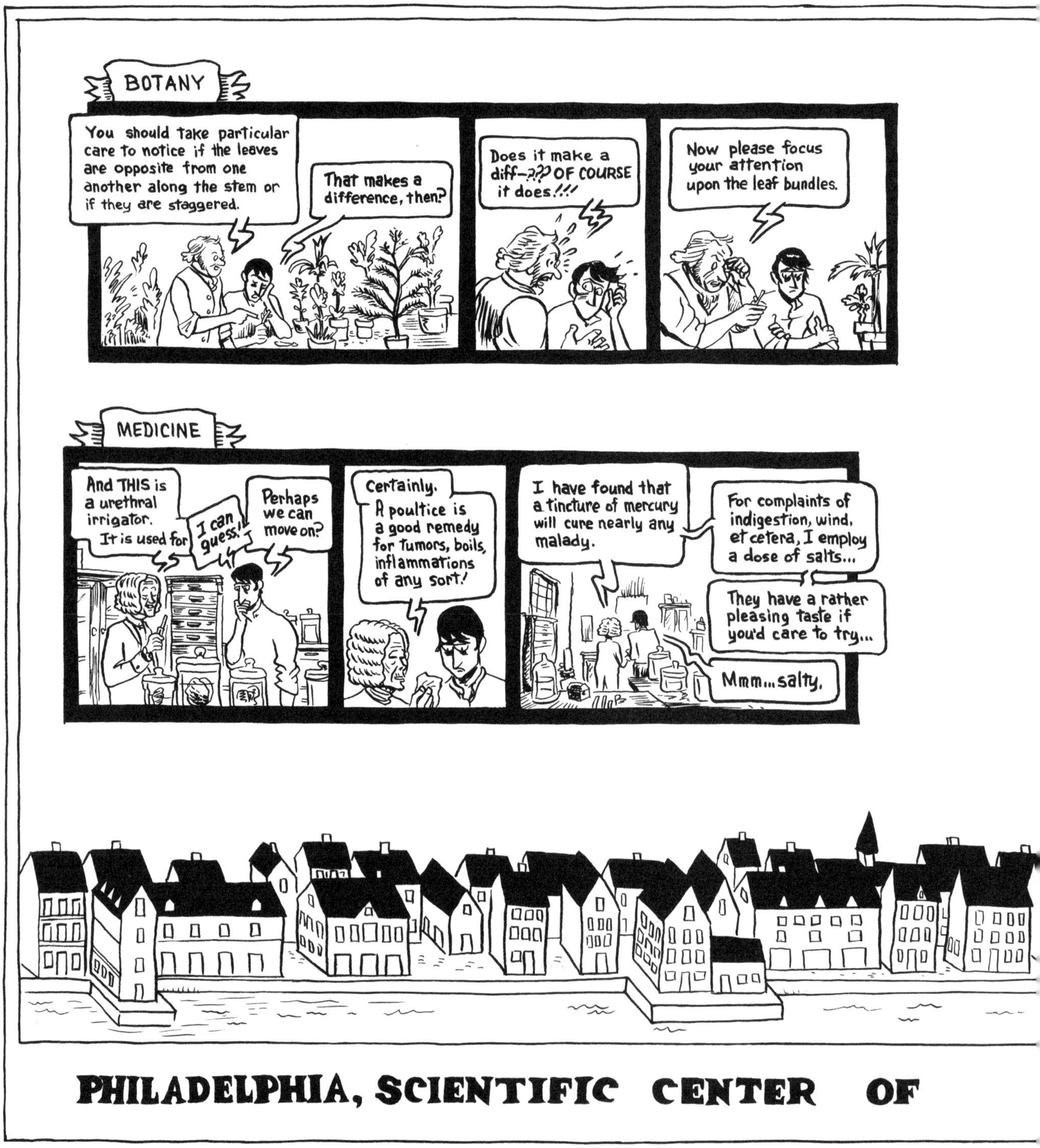

BOTANY
You should take particular care to notice if the leaves are opposite from one another along the stem or if they are staggered.
That makes a difference, then?
Does it make a diff—??? OF COURSE it does!!!
Now please focus your attention upon the leaf bundles.
MEDICINE
And THIS is a urethral irrigator.
It is used for
I can guess!
Perhaps we can move on?
Certainly.
A poultice is a good remedy for tumors, boils, inflammations of any sort!
I have found that a tincture of mercury will cure nearly any malady.
For complaints of indigestion, wind, et cetera, I employ a dose of salts...
They have a rather pleasing taste if you'd care to try...
Mmm... salty.
PHILADELPHIA, SCIENTIFIC CENTER OF

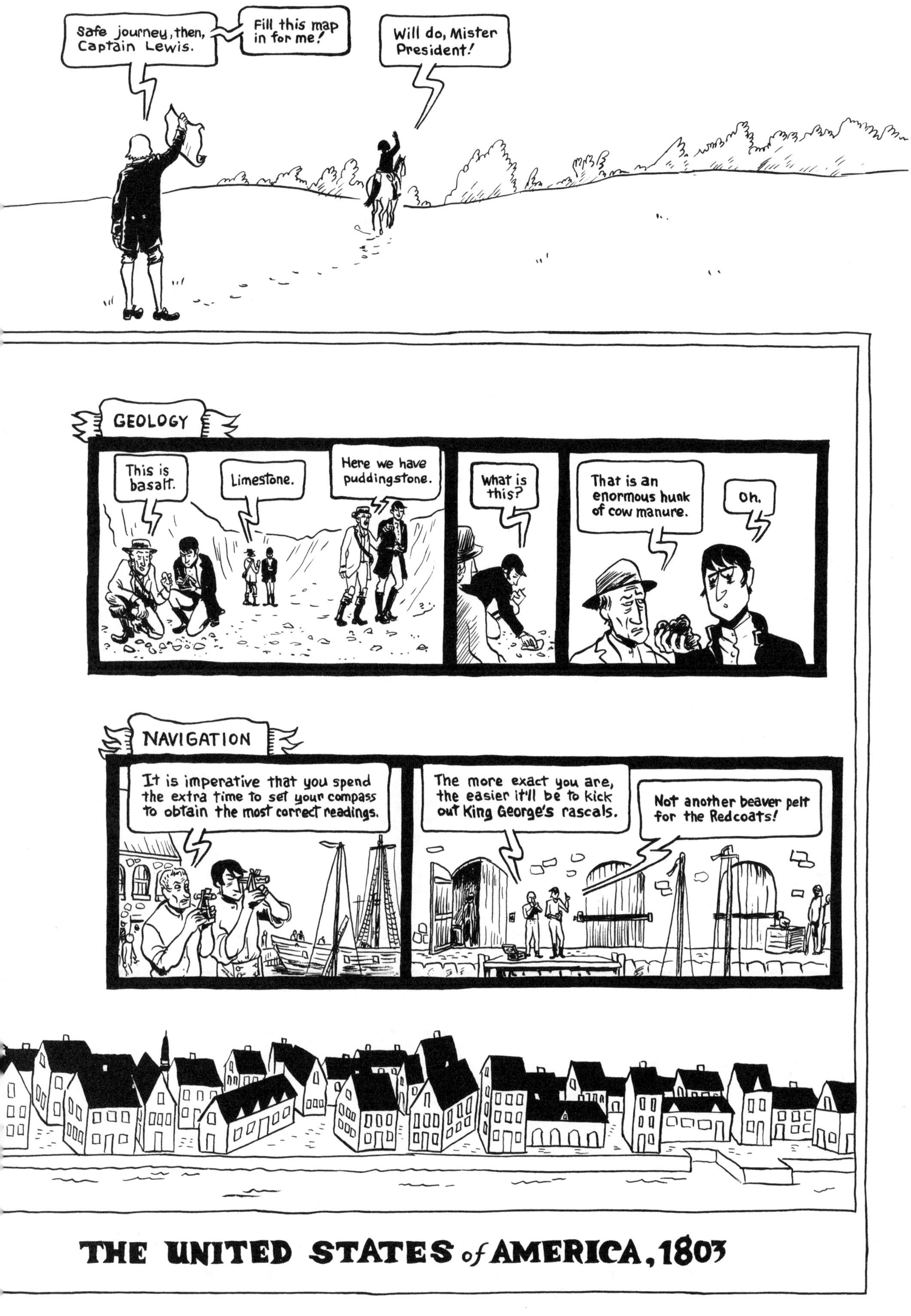
Safe journey, then, Captain Lewis.
Fill this map in for me!
Will do, Mister President!
GEOLOGY
This is basalt.
Limestone.
Here we have puddingstone.
What is this?
That is an enormous hunk of cow manure.
Oh.
NAVIGATION
It is imperative that you spend the extra time to set your compass to obtain the most correct readings.
The more exact you are, the easier it'll be to kick out King George's rascals.
Not another beaver pelt for the Redcoats!
THE UNITED STATES of AMERICA, 1803

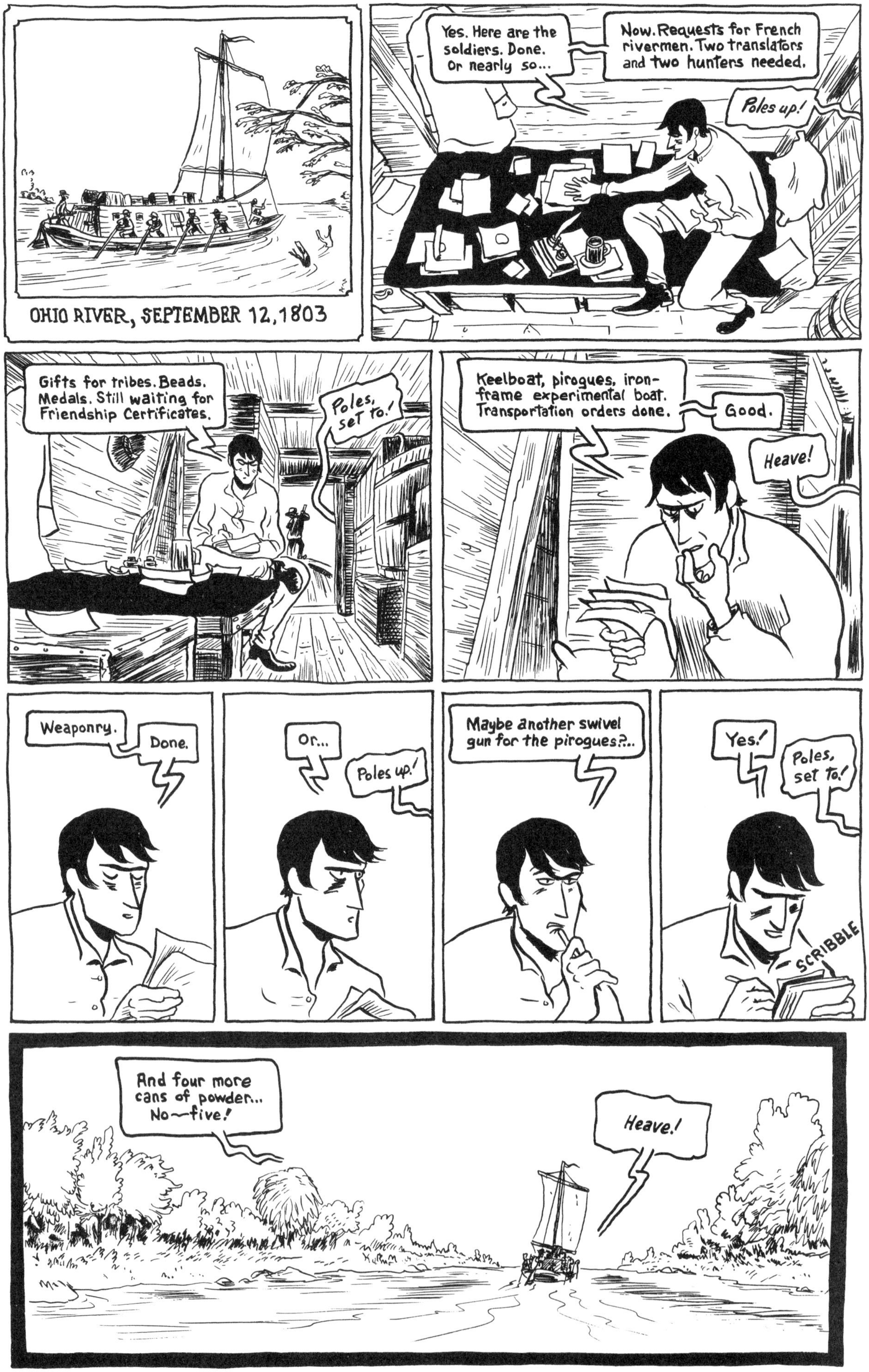
OHIO RIVER, SEPTEMBER 12, 1803
Yes. Here are the soldiers. Done. Or nearly so...
Now. Requests for French rivermen. Two translators and two hunters needed.
Poles up!
Gifts for tribes. Beads. Medals. Still waiting for Friendship Certificates.
Poles, set to!
Keelboat, pirogues, iron-frame experimental boat. Transportation orders done.
Good.
Heave!
Weaponry.
Done.
Or...
Poles up!
Maybe another swivel gun for the pirogues?..
Yes!
Poles, set to!
SCRIBBLE
And four more cans of powder... No—five!
Heave!

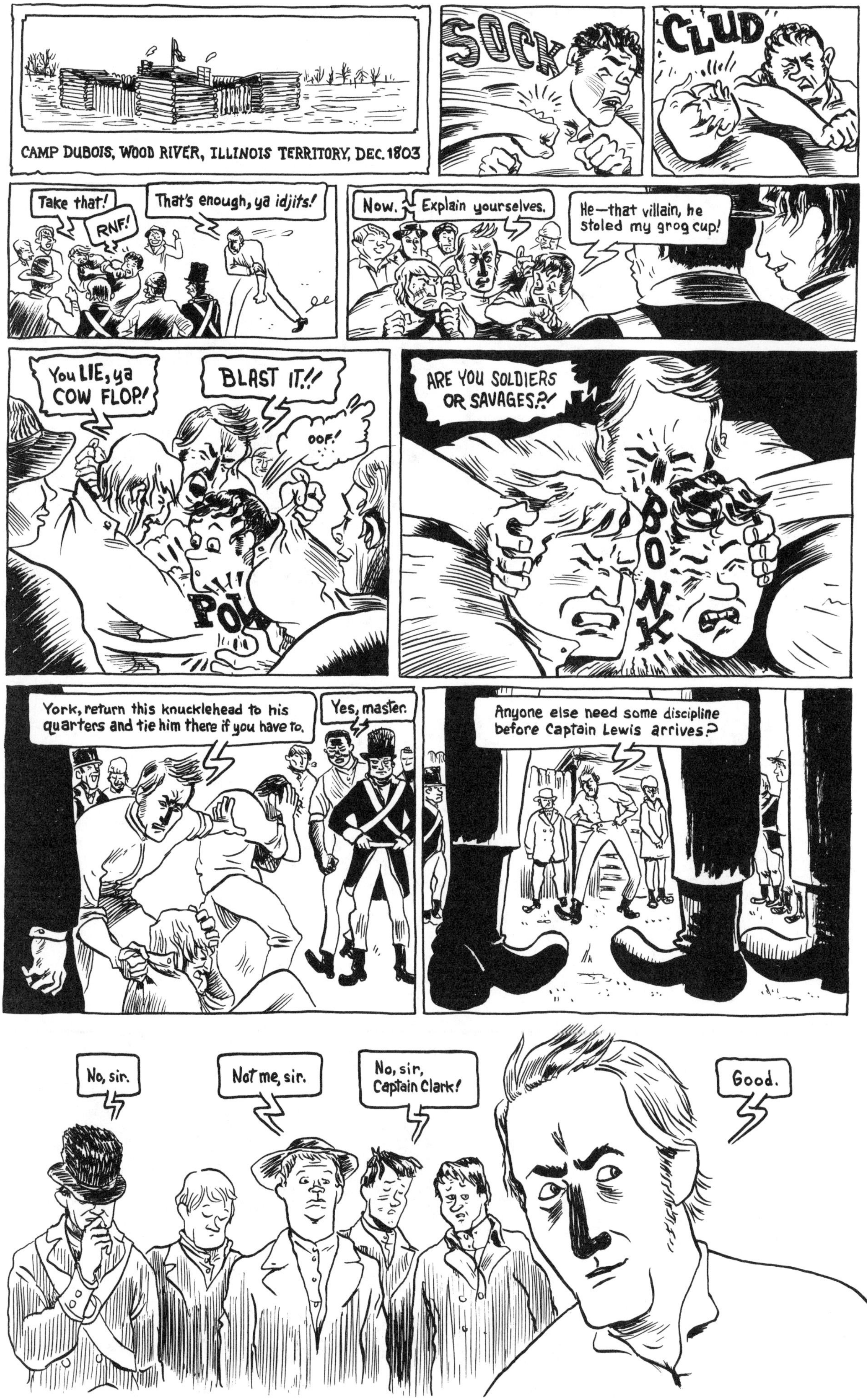

CAMP DUBOIS, WOOD RIVER, ILLINOIS TERRITORY, DEC. 1803
SOCK
CLUD
Take that!
RNF!
That's enough, ya idjits!
Now.
Explain yourselves.
He—that villain, he stoled my grog cup!
You LIE, ya COW FLOP!
BLAST IT!!
OOF!
POW
ARE YOU SOLDIERS OR SAVAGES?!
BONK
York, return this knucklehead to his quarters and tie him there if you have to.
Yes, master.
Anyone else need some discipline before Captain Lewis arrives?
No, sir.
Not me, sir.
No, sir, Captain Clark!
Good.

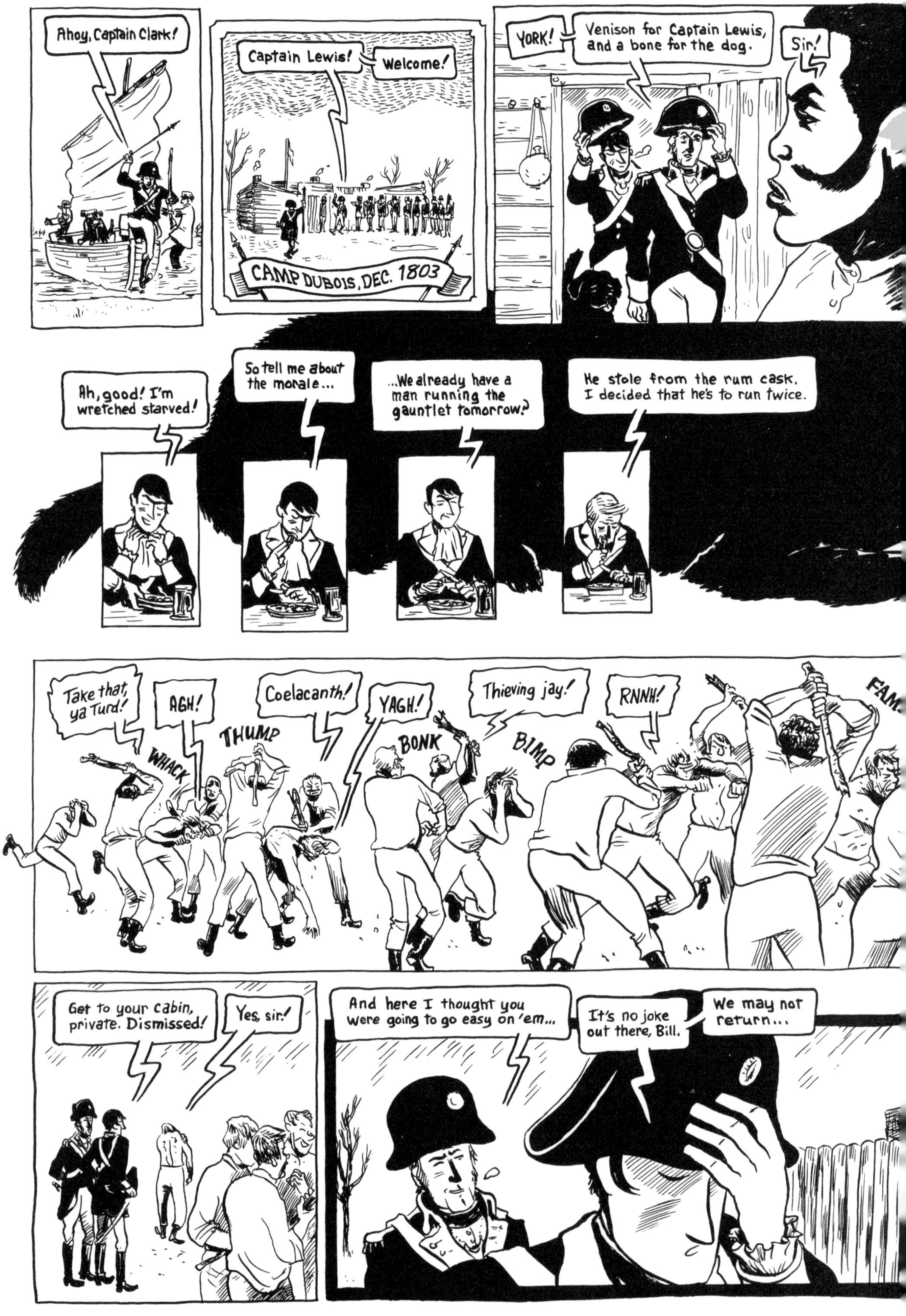

Ahoy, Captain Clark!
Captain Lewis!
Welcome!
CAMP DUBOIS, DEC. 1803
YORK!
Venison for Captain Lewis, and a bone for the dog.
Sir!
Ah, good! I'm wretched starved!
So tell me about the morale...
...We already have a man running the gauntlet tomorrow?
He stole from the rum cask. I decided that he's to run twice.
Take that, ya Turd!
WHACK
AGH!
THUMP
Coelacanth!
YAGH!
BONK
Thieving jay!
BIMP
RNNH!
Get to your cabin, private. Dismissed!
Yes, sir!
And here I thought you were going to go easy on 'em...
It's no joke out there, Bill.
We may not return...

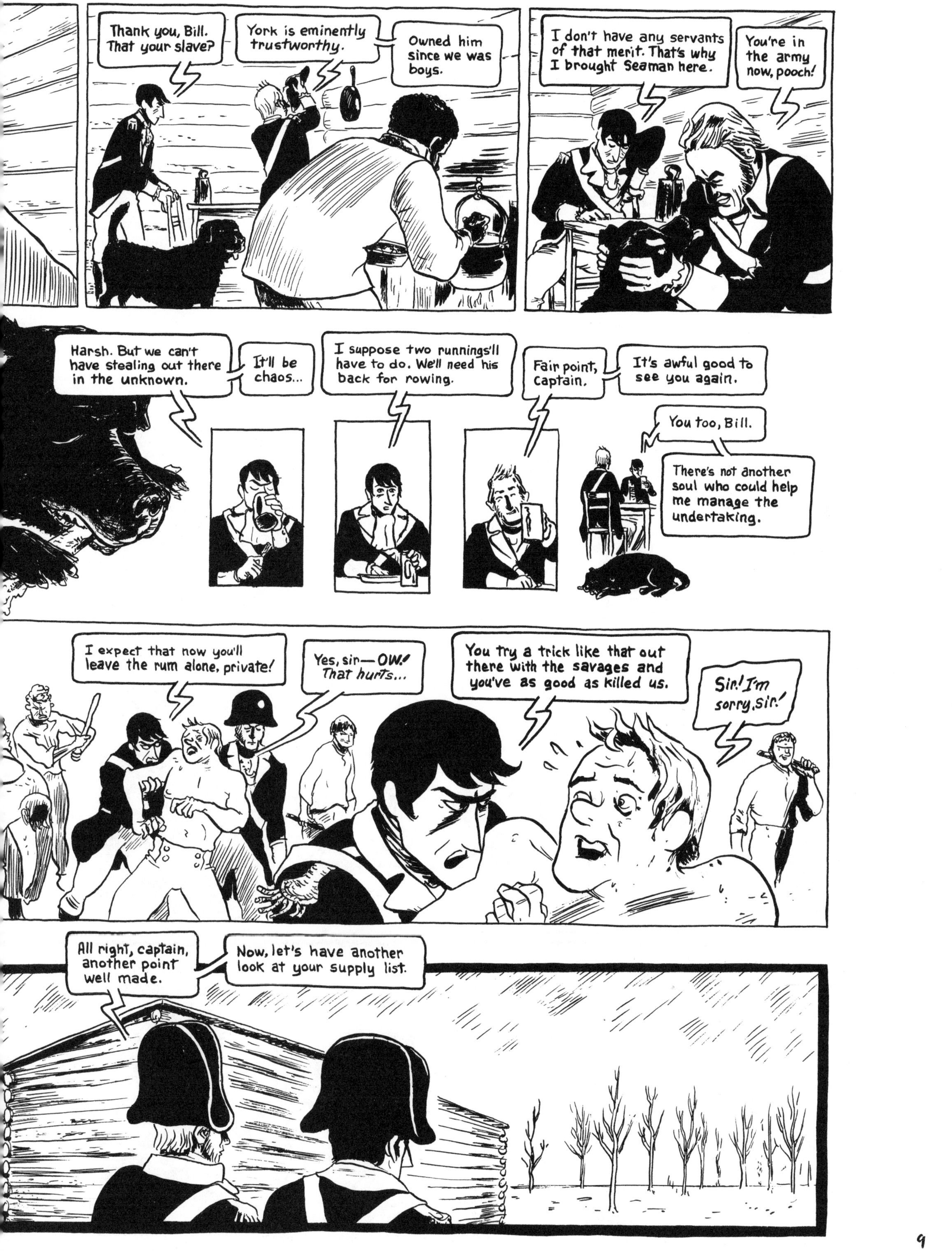
Thank you, Bill. That your slave?
York is eminently trustworthy.
Owned him since we was boys.
I don't have any servants of that merit. That's why I brought Seaman here.
You're in the army now, pooch!
Harsh. But we can't have stealing out there in the unknown.
It'll be chaos...
I suppose two runnings'll have to do. We'll need his back for rowing.
Fair point, Captain.
It's awful good to see you again.
You too, Bill.
There's not another soul who could help me manage the undertaking.
I expect that now you'll leave the rum alone, private!
Yes, sir—OW! That hurts...
You try a trick like that out there with the savages and you've as good as killed us.
Sir! I'm sorry, sir!
All right, captain, another point well made.
Now, let's have another look at your supply list.

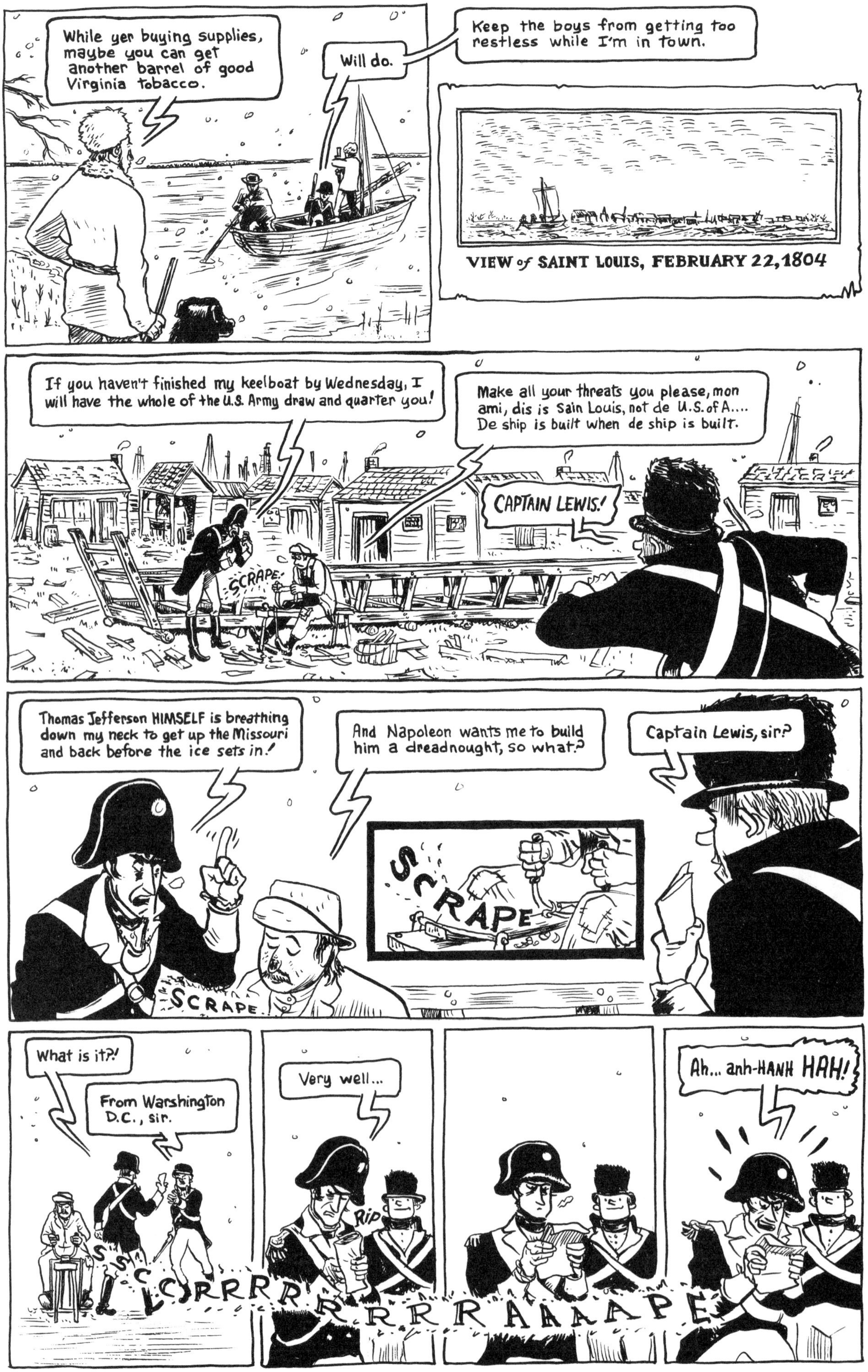
While yer buying supplies, maybe you can get another barrel of good Virginia tobacco.
Will do.
Keep the boys from getting too restless while I'm in town.
VIEW of SAINT LOUIS, FEBRUARY 22, 1804
If you haven't finished my keelboat by Wednesday, I will have the whole of the U.S. Army draw and quarter you!
Make all your threats you please, mon ami, dis is Sain Louis, not de U.S. of A.... De ship is built when de ship is built.
CAPTAIN LEWIS!
SCRAPE
Thomas Jefferson HIMSELF is breathing down my neck to get up the Missouri and back before the ice sets in!
And Napoleon wants me to build him a dreadnought, so what?
Captain Lewis, sir?
SCRAPE
SCRAPE
What is it?!
From Warshington D.C., sir.
Very well...
RIP
Ah... anh-HANH HAH!
SSCCRRRRRRRRRRRAAAAPE

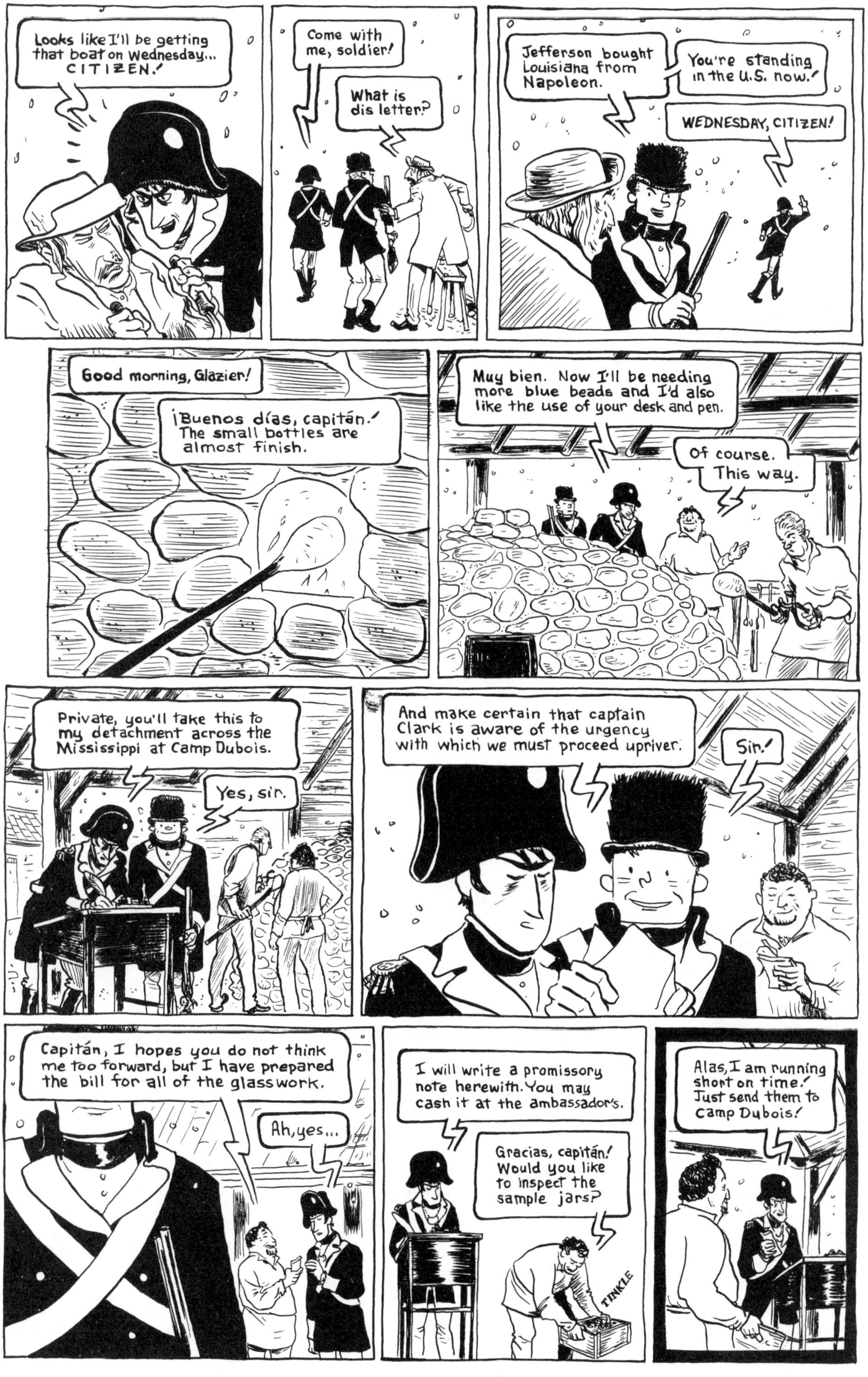

Looks like I'll be getting that boat on Wednesday... CITIZEN!
Come with me, soldier!
What is dis letter?
Jefferson bought Louisiana from Napoleon.
You're standing in the U.S. now!
WEDNESDAY, CITIZEN!
Good morning, Glazier!
¡Buenos días, capitán! The small bottles are almost finish.
Muy bien. Now I'll be needing more blue beads and I'd also like the use of your desk and pen.
Of course. This way.
Private, you'll take this to my detachment across the Mississippi at Camp Dubois.
Yes, sir.
And make certain that captain Clark is aware of the urgency with which we must proceed upriver.
Sir!
Capitán, I hopes you do not think me too forward, but I have prepared the bill for all of the glasswork.
Ah, yes...
I will write a promissory note herewith. You may cash it at the ambassador's.
Gracias, capitán! Would you like to inspect the sample jars?
TINKLE
Alas, I am running short on time! Just send them to Camp Dubois!

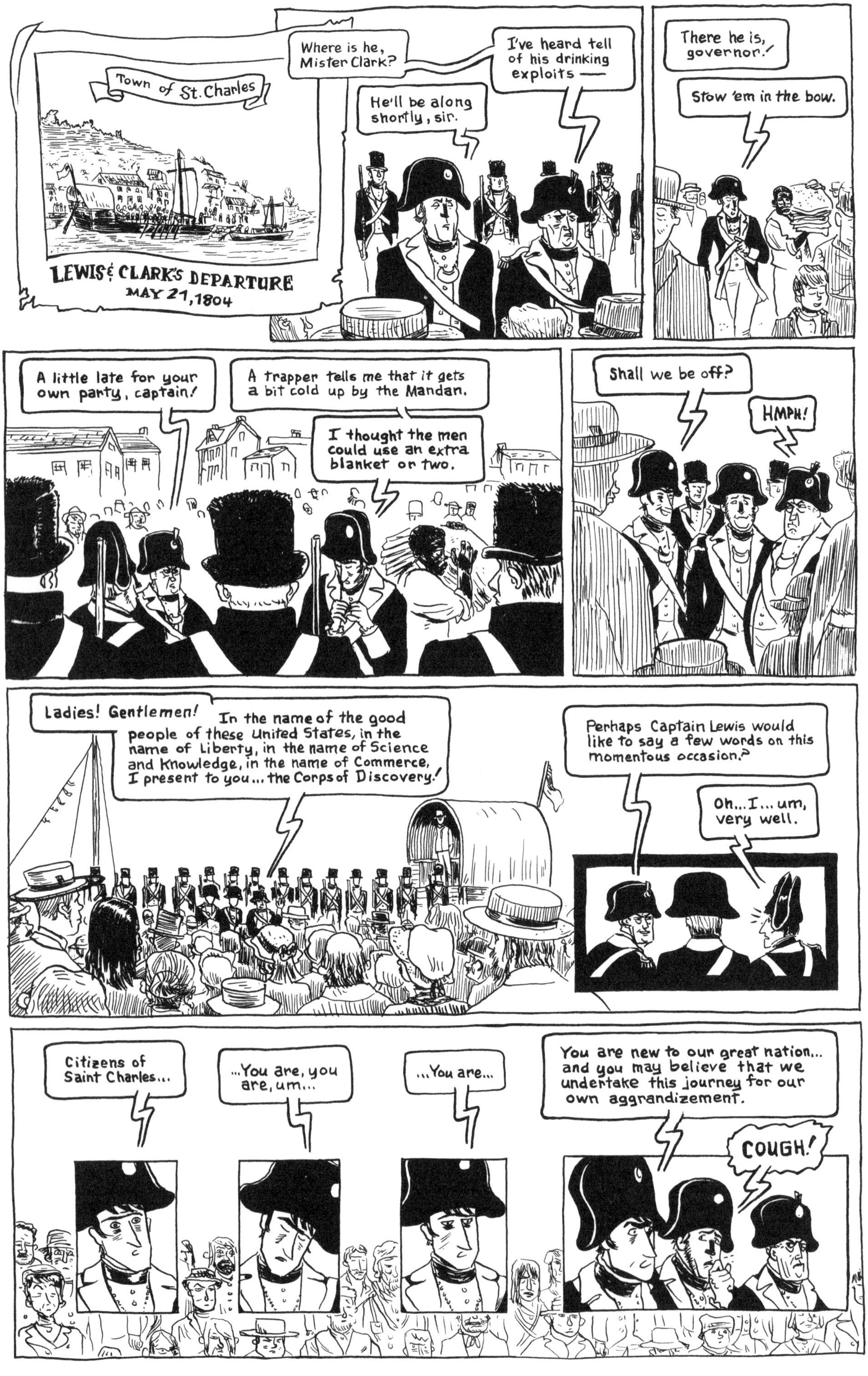
Town of St. Charles
LEWIS & CLARK'S DEPARTURE
MAY 21, 1804
Where is he, Mister Clark?
He'll be along shortly, sir.
I've heard tell of his drinking exploits —
There he is, governor!
Stow 'em in the bow.
A little late for your own party, captain!
A trapper tells me that it gets a bit cold up by the Mandan.
I thought the men could use an extra blanket or two.
Shall we be off?
HMPH!
Ladies! Gentlemen! In the name of the good people of these United States, in the name of Liberty, in the name of Science and Knowledge, in the name of Commerce, I present to you... the Corps of Discovery!
Perhaps Captain Lewis would like to say a few words on this momentous occasion?
Oh... I... um, very well.
Citizens of Saint Charles...
...You are, you are, um...
...You are...
You are new to our great nation... and you may believe that we undertake this journey for our own aggrandizement.
COUGH!

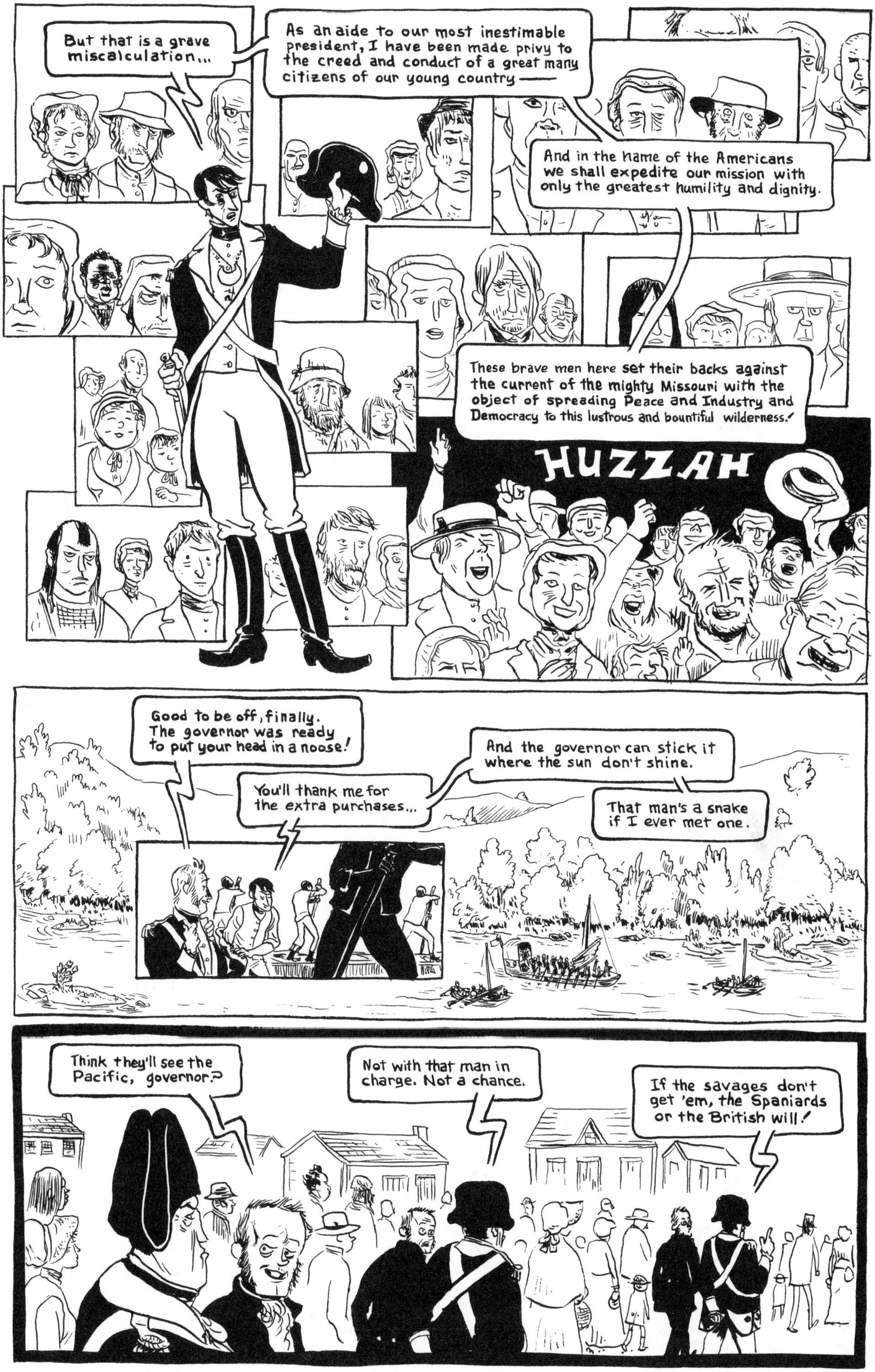

But that is a grave miscalculation...
As an aide to our most inestimable president, I have been made privy to the creed and conduct of a great many citizens of our young country —
And in the name of the Americans we shall expedite our mission with only the greatest humility and dignity.
These brave men here set their backs against the current of the mighty Missouri with the object of spreading Peace and Industry and Democracy to this lustrous and bountiful wilderness!
HUZZAH
Good to be off, finally. The governor was ready to put your head in a noose!
You'll thank me for the extra purchases...
And the governor can stick it where the sun don't shine.
That man's a snake if I ever met one.
Think they'll see the Pacific, governor?
Not with that man in charge. Not a chance.
If the savages don't get 'em, the Spaniards or the British will!

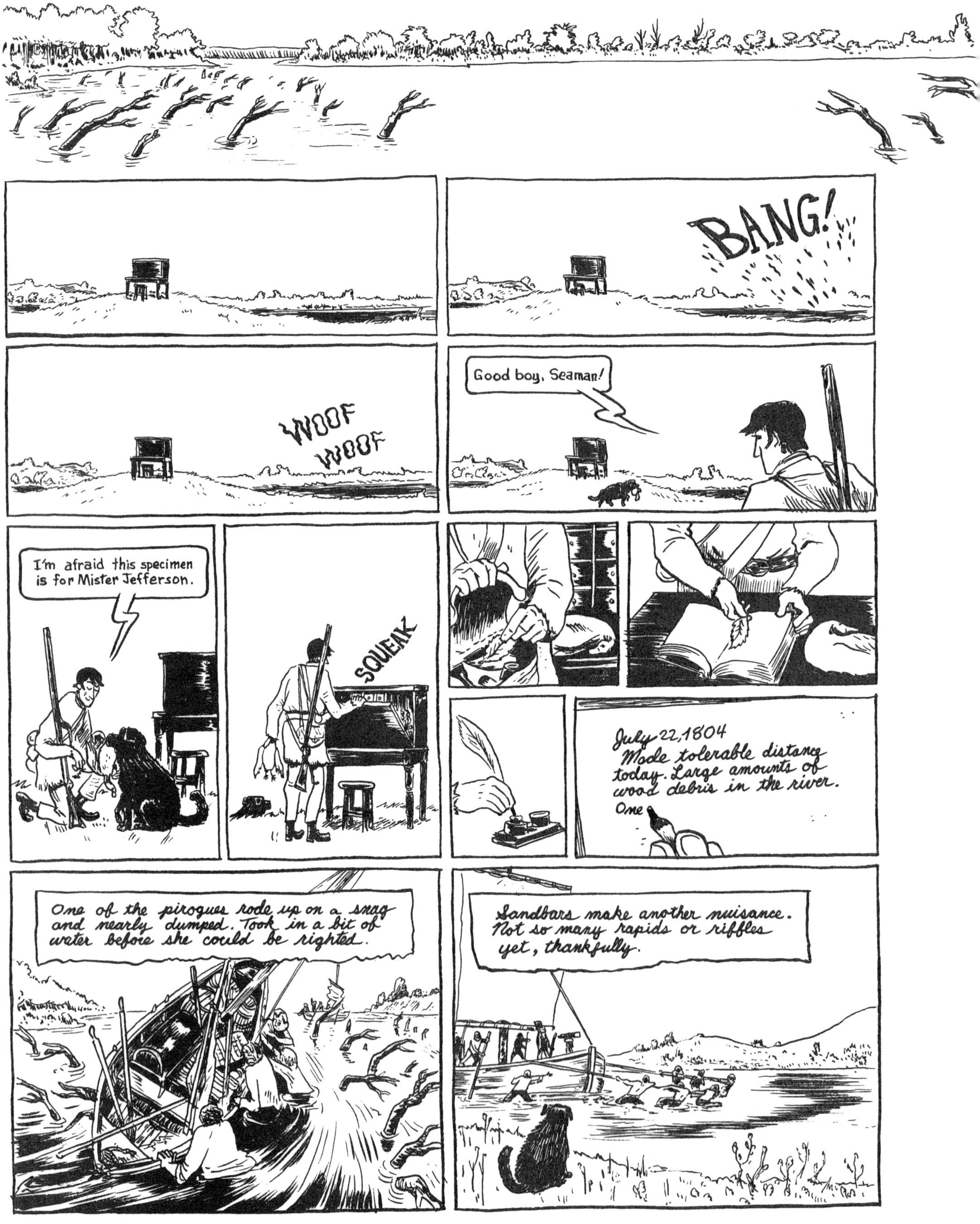
BANG!
WOOF
WOOF
Good boy, Seaman!
I'm afraid this specimen is for Mister Jefferson.
SQUEAK
July 22, 1804
Made tolerable distance today. Large amounts of wood debris in the river.
One
One of the pirogues rode up on a snag and nearly dumped. Took in a bit of water before she could be righted.
Sandbars make another nuisance. Not so many rapids or riffles yet, thankfully.

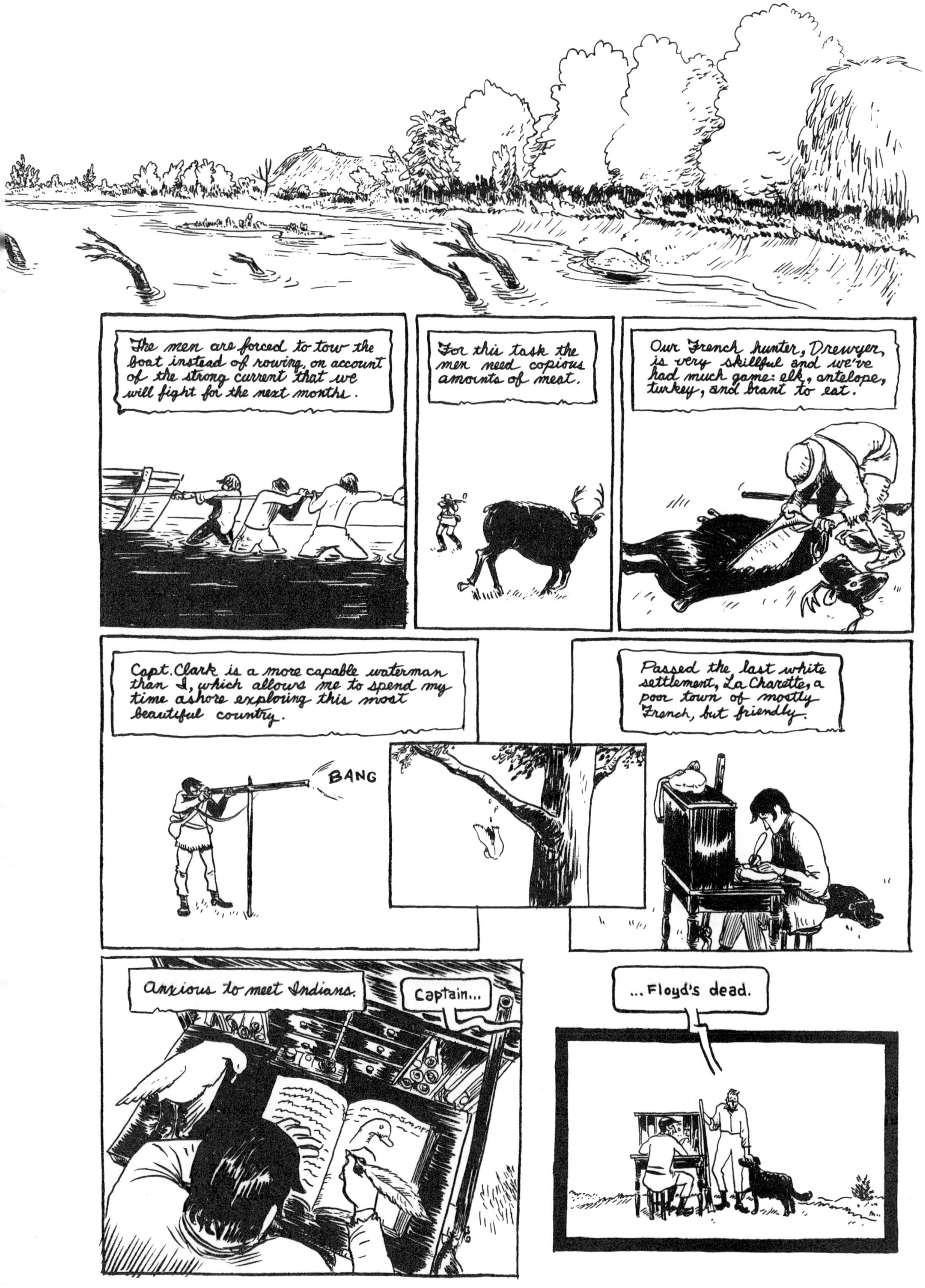

The men are forced to tow the boat instead of rowing, on account of the strong current that we will fight for the next months.
For this task the men need copious amounts of meat.
Our French hunter, Drewyer, is very skillful and we've had much game: elk, antelope, turkey, and brant to eat.
Capt. Clark is a more capable waterman than I, which allows me to spend my time ashore exploring this most beautiful country.
BANG
Passed the last white settlement, La Charette, a poor town of mostly French, but friendly.
Anxious to meet Indians.
Captain...
...Floyd's dead.

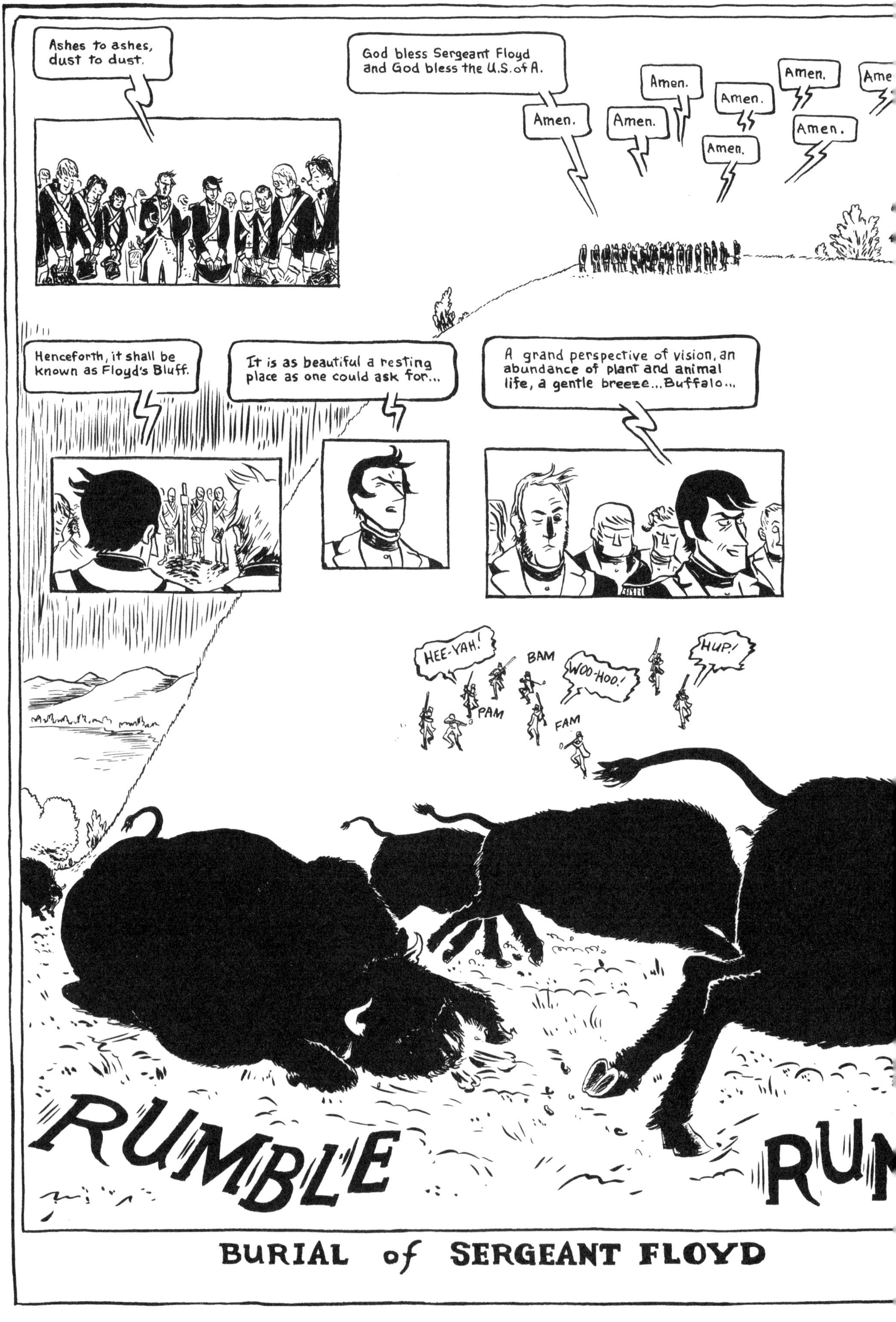
Ashes to ashes, dust to dust.
God bless Sergeant Floyd and God bless the U.S. of A.
Amen.
Amen.
Amen.
Amen.
Amen.
Amen.
Amen.
Henceforth, it shall be known as Floyd's Bluff.
It is as beautiful a resting place as one could ask for...
A grand perspective of vision, an abundance of plant and animal life, a gentle breeze... Buffalo...
HEE-YAH!
BAM
WOO-HOO!
HUP!
PAM
FAM
RUMBLE
RUM
BURIAL of SERGEANT FLOYD

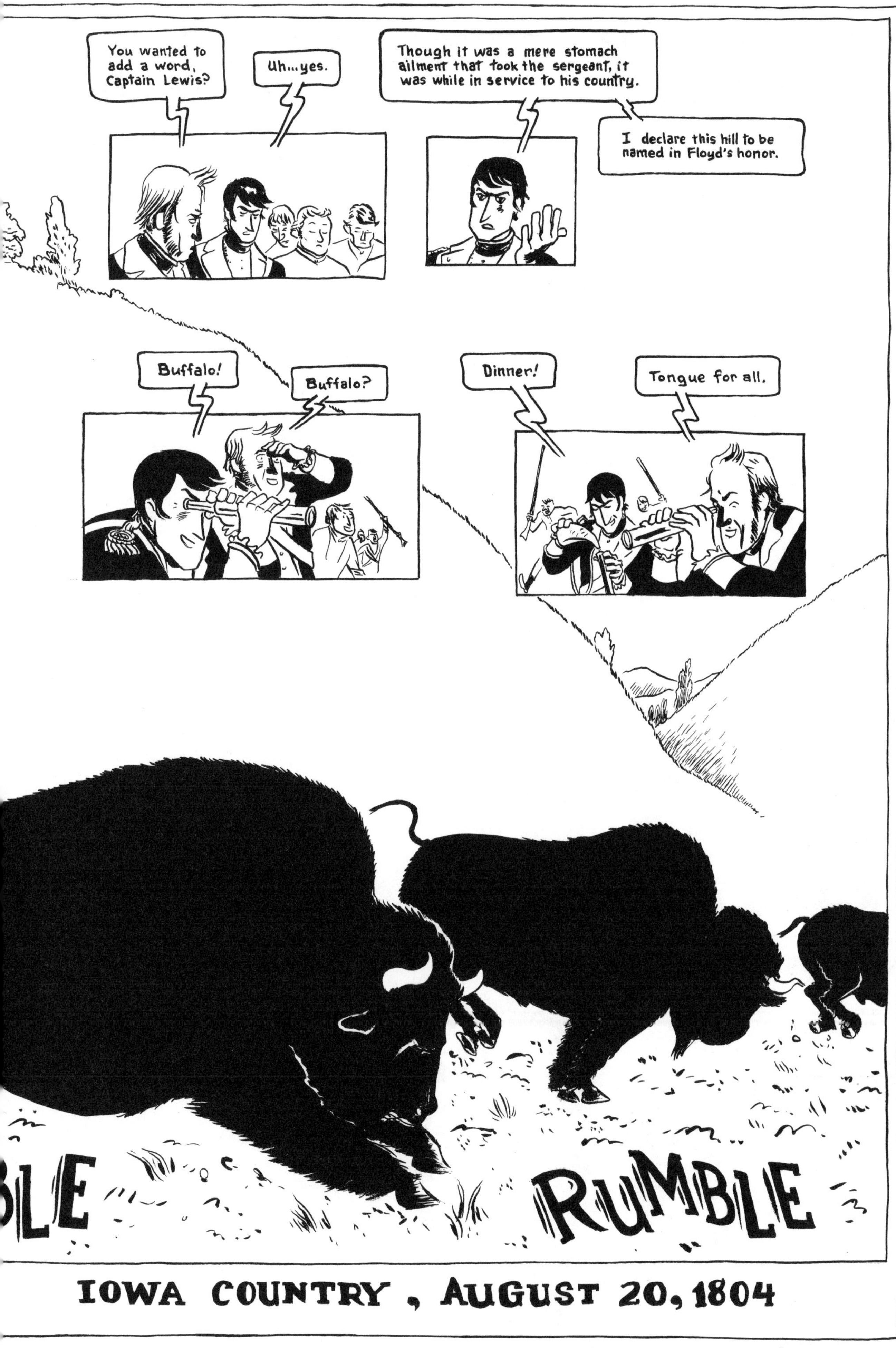
You wanted to add a word, Captain Lewis?
Uh...yes.
Though it was a mere stomach ailment that took the sergeant, it was while in service to his country.
I declare this hill to be named in Floyd's honor.
Buffalo!
Buffalo?
Dinner!
Tongue for all.
BLE
RUMBLE
IOWA COUNTRY, AUGUST 20, 1804

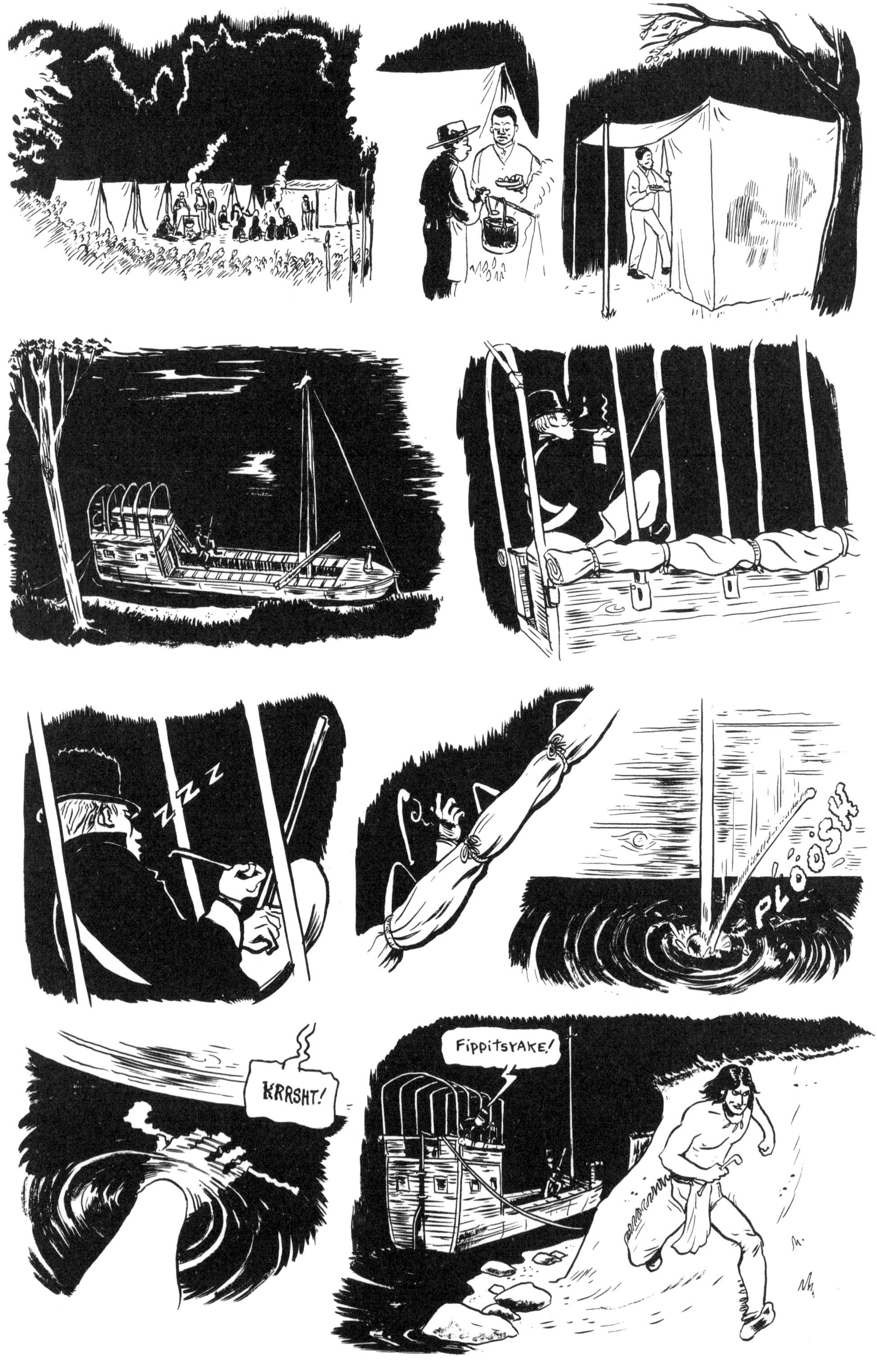
ZZZ
PLOOSH
KRRSHT!
Fippitsrake!

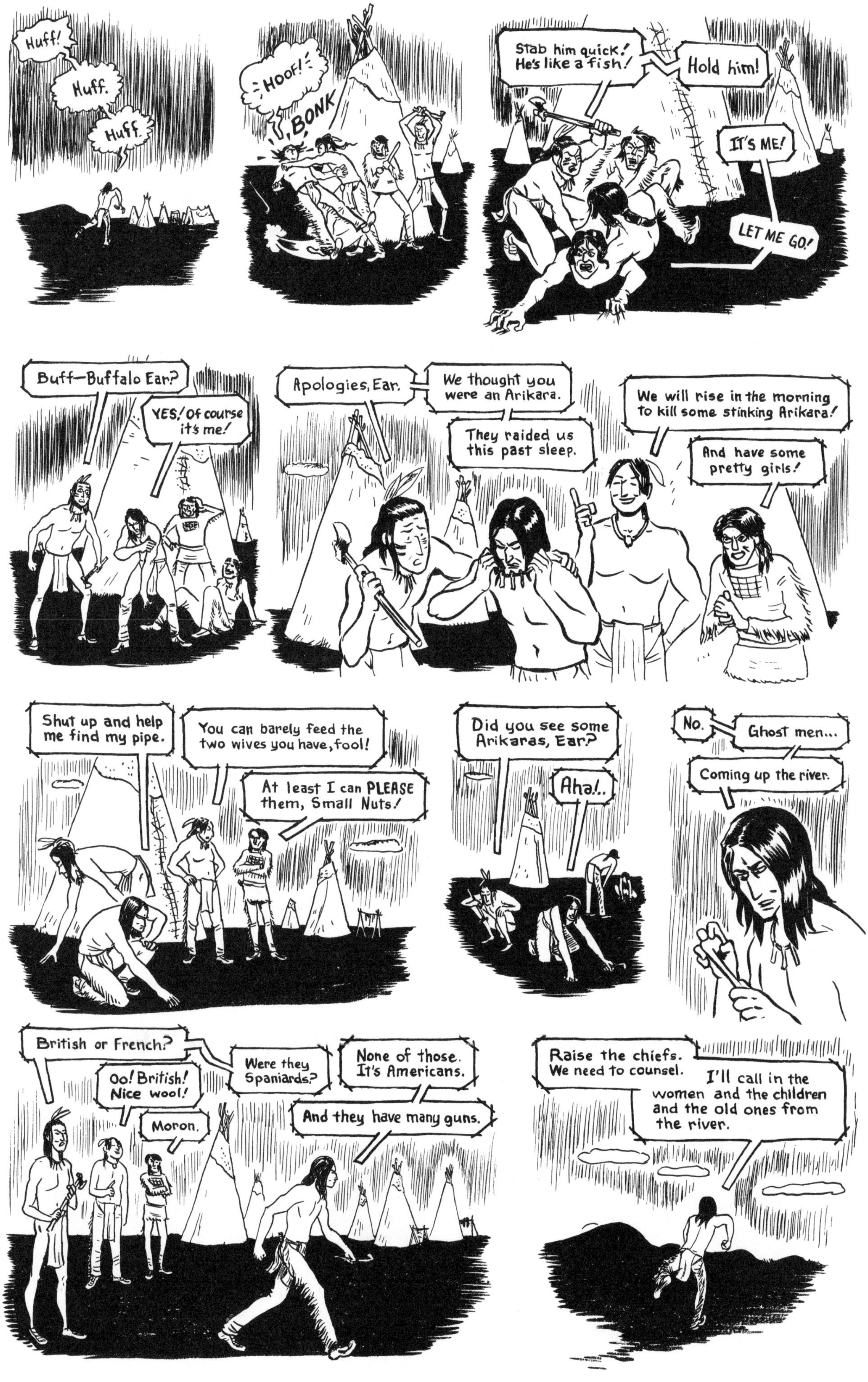
Huff!
Huff.
Huff.
HOOF!
BONK
Stab him quick! He's like a fish!
Hold him!
IT'S ME!
LET ME GO!
Buff—Buffalo Ear?
YES! Of course it's me!
Apologies, Ear.
We thought you were an Arikara.
They raided us this past sleep.
We will rise in the morning to kill some stinking Arikara!
And have some pretty girls!
Shut up and help me find my pipe.
You can barely feed the two wives you have, fool!
At least I can PLEASE them, Small Nuts!
Did you see some Arikaras, Ear?
Aha!..
No.
Ghost men...
Coming up the river.
British or French?
Oo! British! Nice wool!
Moron.
Were they Spaniards?
None of those. It's Americans.
And they have many guns.
Raise the chiefs. We need to counsel.
I'll call in the women and the children and the old ones from the river.

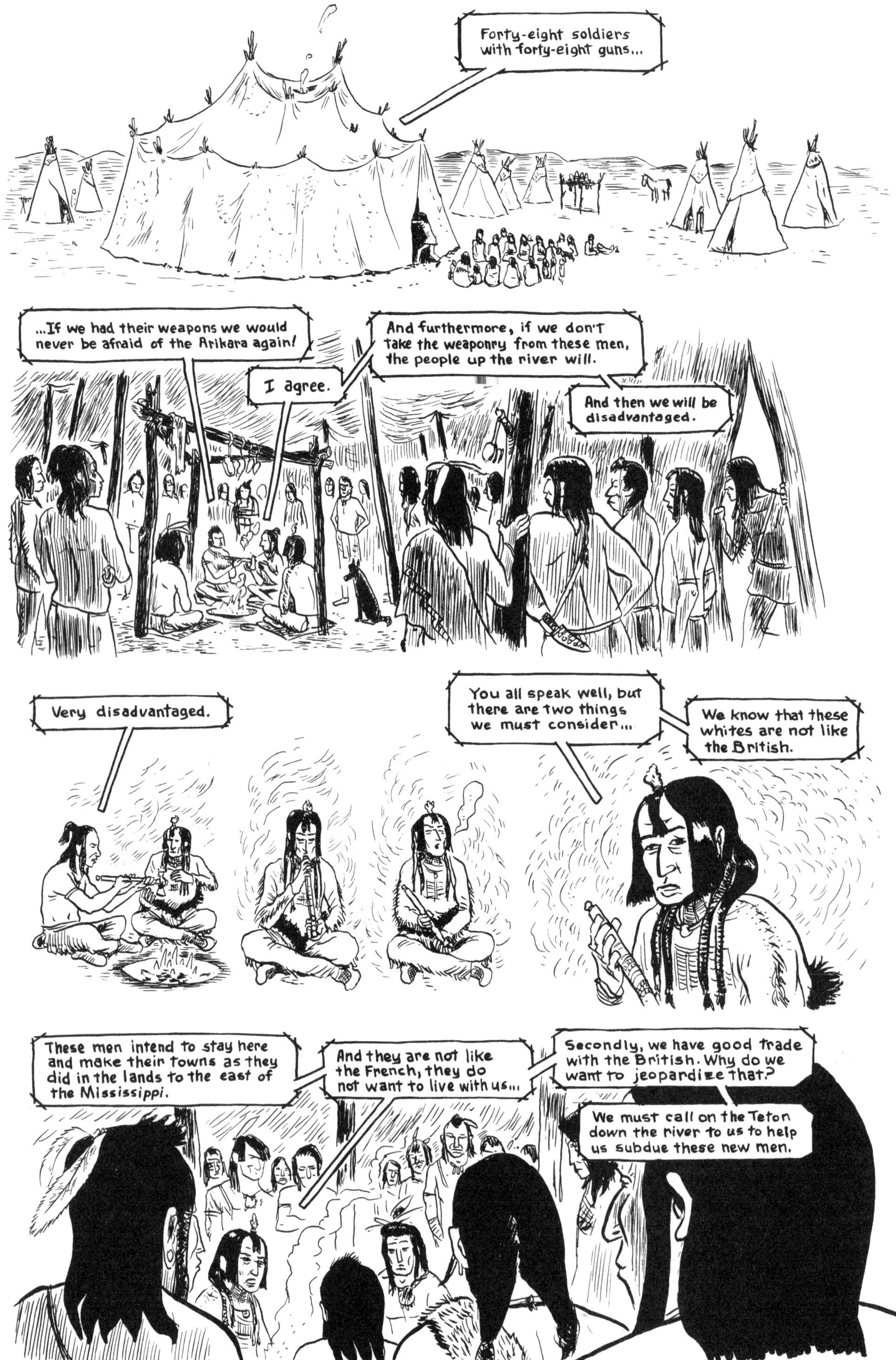

Forty-eight soldiers with forty-eight guns...
...If we had their weapons we would never be afraid of the Arikara again!
I agree.
And furthermore, if we don't take the weaponry from these men, the people up the river will.
And then we will be disadvantaged.
Very disadvantaged.
You all speak well, but there are two things we must consider...
We know that these whites are not like the British.
These men intend to stay here and make their towns as they did in the lands to the east of the Mississippi.
And they are not like the French, they do not want to live with us...
Secondly, we have good trade with the British. Why do we want to jeopardize that?
We must call on the Teton down the river to us to help us subdue these new men.

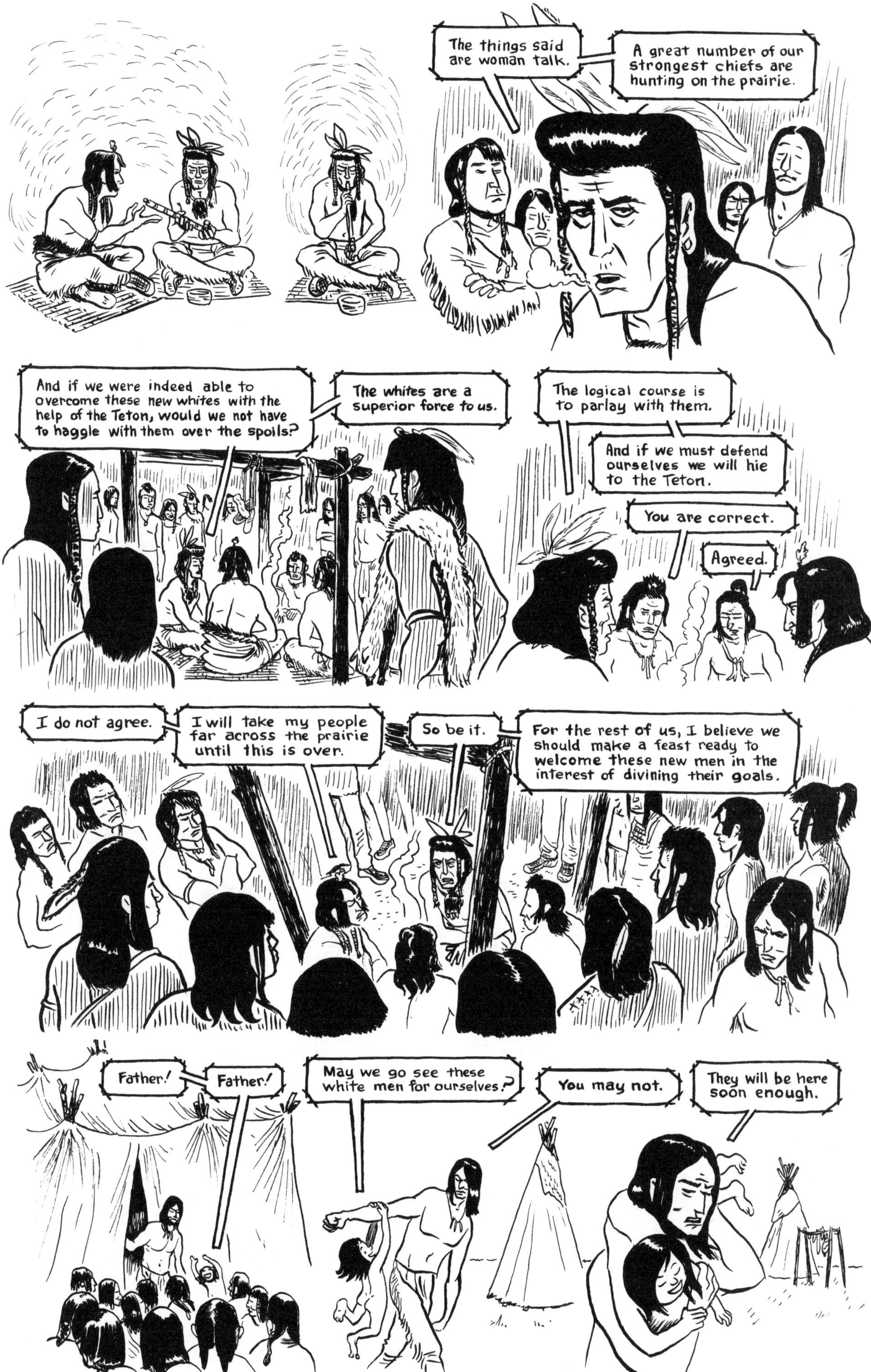
The things said are woman talk.
A great number of our strongest chiefs are hunting on the prairie.
And if we were indeed able to overcome these new whites with the help of the Teton, would we not have to haggle with them over the spoils?
The whites are a superior force to us.
The logical course is to parlay with them.
And if we must defend ourselves we will hie to the Teton.
You are correct.
Agreed.
I do not agree.
I will take my people far across the prairie until this is over.
So be it.
For the rest of us, I believe we should make a feast ready to welcome these new men in the interest of divining their goals.
Father!
Father!
May we go see these white men for ourselves?
You may not.
They will be here soon enough.

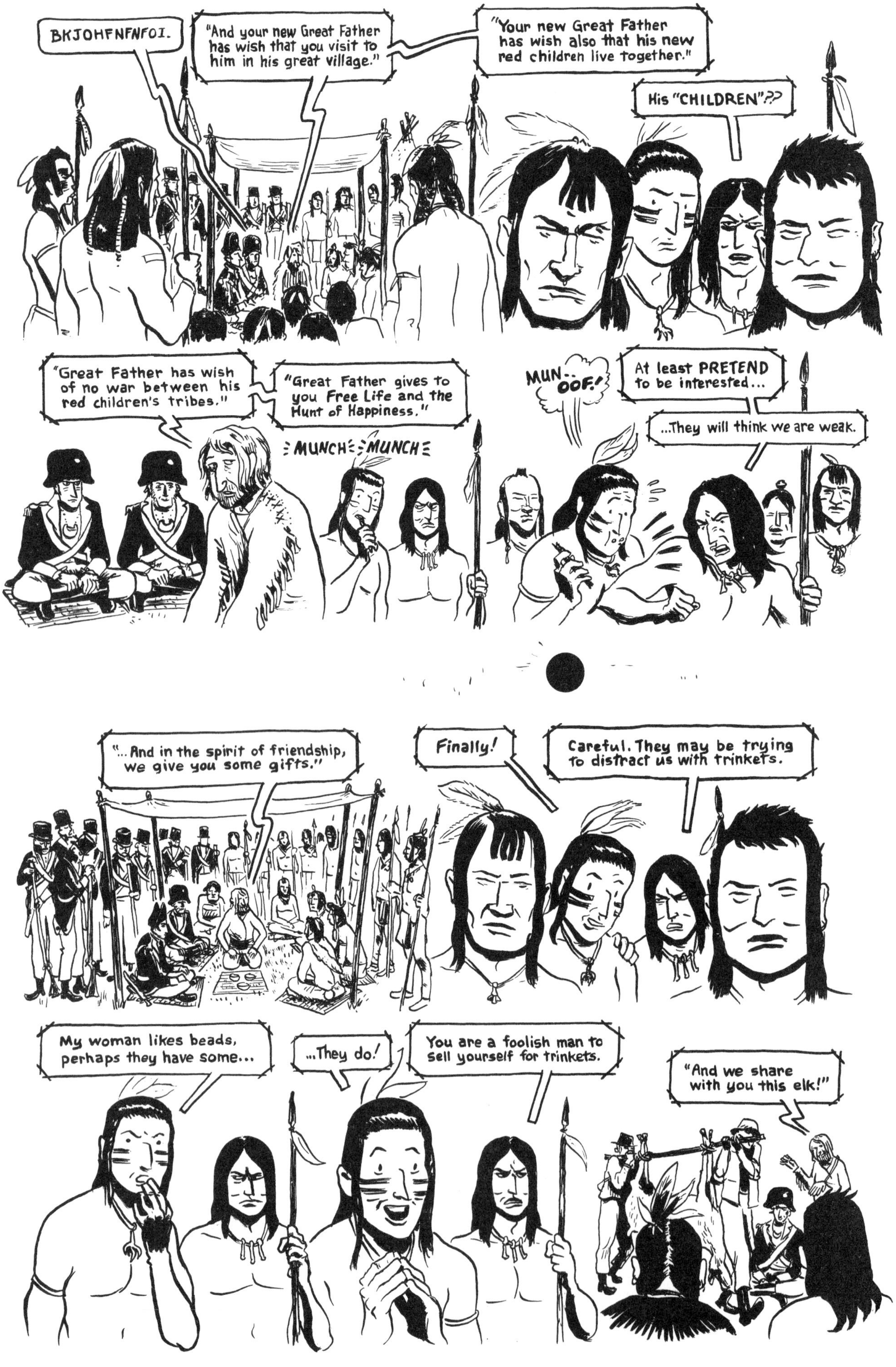
BKJOHFNFNFOI.
"And your new Great Father has wish that you visit to him in his great village."
"Your new Great Father has wish also that his new red children live together."
His "CHILDREN"??
"Great Father has wish of no war between his red children's tribes."
"Great Father gives to you Free Life and the Hunt of Happiness."
MUNCH MUNCH
MUN.. OOF!
At least PRETEND to be interested...
...They will think we are weak.
"...And in the spirit of friendship, we give you some gifts."
Finally!
Careful. They may be trying to distract us with trinkets.
My woman likes beads, perhaps they have some...
...They do!
You are a foolish man to sell yourself for trinkets.
"And we share with you this elk!"

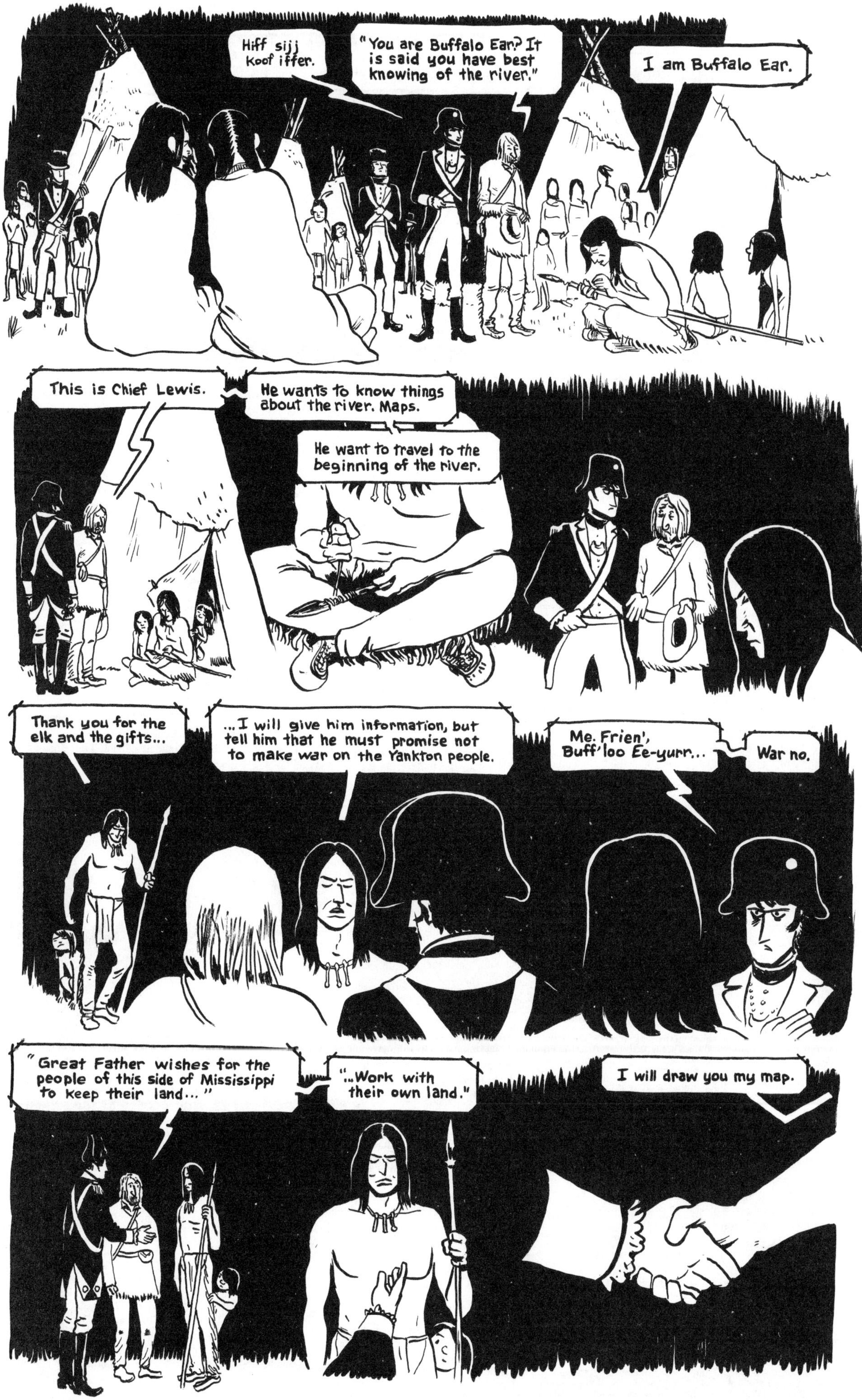
Hiff sijj koof iffer.
"You are Buffalo Ear? It is said you have best knowing of the river."
I am Buffalo Ear.
This is Chief Lewis.
He wants to know things about the river. Maps.
He want to travel to the beginning of the river.
Thank you for the elk and the gifts...
...I will give him information, but tell him that he must promise not to make war on the Yankton people.
Me. Frien', Buff'loo Ee-yurr...
War no.
"Great Father wishes for the people of this side of Mississippi to keep their land..."
"...Work with their own land."
I will draw you my map.

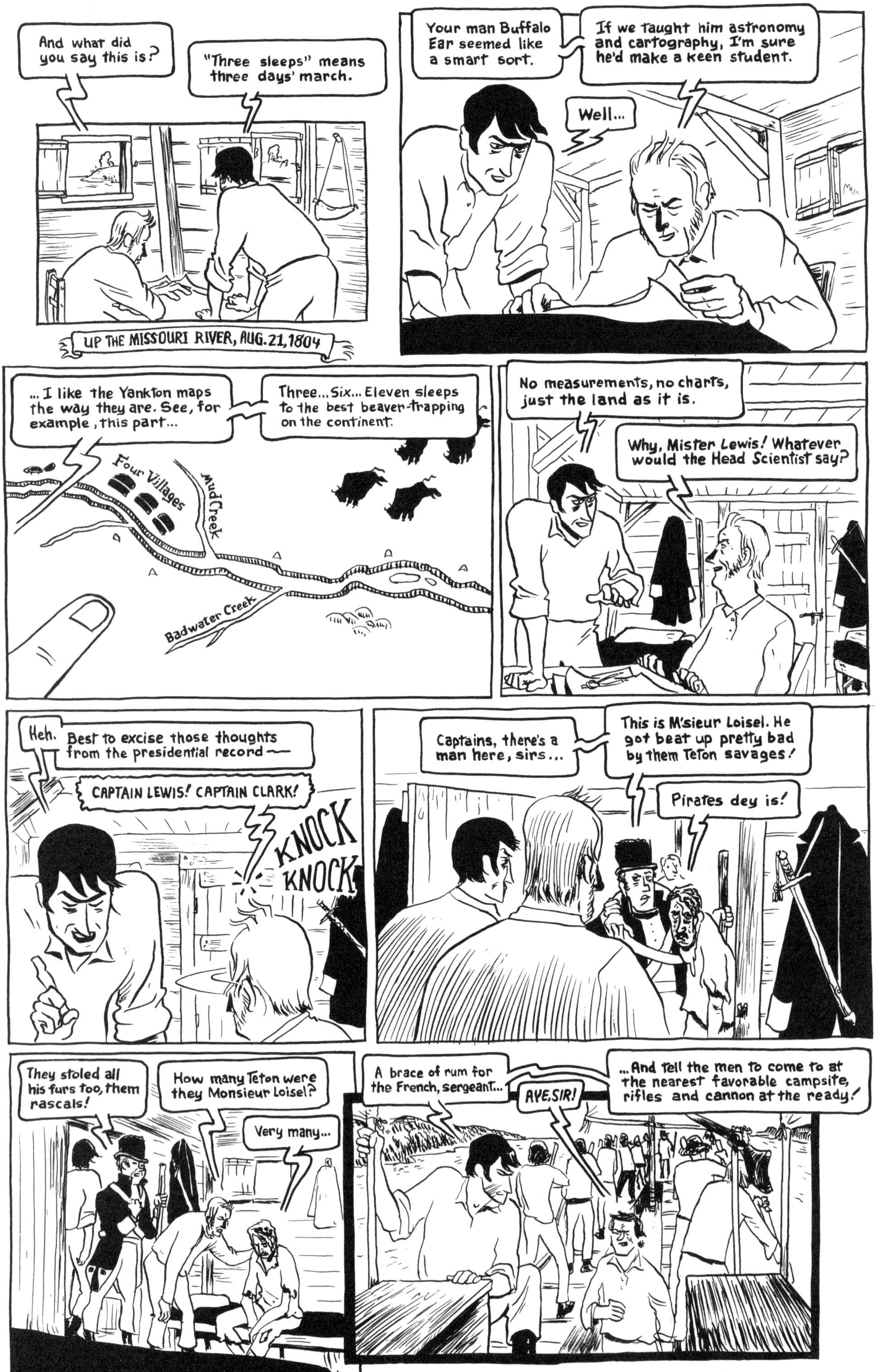
And what did you say this is?
"Three sleeps" means three days' march.
UP THE MISSOURI RIVER, AUG. 21, 1804
Your man Buffalo Ear seemed like a smart sort.
If we taught him astronomy and cartography, I'm sure he'd make a keen student.
Well...
... I like the Yankton maps the way they are. See, for example, this part...
Three... Six... Eleven sleeps to the best beaver-trapping on the continent.
Four Villages
Mud Creek
Badwater Creek
No measurements, no charts, just the land as it is.
Why, Mister Lewis! Whatever would the Head Scientist say?
Heh.
Best to excise those thoughts from the presidential record —
CAPTAIN LEWIS! CAPTAIN CLARK!
KNOCK KNOCK
Captains, there's a man here, sirs...
This is M'sieur Loisel. He got beat up pretty bad by them Teton savages!
Pirates dey is!
They stoled all his furs too, them rascals!
How many Teton were they Monsieur Loisel?
Very many...
A brace of rum for the French, sergeant...
AYE, SIR!
...And tell the men to come to at the nearest favorable campsite, rifles and cannon at the ready!

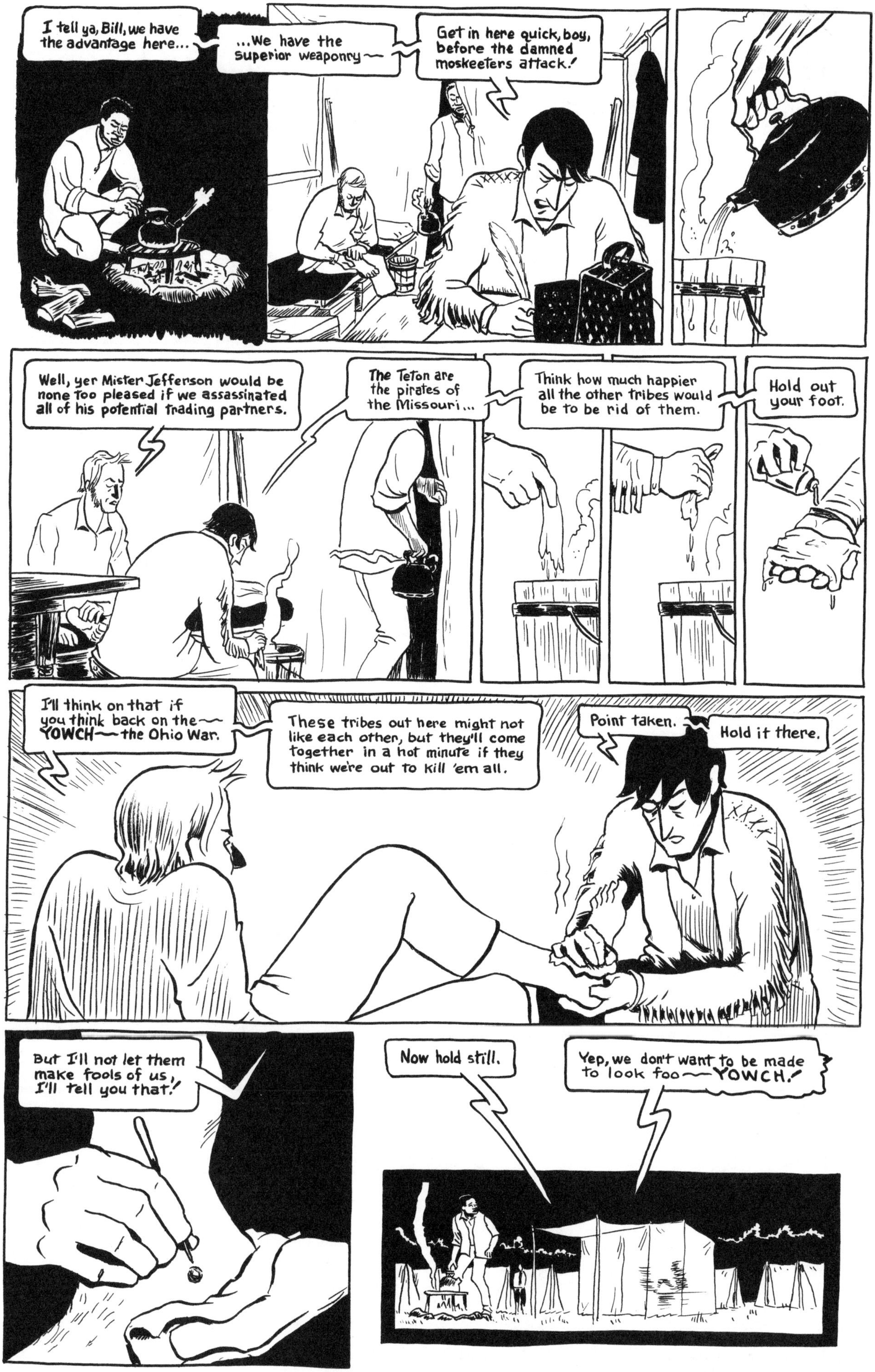
I tell ya, Bill, we have the advantage here...
...We have the superior weaponry—
Get in here quick, boy, before the damned moskeeters attack!
Well, yer Mister Jefferson would be none too pleased if we assassinated all of his potential trading partners.
The Teton are the pirates of the Missouri...
Think how much happier all the other tribes would be to be rid of them.
Hold out your foot.
I'll think on that if you think back on the— YOWCH— the Ohio War.
These tribes out here might not like each other, but they'll come together in a hot minute if they think we're out to kill 'em all.
Point taken.
Hold it there.
But I'll not let them make fools of us, I'll tell you that!
Now hold still.
Yep, we don't want to be made to look foo—YOWCH!

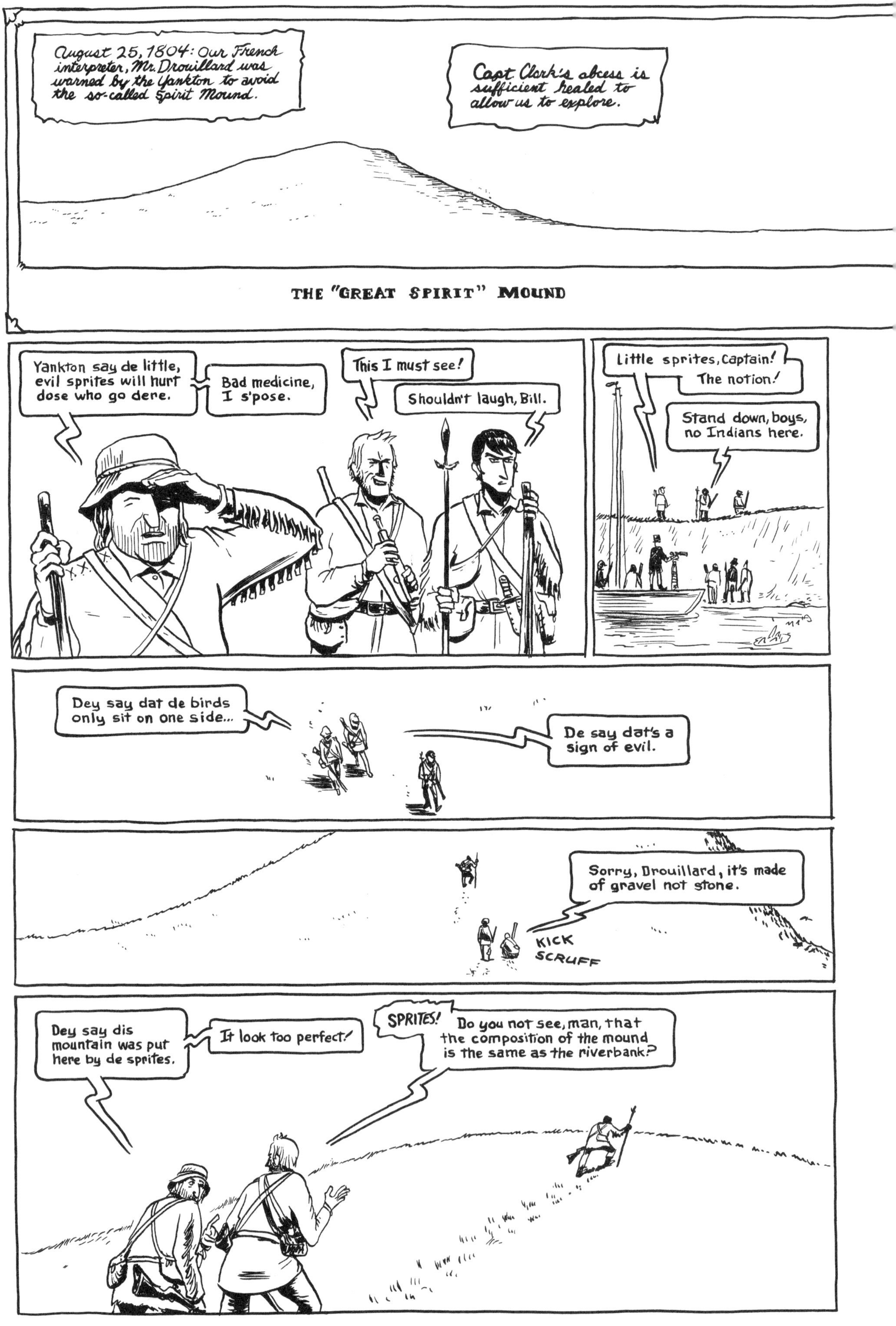
August 25, 1804: Our French interpreter, Mr. Drouillard was warned by the Yankton to avoid the so-called Spirit Mound.
Capt Clark's abcess is sufficient healed to allow us to explore.
THE "GREAT SPIRIT" MOUND
Yankton say de little, evil sprites will hurt dose who go dere.
Bad medicine, I s'pose.
This I must see!
Shouldn't laugh, Bill.
Little sprites, Captain!
The notion!
Stand down, boys, no Indians here.
Dey say dat de birds only sit on one side...
De say dat's a sign of evil.
Sorry, Drouillard, it's made of gravel not stone.
KICK
SCRUFF
Dey say dis mountain was put here by de sprites.
It look too perfect!
SPRITES! Do you not see, man, that the composition of the mound is the same as the riverbank?

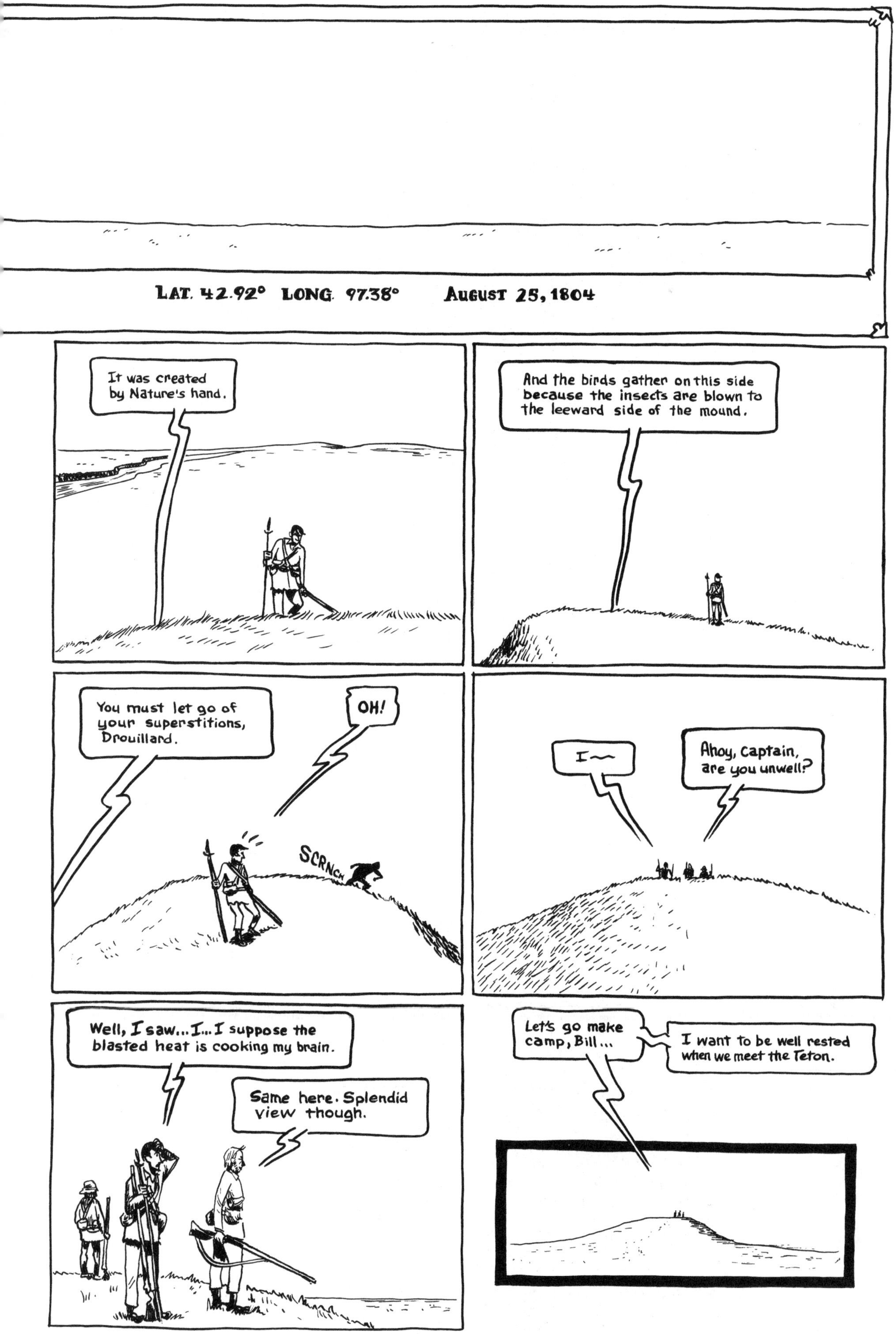
LAT. 42.92° LONG. 97.38° AUGUST 25, 1804
It was created by Nature's hand.
And the birds gather on this side because the insects are blown to the leeward side of the mound.
You must let go of your superstitions, Drouillard.
OH!
SCRNCH
I~
Ahoy, captain, are you unwell?
Well, I saw... I... I suppose the blasted heat is cooking my brain.
Same here. Splendid view though.
Let's go make camp, Bill...
I want to be well rested when we meet the Teton.

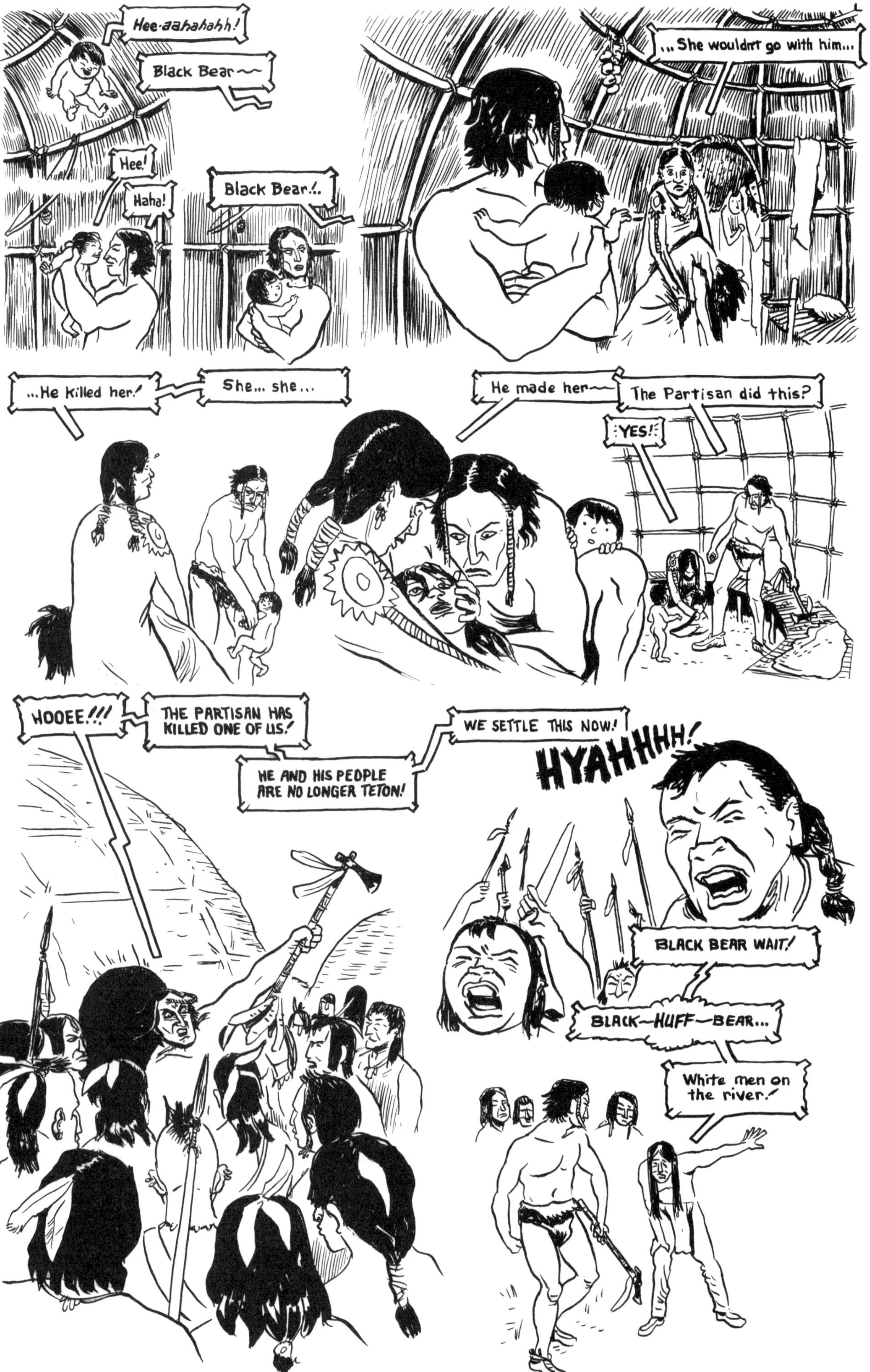
Hee-aahahahh!
Black Bear~~
Hee!
Haha!
Black Bear!..
...She wouldn't go with him...
...He killed her!
She... she...
He made her~~
The Partisan did this?
YES!
HOOEE!!!
THE PARTISAN HAS KILLED ONE OF US!
HE AND HIS PEOPLE ARE NO LONGER TETON!
WE SETTLE THIS NOW!
HYAHHHH!
BLACK BEAR WAIT!
BLACK—HUFF—BEAR...
White men on the river!

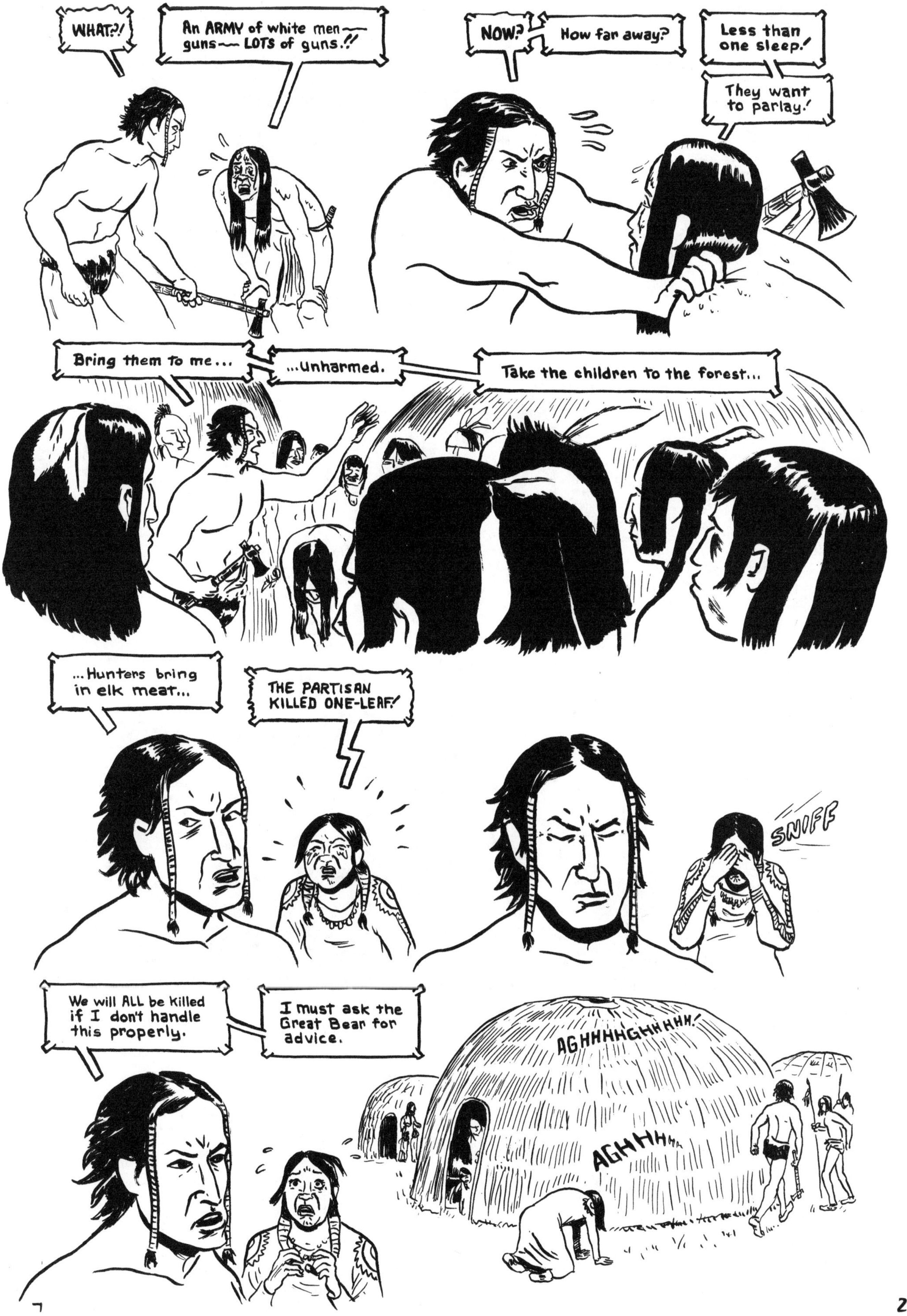
WHAT?!
An ARMY of white men—guns—LOTS of guns.!!
NOW?
How far away?
Less than one sleep.!
They want to parlay.!
Bring them to me...
...unharmed.
Take the children to the forest...
...Hunters bring in elk meat...
THE PARTISAN KILLED ONE-LEAF!
SNIFF
We will ALL be killed if I don't handle this properly.
I must ask the Great Bear for advice.
AGHHHHGHHHHH!
AGHHHhh

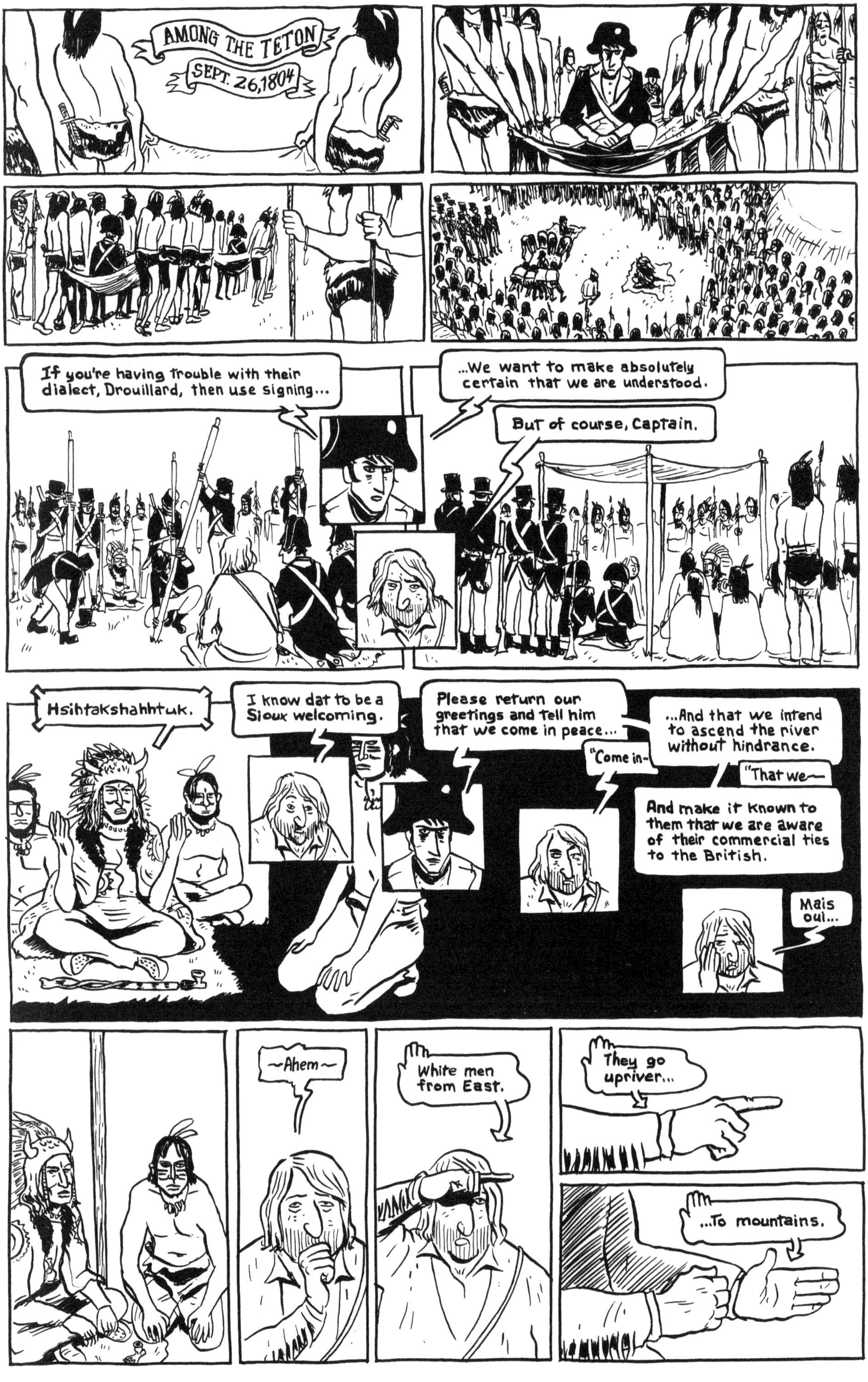
AMONG THE TETON
SEPT. 26,1804
If you're having trouble with their dialect, Drouillard, then use signing...
...We want to make absolutely certain that we are understood.
But of course, Captain.
Hsihtakshahhtuk.
I know dat to be a Sioux welcoming.
Please return our greetings and tell him that we come in peace...
"Come in-
...And that we intend to ascend the river without hindrance.
"That we—
And make it known to them that we are aware of their commercial ties to the British.
Mais oui...
~Ahem~
White men from East.
They go upriver...
...To mountains.

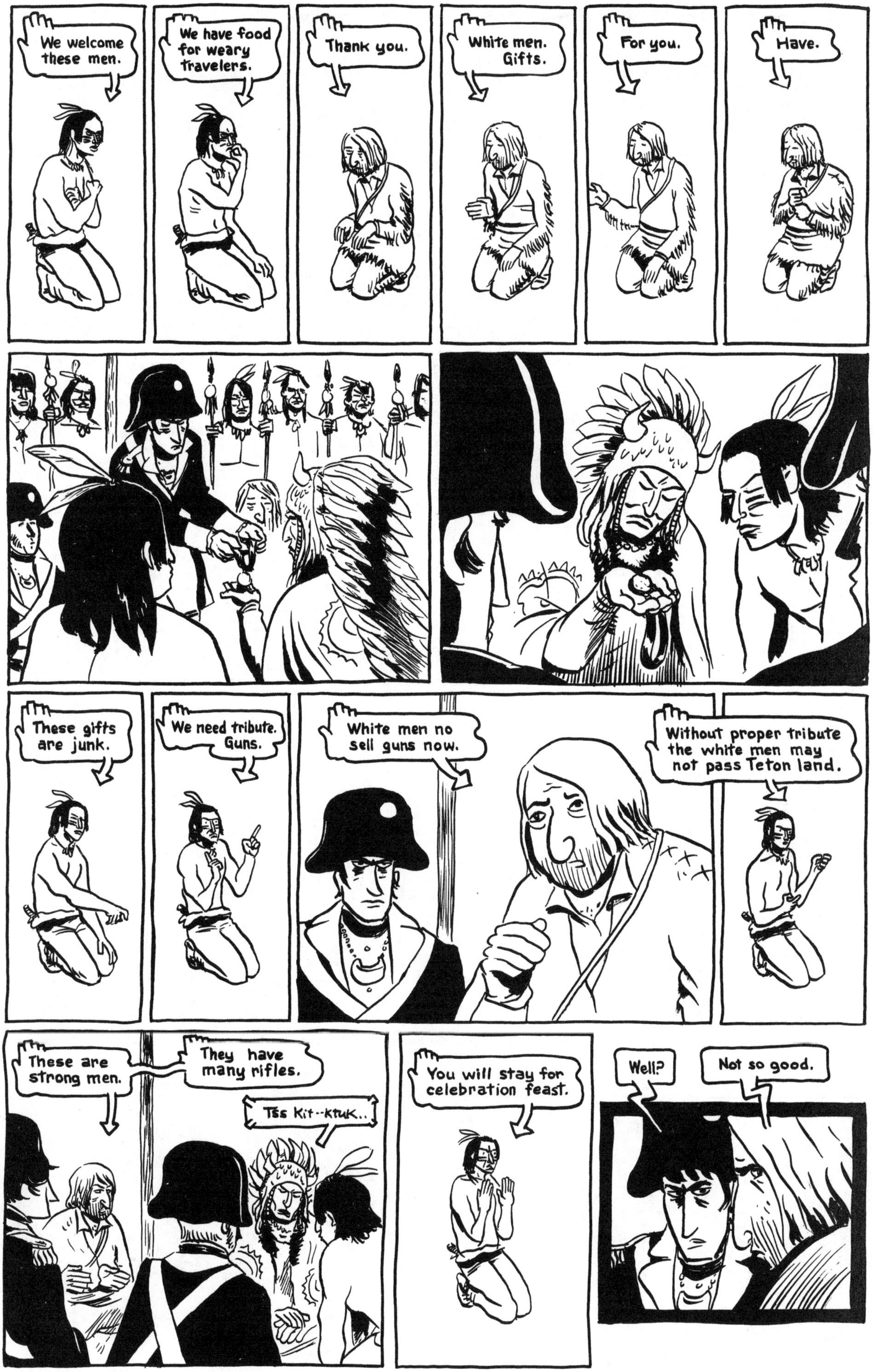
We welcome these men.
We have food for weary travelers.
Thank you.
White men. Gifts.
For you.
Have.
These gifts are junk.
We need tribute. Guns.
White men no sell guns now.
Without proper tribute the white men may not pass Teton land.
These are strong men.
They have many rifles.
Tss Kit--ktuk..
You will stay for celebration feast.
Well?
Not so good.

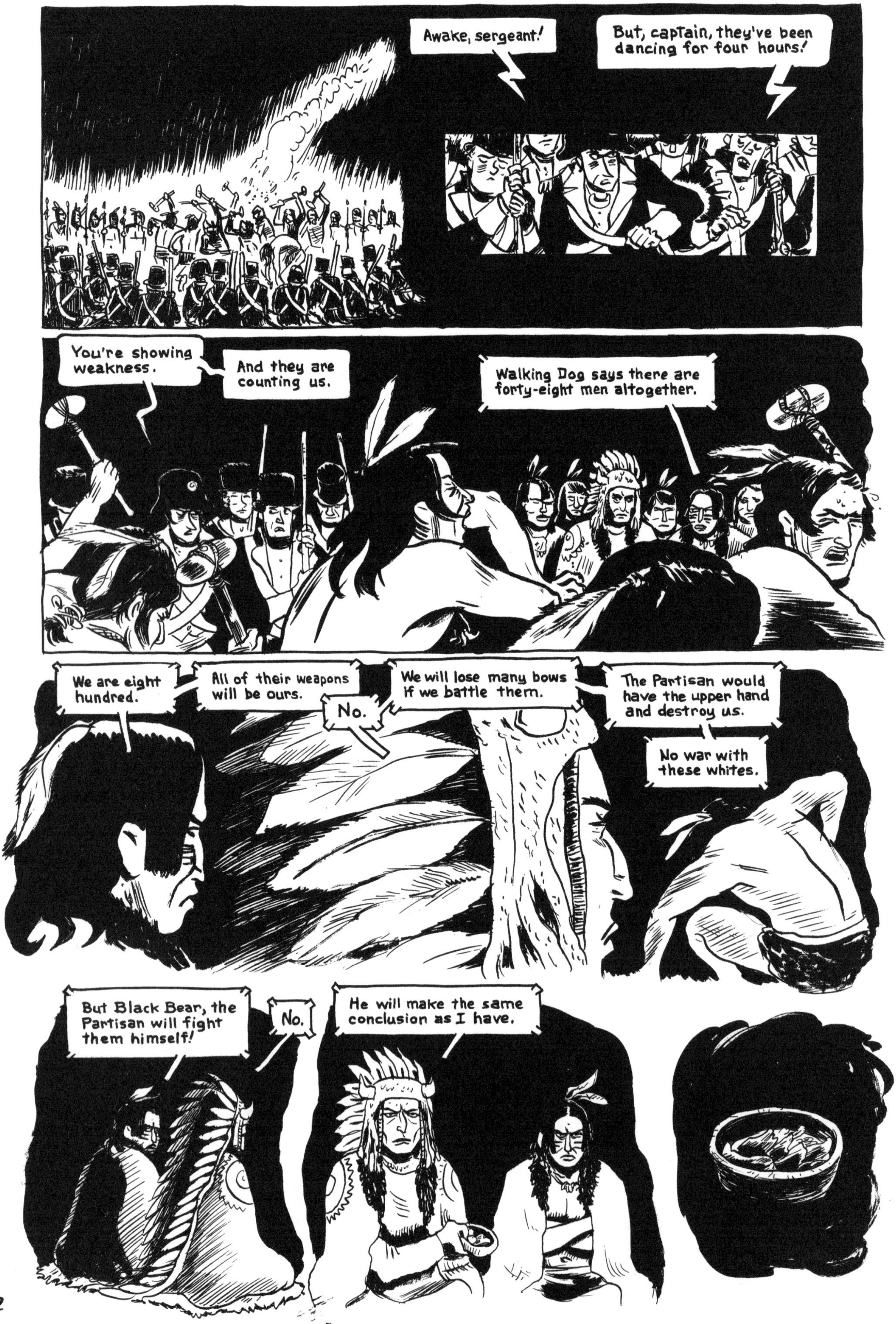
Awake, sergeant!
But, captain, they've been dancing for four hours!
You're showing weakness.
And they are counting us.
Walking Dog says there are forty-eight men altogether.
We are eight hundred.
All of their weapons will be ours.
No.
We will lose many bows if we battle them.
The Partisan would have the upper hand and destroy us.
No war with these whites.
But Black Bear, the Partisan will fight them himself!
No.
He will make the same conclusion as I have.

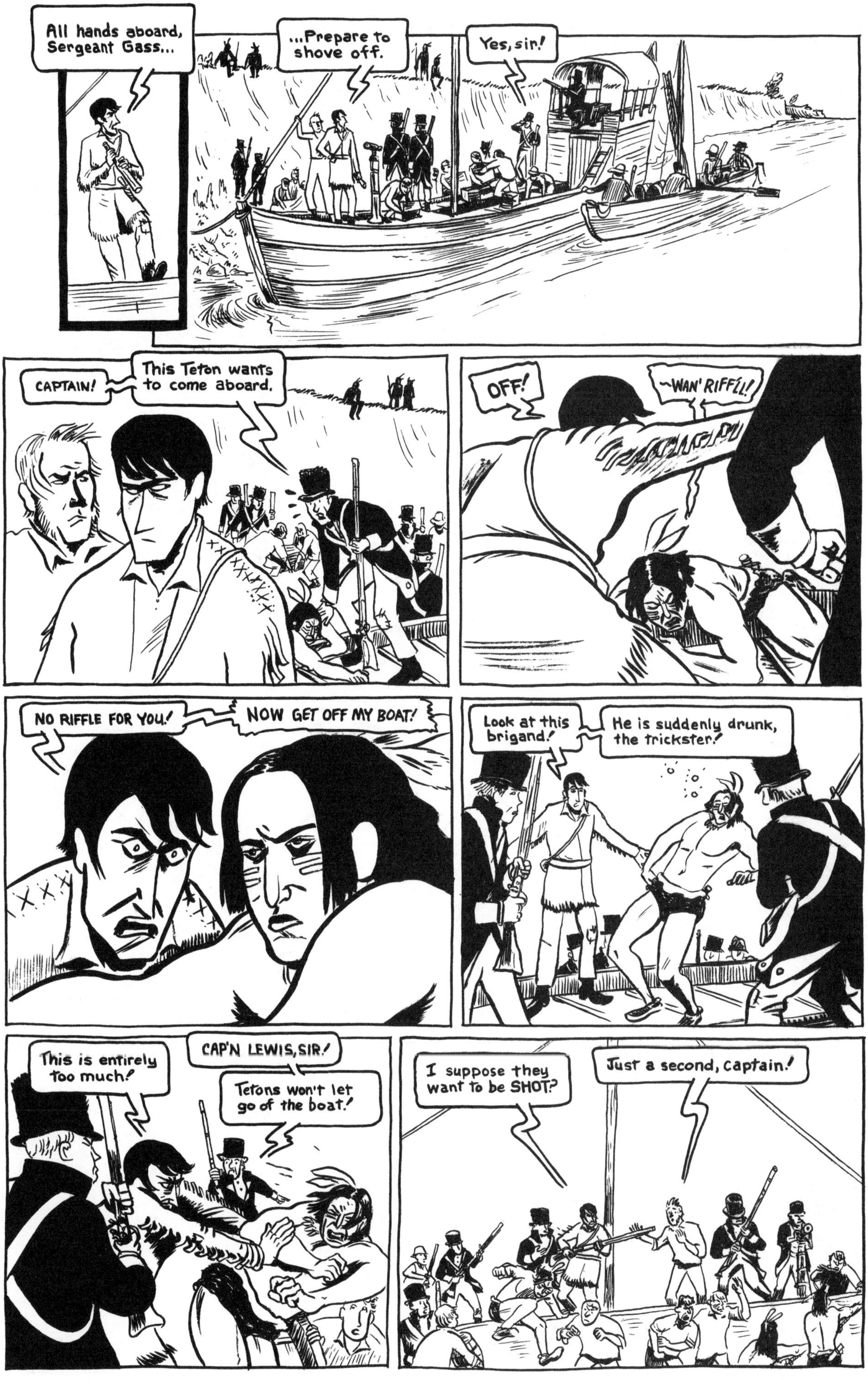
All hands aboard, Sergeant Gass...
...Prepare to shove off.
Yes, sir!
CAPTAIN!
This Teton wants to come aboard.
OFF!
~WAN' RIFFLE!
NO RIFFLE FOR YOU!
NOW GET OFF MY BOAT!
Look at this brigand!
He is suddenly drunk, the trickster!
This is entirely too much!
CAP'N LEWIS, SIR!
Tetons won't let go of the boat!
I suppose they want to be SHOT?
Just a second, captain!

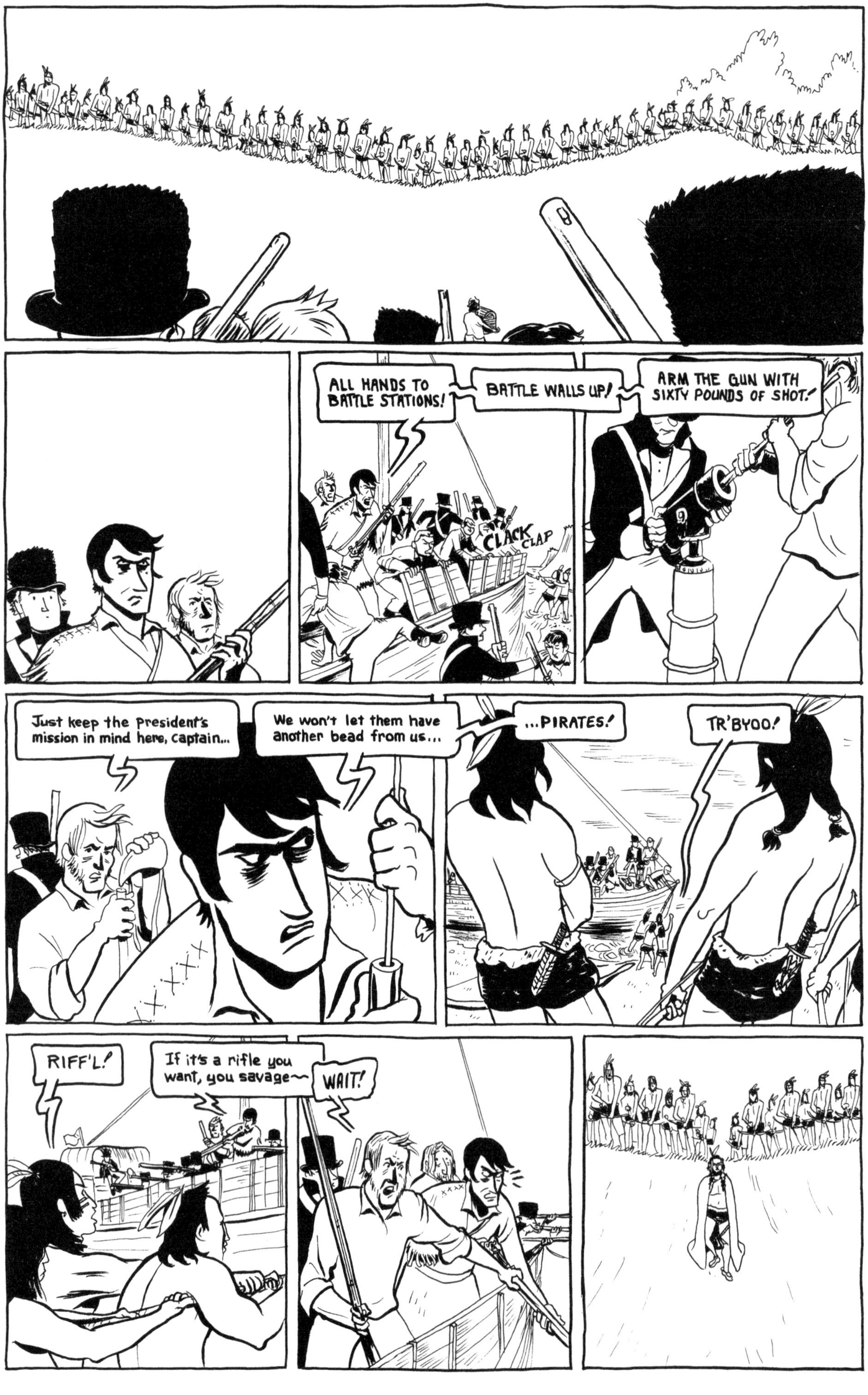
ALL HANDS TO BATTLE STATIONS!
BATTLE WALLS UP!
CLACK CLAP
ARM THE GUN WITH SIXTY POUNDS OF SHOT!
Just keep the president's mission in mind here, captain...
We won't let them have another bead from us...
...PIRATES!
TR'BYOO!
RIFF'L!
If it's a rifle you want, you savage~
WAIT!

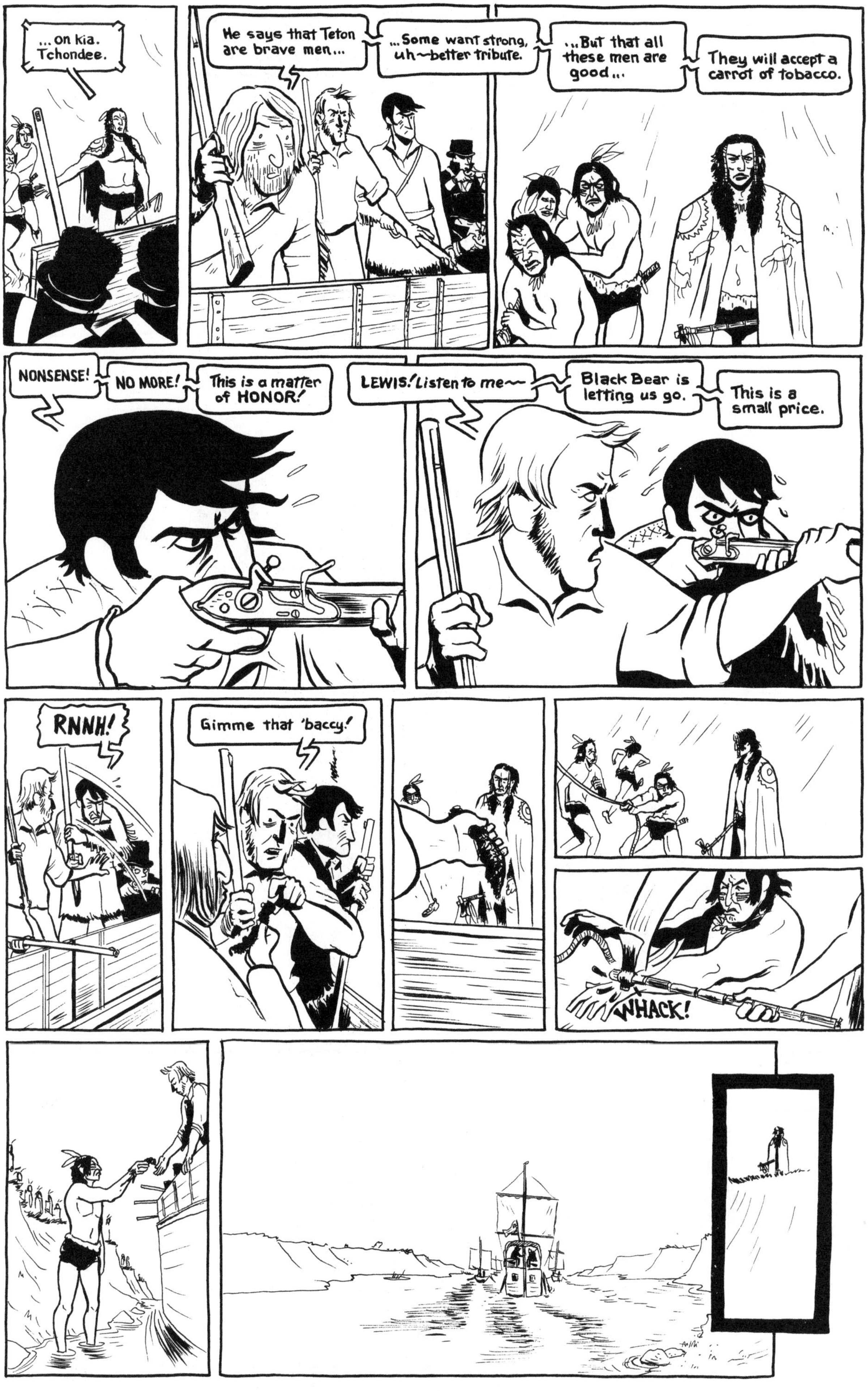
...on kia. Tchondee.
He says that Teton are brave men...
...Some want strong, uh~better tribute.
...But that all these men are good...
They will accept a carrot of tobacco.
NONSENSE!
NO MORE!
This is a matter of HONOR!
LEWIS! Listen to me~~
Black Bear is letting us go.
This is a small price.
RNNH!
Gimme that 'baccy!
WHACK!

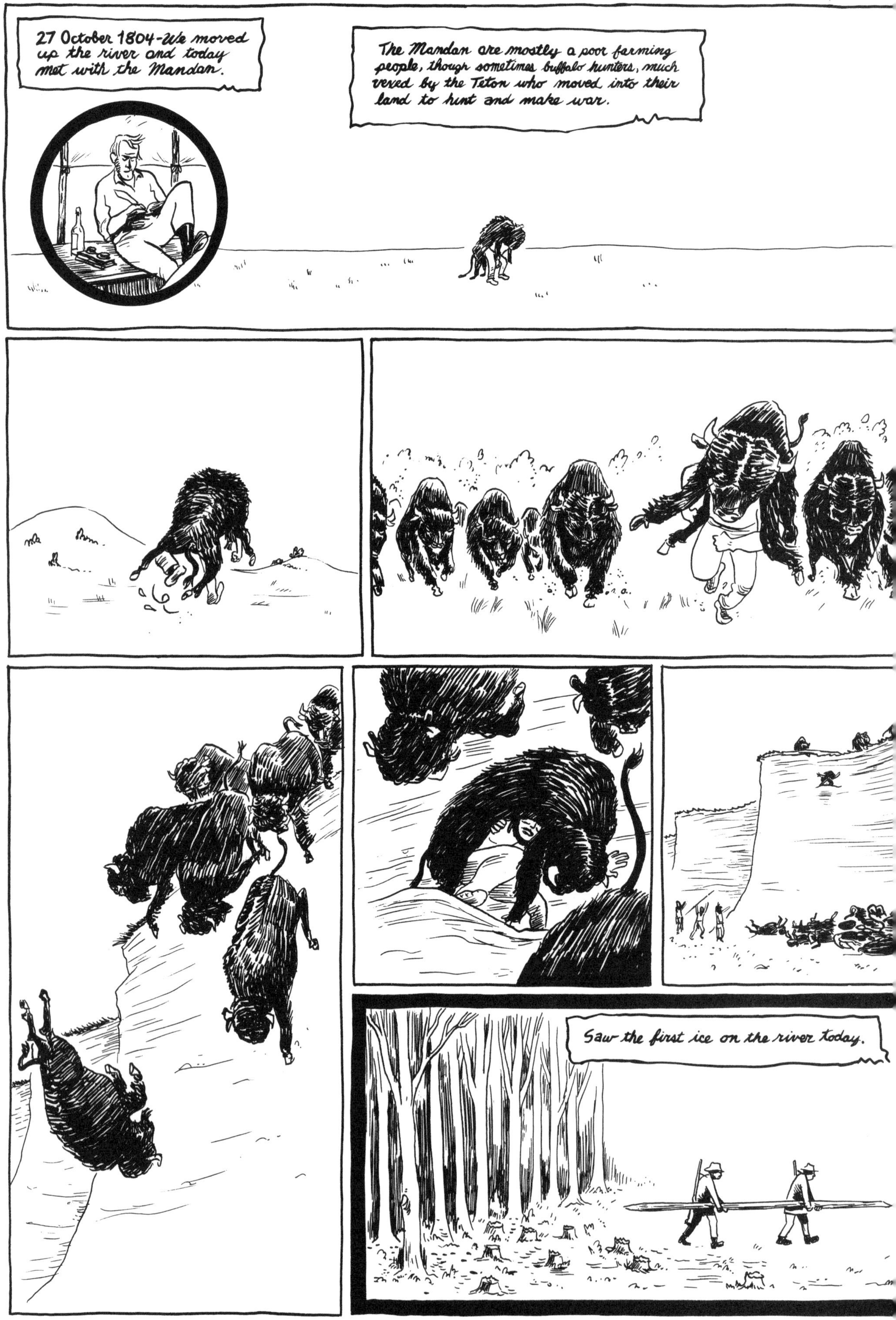
27 October 1804-We moved up the river and today met with the Mandan.
The Mandan are mostly a poor farming people, though sometimes buffalo hunters, much vexed by the Teton who moved into their land to hunt and make war.
Saw the first ice on the river today.

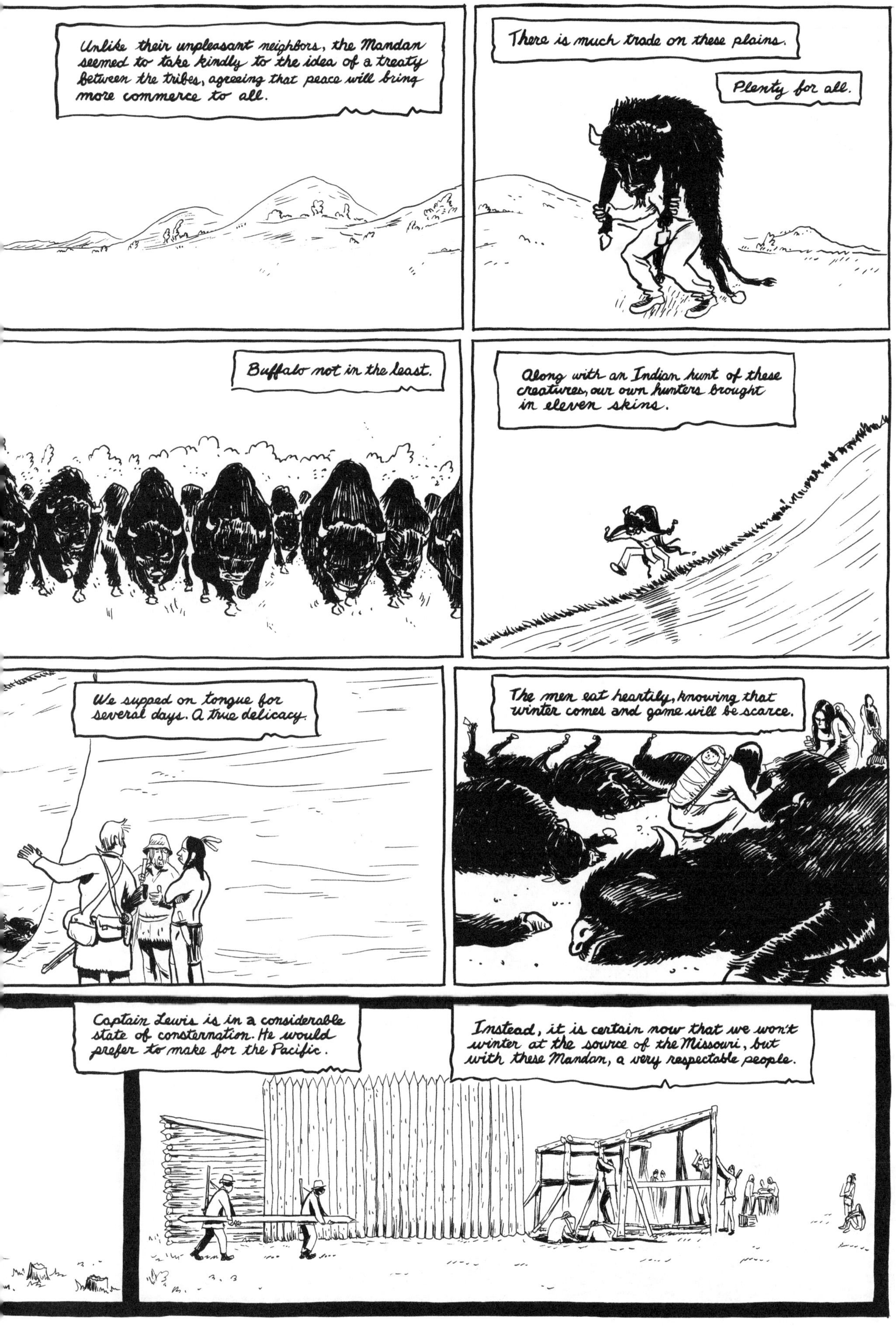
Unlike their unpleasant neighbors, the Mandan seemed to take kindly to the idea of a treaty between the tribes, agreeing that peace will bring more commerce to all.
There is much trade on these plains.
Plenty for all.
Buffalo not in the least.
Along with an Indian hunt of these creatures, our own hunters brought in eleven skins.
We supped on tongue for several days. A true delicacy.
The men eat heartily, knowing that winter comes and game will be scarce.
Captain Lewis is in a considerable state of consternation. He would prefer to make for the Pacific.
Instead, it is certain now that we won't winter at the source of the Missouri, but with these Mandan, a very respectable people.

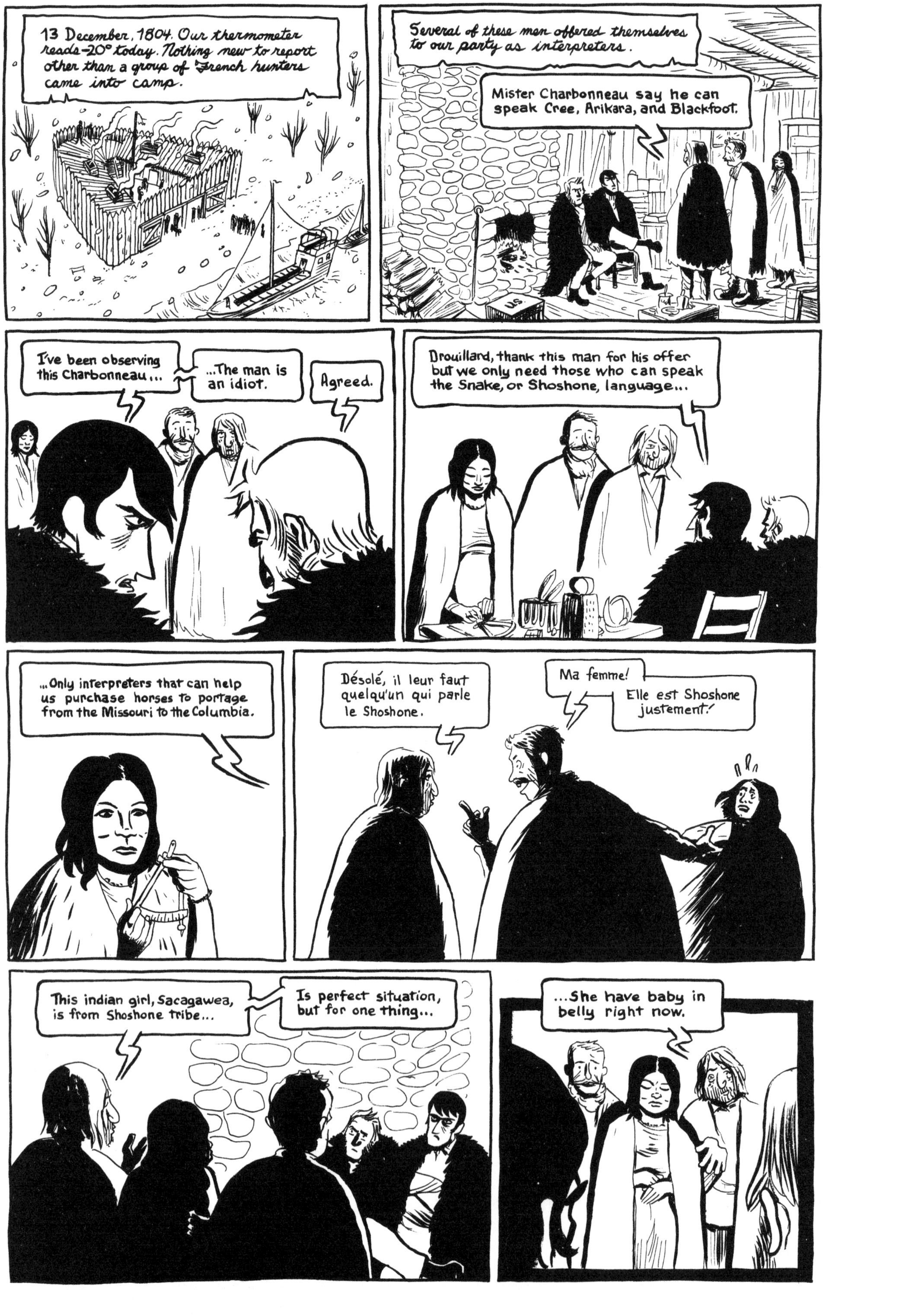
13 December, 1804. Our thermometer reads -20° today. Nothing new to report other than a group of French hunters came into camp.
US
Several of these men offered themselves to our party as interpreters.
Mister Charbonneau say he can speak Cree, Arikara, and Blackfoot.
I've been observing this Charbonneau...
...The man is an idiot.
Agreed.
Drouillard, thank this man for his offer but we only need those who can speak the Snake, or Shoshone, language...
...Only interpreters that can help us purchase horses to portage from the Missouri to the Columbia.
Désolé, il leur faut quelqu'un qui parle le Shoshone.
Ma femme!
Elle est Shoshone justement!
This indian girl, Sacagawea, is from Shoshone tribe...
Is perfect situation, but for one thing...
...She have baby in belly right now.

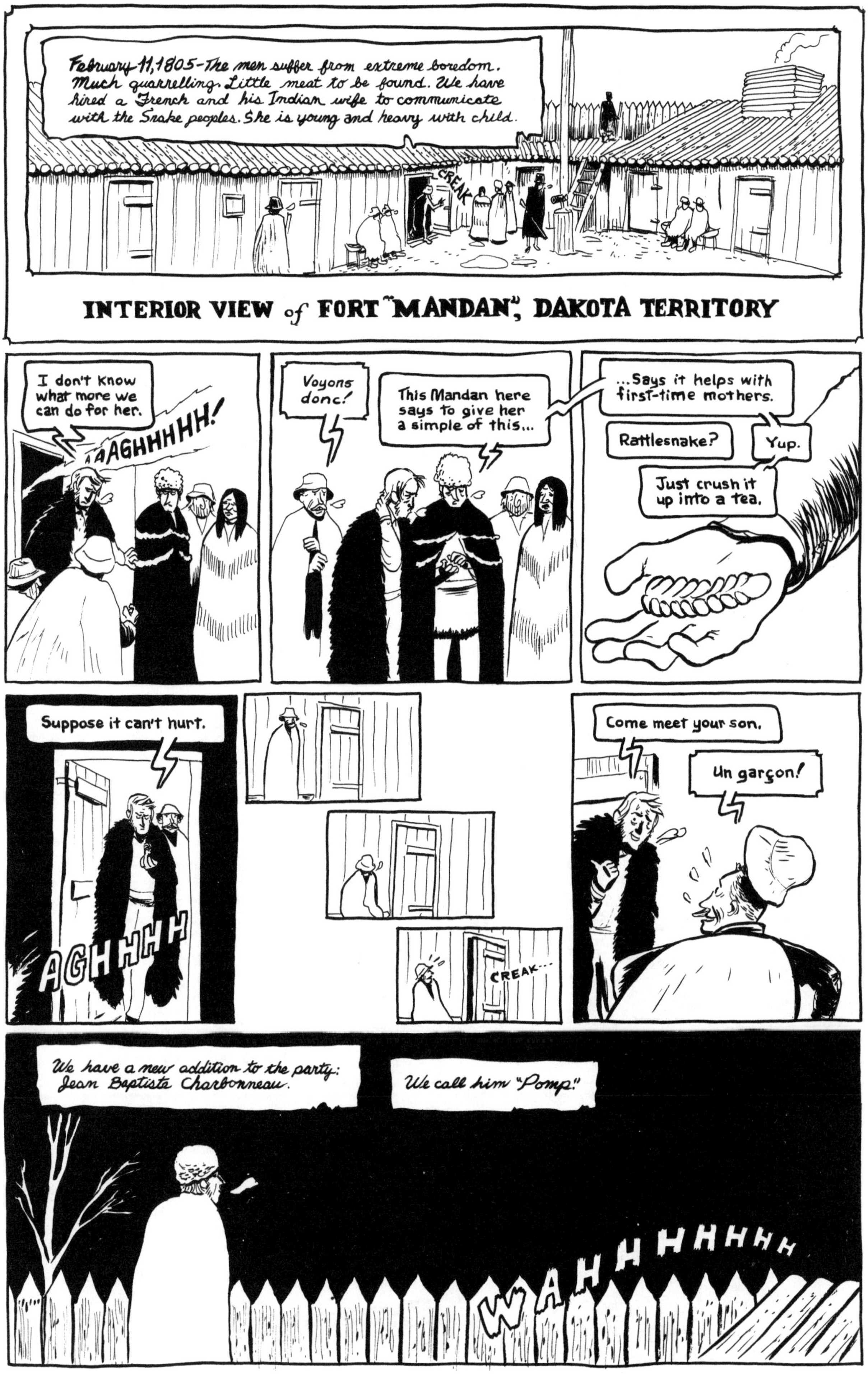
February 11, 1805 - The men suffer from extreme boredom. Much quarrelling. Little meat to be found. We have hired a French and his Indian wife to communicate with the Snake peoples. She is young and heavy with child.
CREAK
INTERIOR VIEW of FORT "MANDAN", DAKOTA TERRITORY
I don't know what more we can do for her.
AAAGHHHHH!
Voyons donc!
This Mandan here says to give her a simple of this...
...Says it helps with first-time mothers.
Rattlesnake?
Yup.
Just crush it up into a tea.
Suppose it can't hurt.
AGHHHH
CREAK...
Come meet your son.
Un garçon!
We have a new addition to the party: Jean Baptiste Charbonneau.
We call him "Pomp."
WAHHHHHHHH

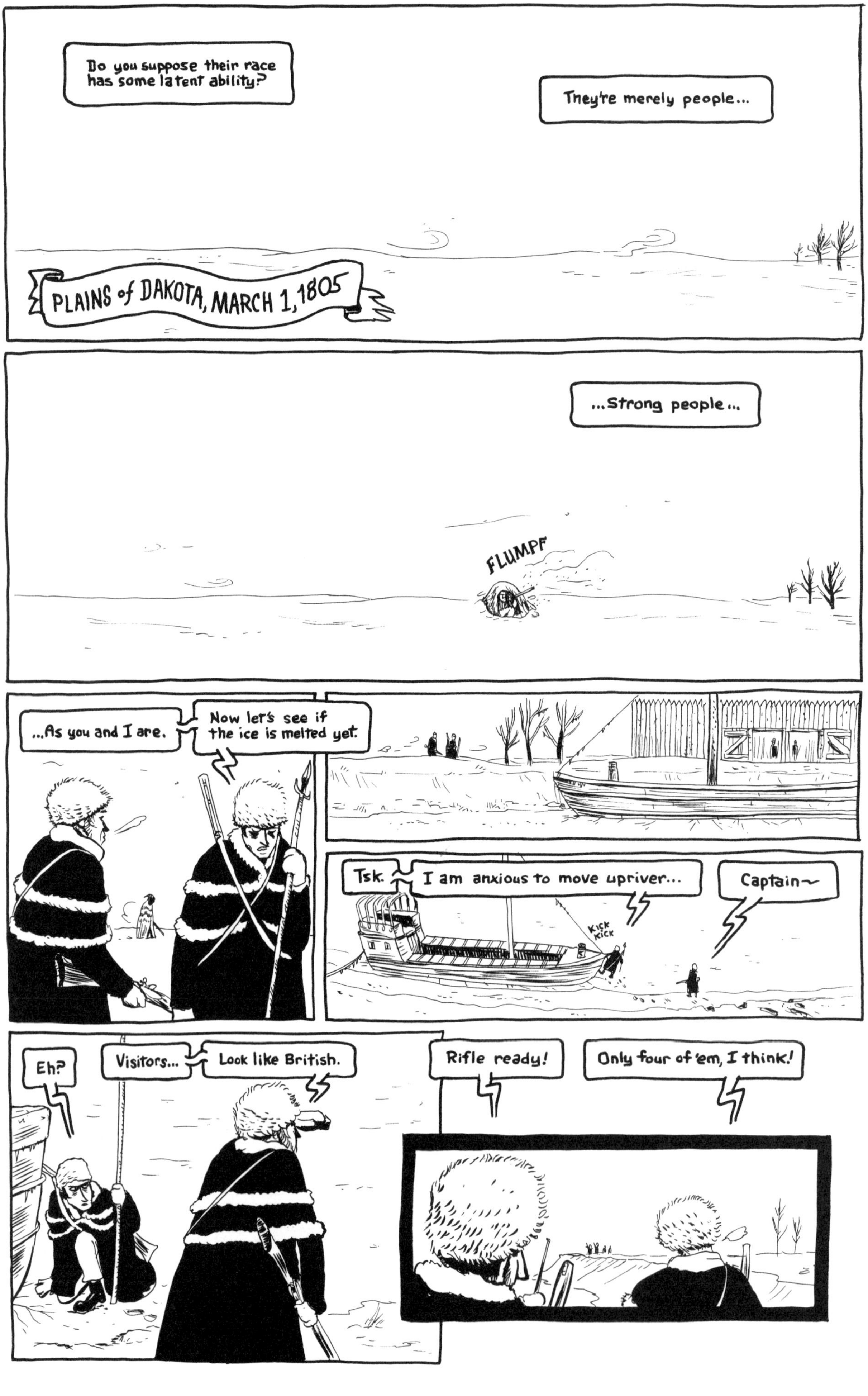

Do you suppose their race has some latent ability?
They're merely people...
PLAINS of DAKOTA, MARCH 1, 1805
...Strong people...
FLUMPF
...As you and I are.
Now let's see if the ice is melted yet.
Tsk.
I am anxious to move upriver...
KICK KICK
Captain~
Eh?
Visitors...
Look like British.
Rifle ready!
Only four of 'em, I think!

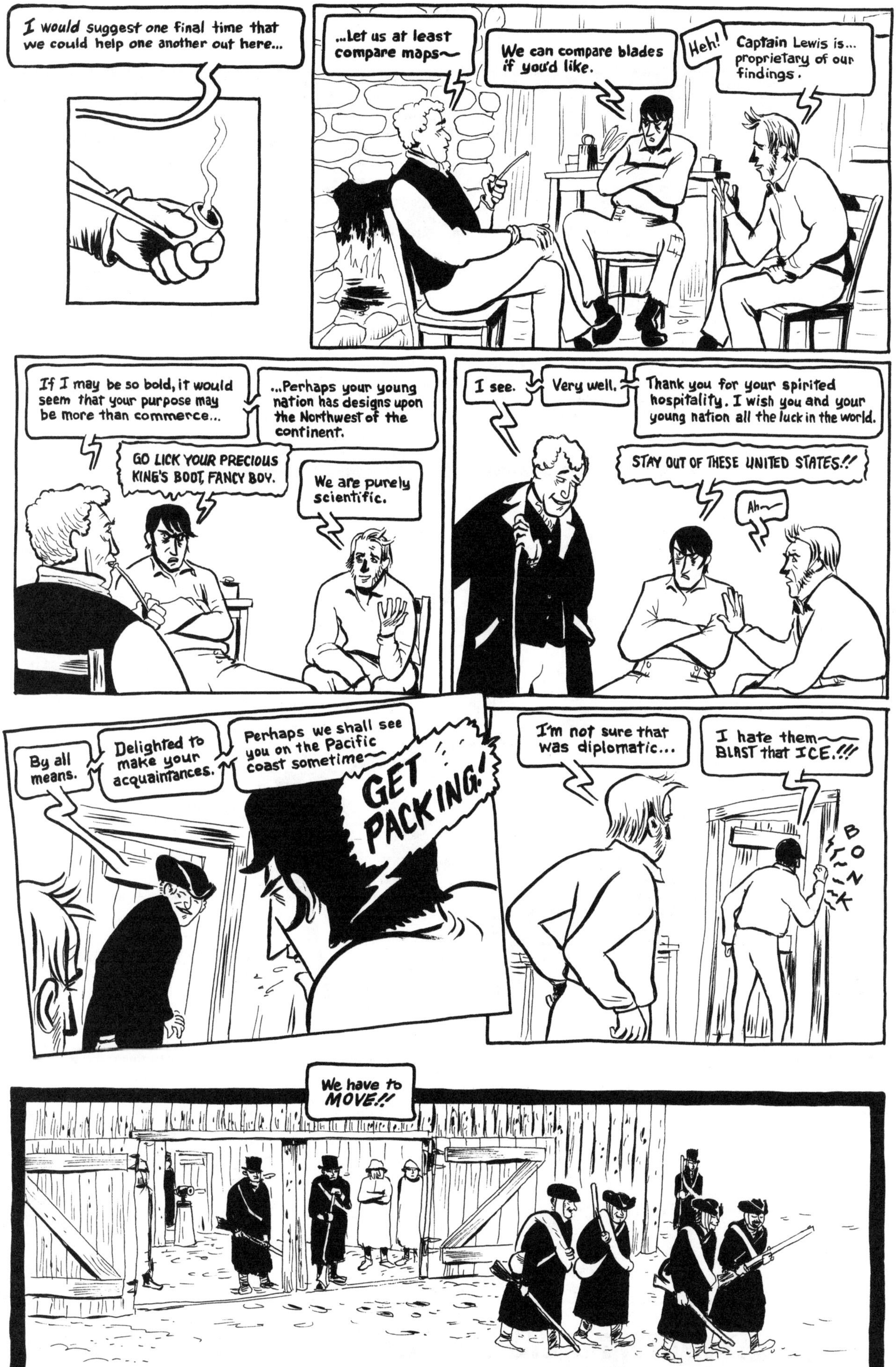
I would suggest one final time that we could help one another out here...
...Let us at least compare maps~
We can compare blades if you'd like.
Heh!
Captain Lewis is... proprietary of our findings.
If I may be so bold, it would seem that your purpose may be more than commerce...
...Perhaps your young nation has designs upon the Northwest of the continent.
GO LICK YOUR PRECIOUS KING'S BOOT, FANCY BOY.
We are purely scientific.
I see.
Very well.
Thank you for your spirited hospitality. I wish you and your young nation all the luck in the world.
STAY OUT OF THESE UNITED STATES!!!
Ah~
By all means.
Delighted to make your acquaintances.
Perhaps we shall see you on the Pacific coast sometime~
GET PACKING!
I'm not sure that was diplomatic...
I hate them~ BLAST that ICE!!!
BONK
We have to MOVE!!

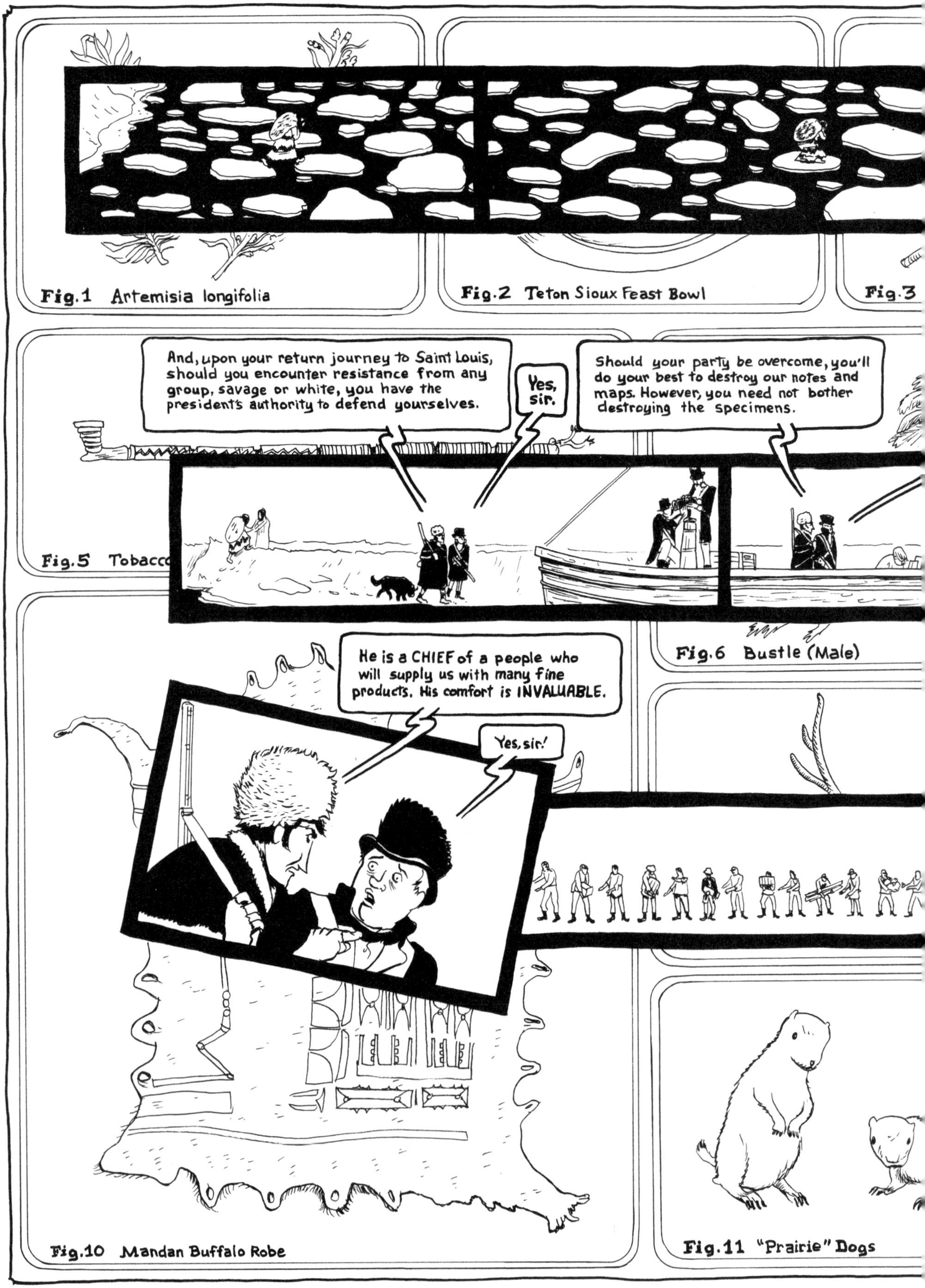
Fig.1 Artemisia longifolia
Fig.2 Teton Sioux Feast Bowl
Fig.3
Fig.5 Tobacco
And, upon your return journey to Saint Louis, should you encounter resistance from any group, savage or white, you have the president's authority to defend yourselves.
Yes, sir.
Should your party be overcome, you'll do your best to destroy our notes and maps. However, you need not bother destroying the specimens.
Fig.6 Bustle (Male)
He is a CHIEF of a people who will supply us with many fine products. His comfort is INVALUABLE.
Yes, sir!
Fig.10 Mandan Buffalo Robe
Fig.11 "Prairie" Dogs

A SAMPLING of CAPT. M. LEWIS'S DISCOVERIES for PRES.

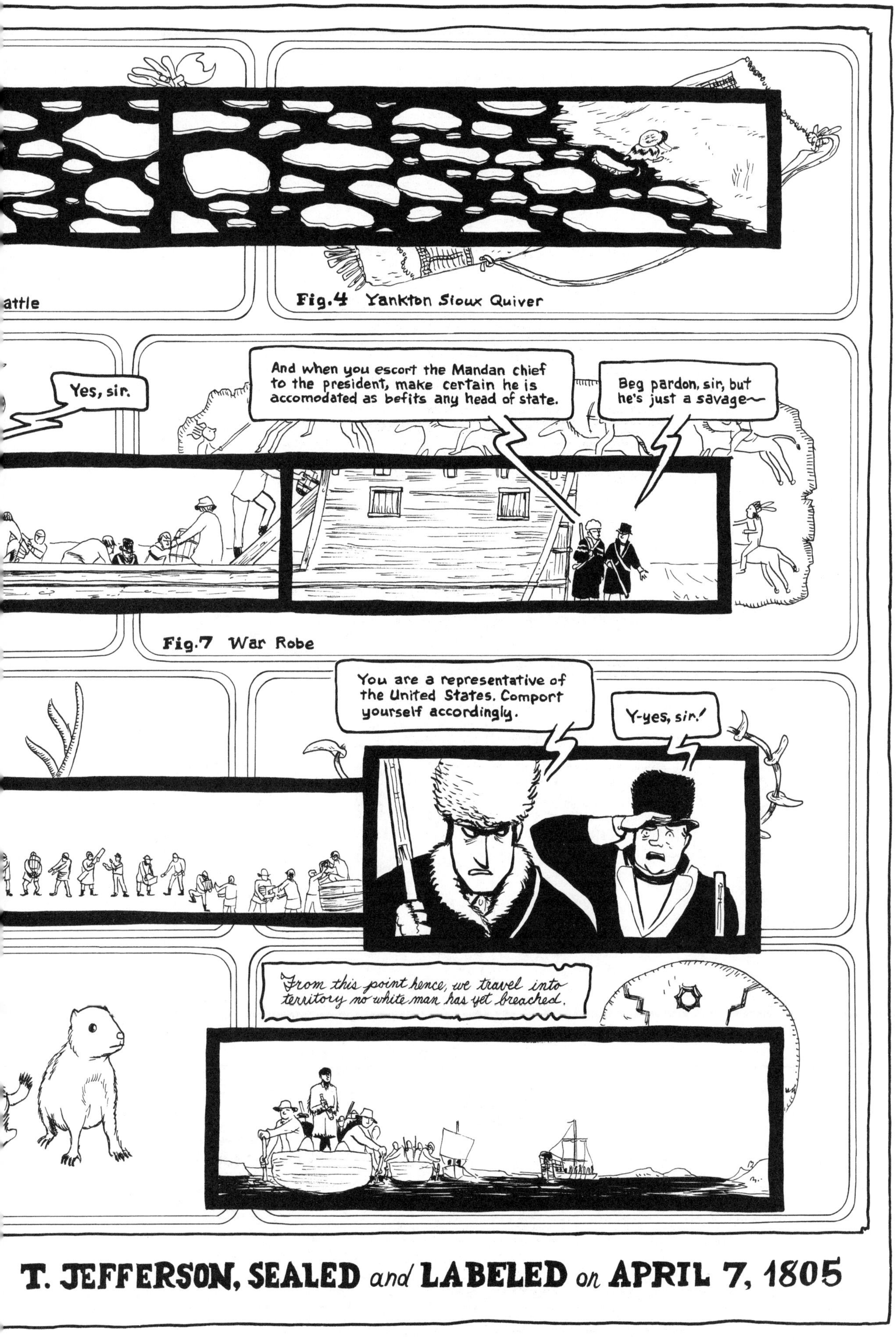

attle
Fig.4 Yankton Sioux Quiver
Yes, sir.
And when you escort the Mandan chief to the president, make certain he is accomodated as befits any head of state.
Beg pardon, sir, but he's just a savage~
Fig.7 War Robe
You are a representative of the United States. Comport yourself accordingly.
Y-yes, sir!
From this point hence, we travel into territory no white man has yet breached.

T. JEFFERSON, SEALED *and* LABELED *on* APRIL 7, 1805

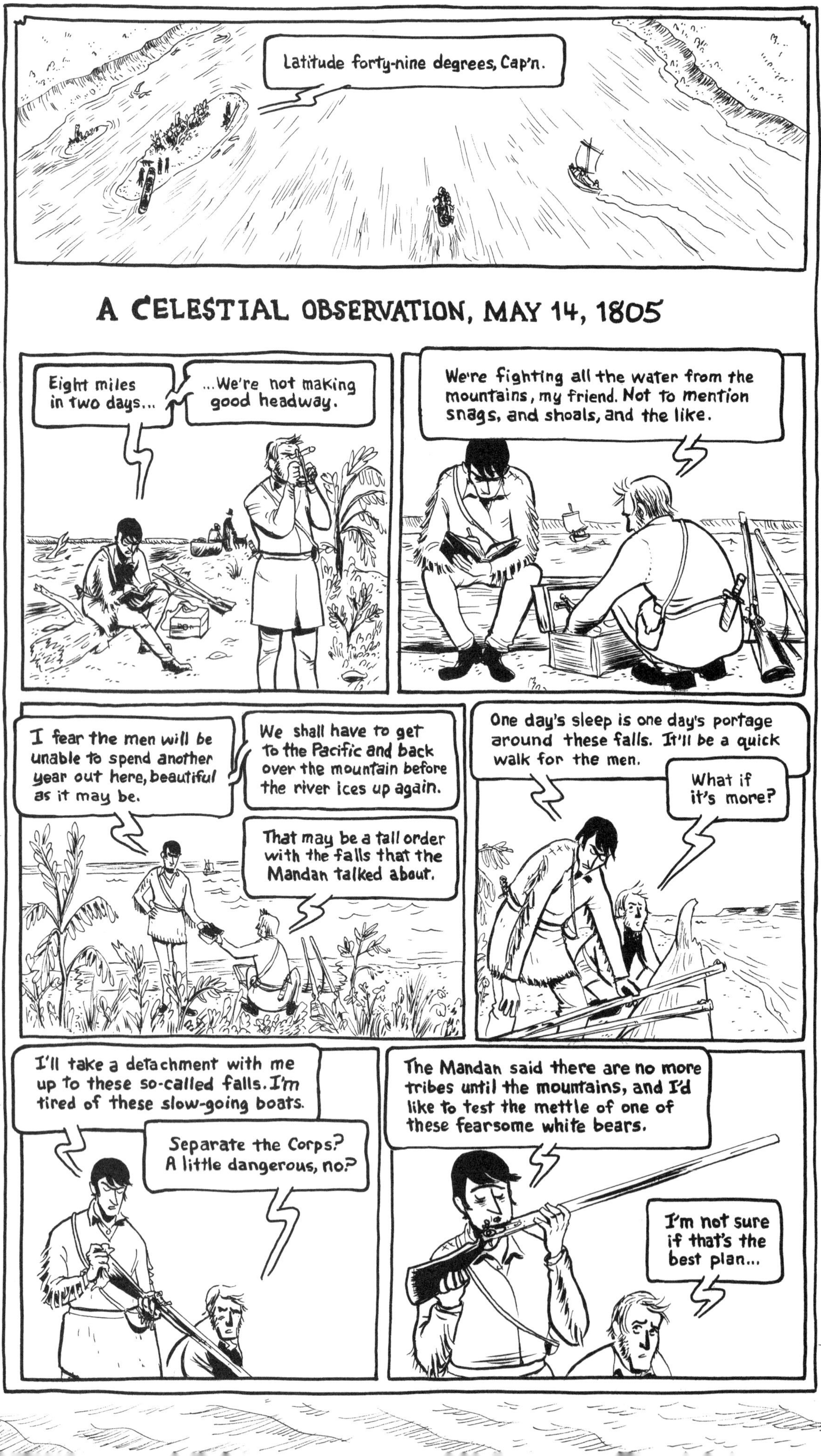
Latitude forty-nine degrees, Cap'n.
A CELESTIAL OBSERVATION, MAY 14, 1805
Eight miles in two days...
...We're not making good headway.
We're fighting all the water from the mountains, my friend. Not to mention snags, and shoals, and the like.
I fear the men will be unable to spend another year out here, beautiful as it may be.
We shall have to get to the Pacific and back over the mountain before the river ices up again.
That may be a tall order with the falls that the Mandan talked about.
One day's sleep is one day's portage around these falls. It'll be a quick walk for the men.
What if it's more?
I'll take a detachment with me up to these so-called falls. I'm tired of these slow-going boats.
Separate the Corps? A little dangerous, no?
The Mandan said there are no more tribes until the mountains, and I'd like to test the mettle of one of these fearsome white bears.
I'm not sure if that's the best plan...

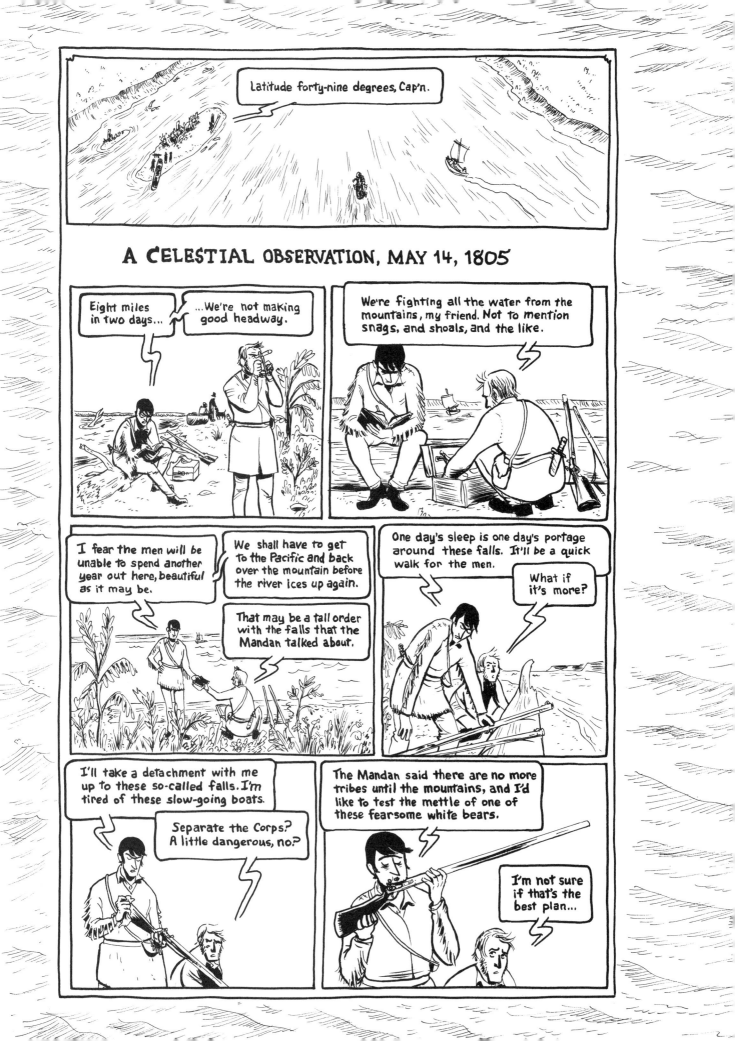

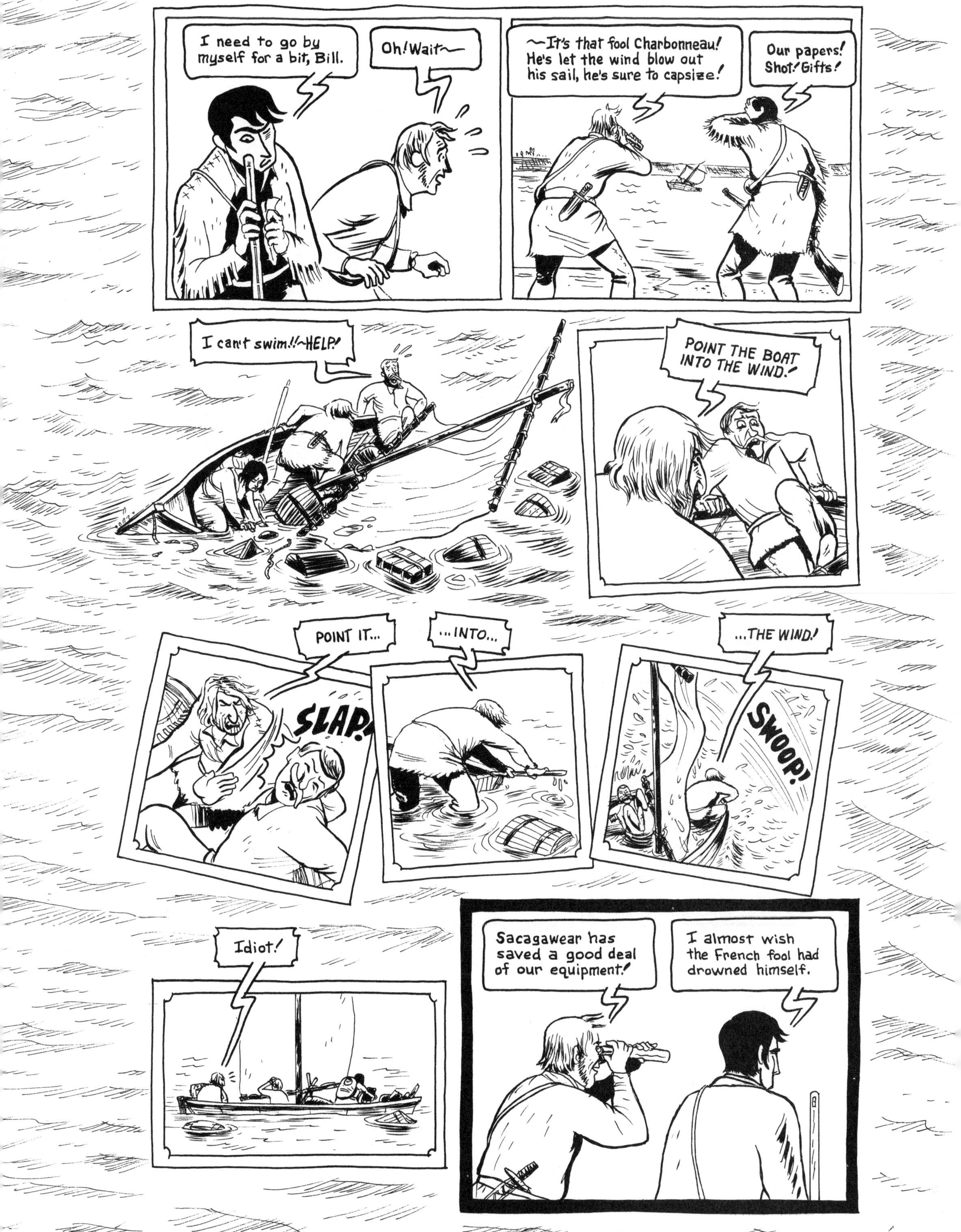
I need to go by myself for a bit, Bill.
Oh! Wait~
~It's that fool Charbonneau! He's let the wind blow out his sail, he's sure to capsize!
Our papers! Shot! Gifts!
I can't swim!! ~HELP!
POINT THE BOAT INTO THE WIND!
POINT IT...
SLAP!
...INTO...
...THE WIND!
SWOOP!
Idiot!
Sacagawear has saved a good deal of our equipment!
I almost wish the French fool had drowned himself.

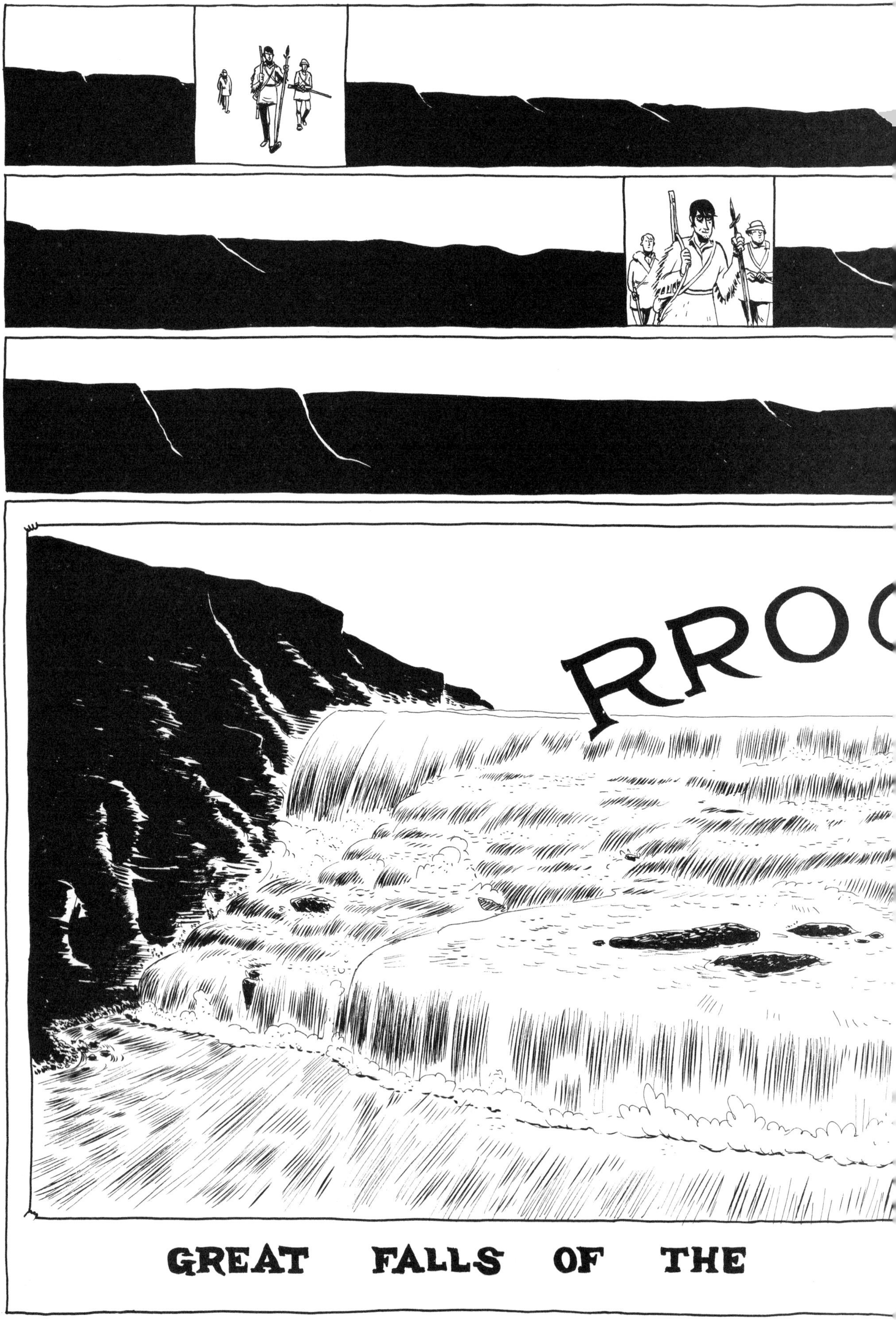
RROO
GREAT FALLS OF THE

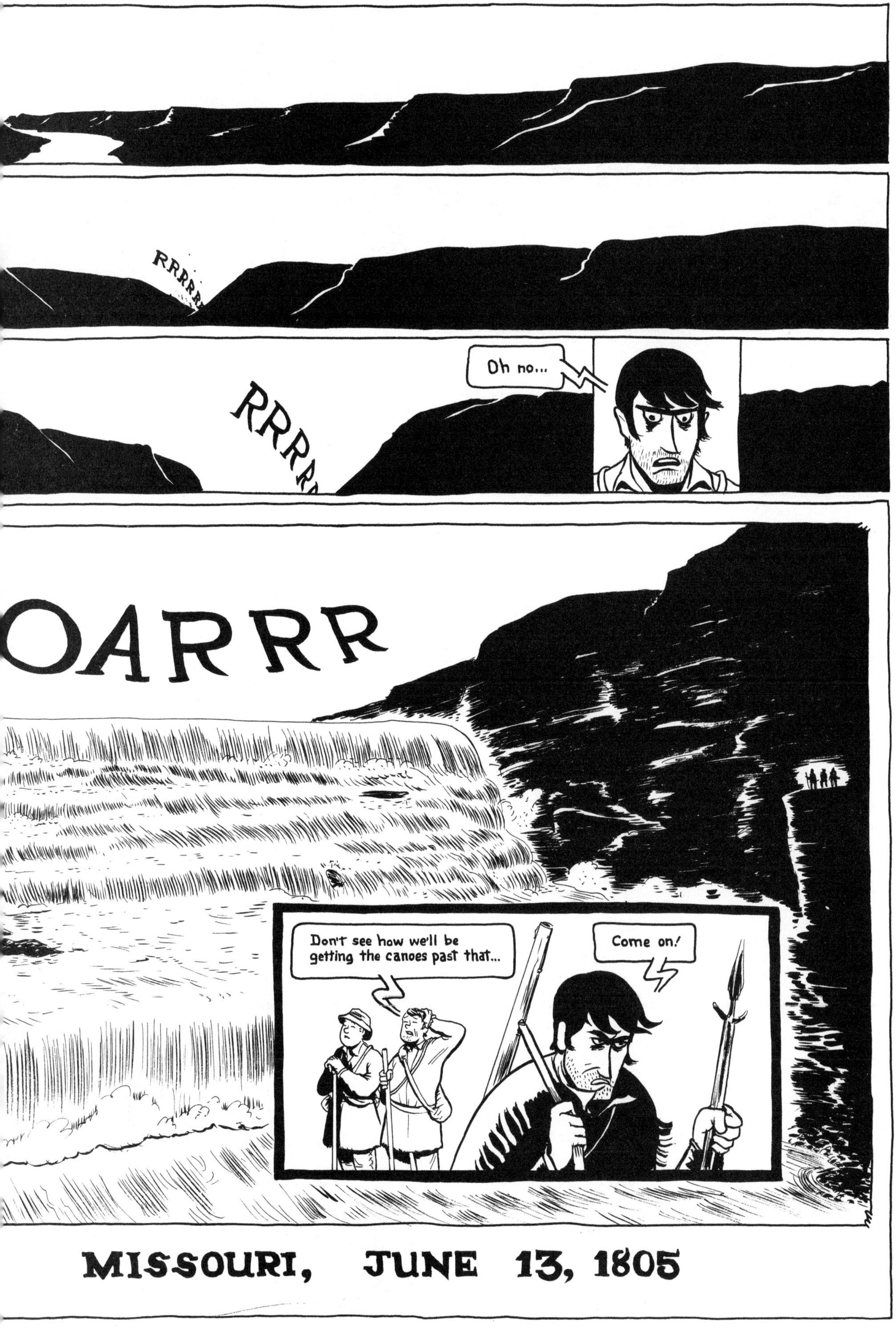

RRRRR
RRRRR
Oh no...
OARRR
Don't see how we'll be getting the canoes past that...
Come on!
MISSOURI, JUNE 13, 1805

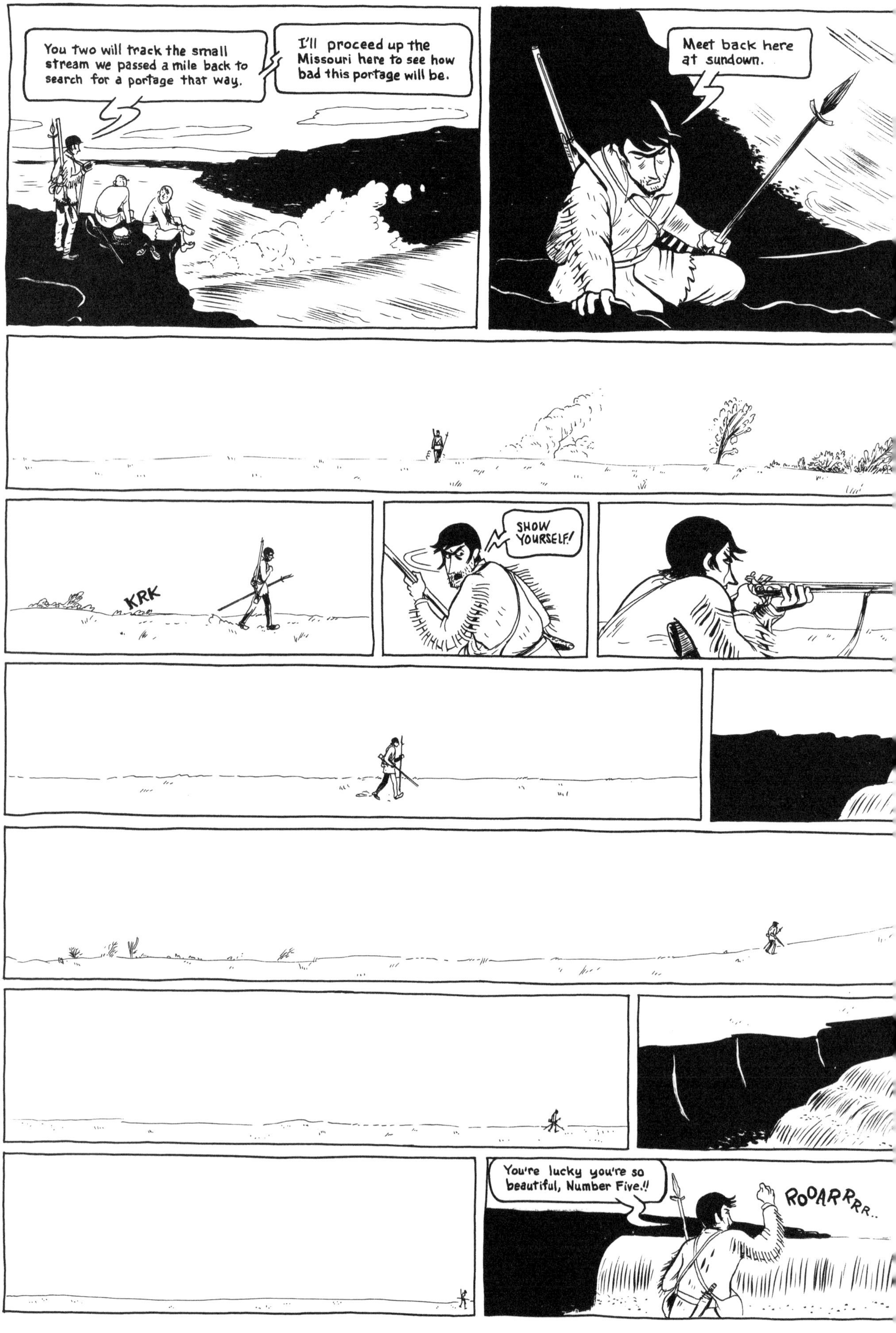
You two will track the small stream we passed a mile back to search for a portage that way.
I'll proceed up the Missouri here to see how bad this portage will be.
Meet back here at sundown.
KRK
SHOW YOURSELF!
You're lucky you're so beautiful, Number Five.!!
ROOARRRR..

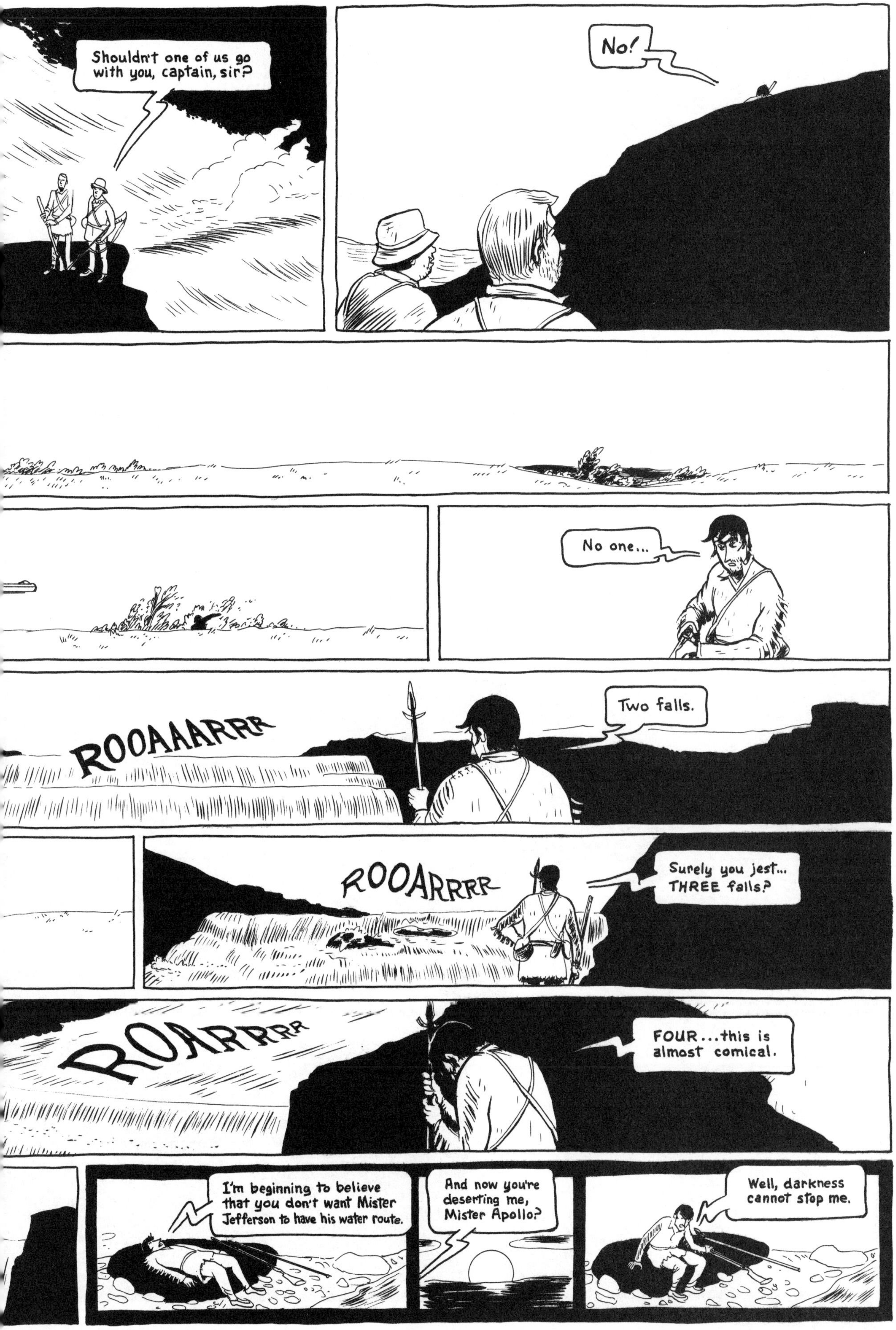
Shouldn't one of us go with you, captain, sir?
No!
No one...
ROOAAARRR
Two falls.
ROOARRRR
Surely you jest... THREE falls?
ROARRRRR
FOUR...this is almost comical.
I'm beginning to believe that you don't want Mister Jefferson to have his water route.
And now you're deserting me, Mister Apollo?
Well, darkness cannot stop me.

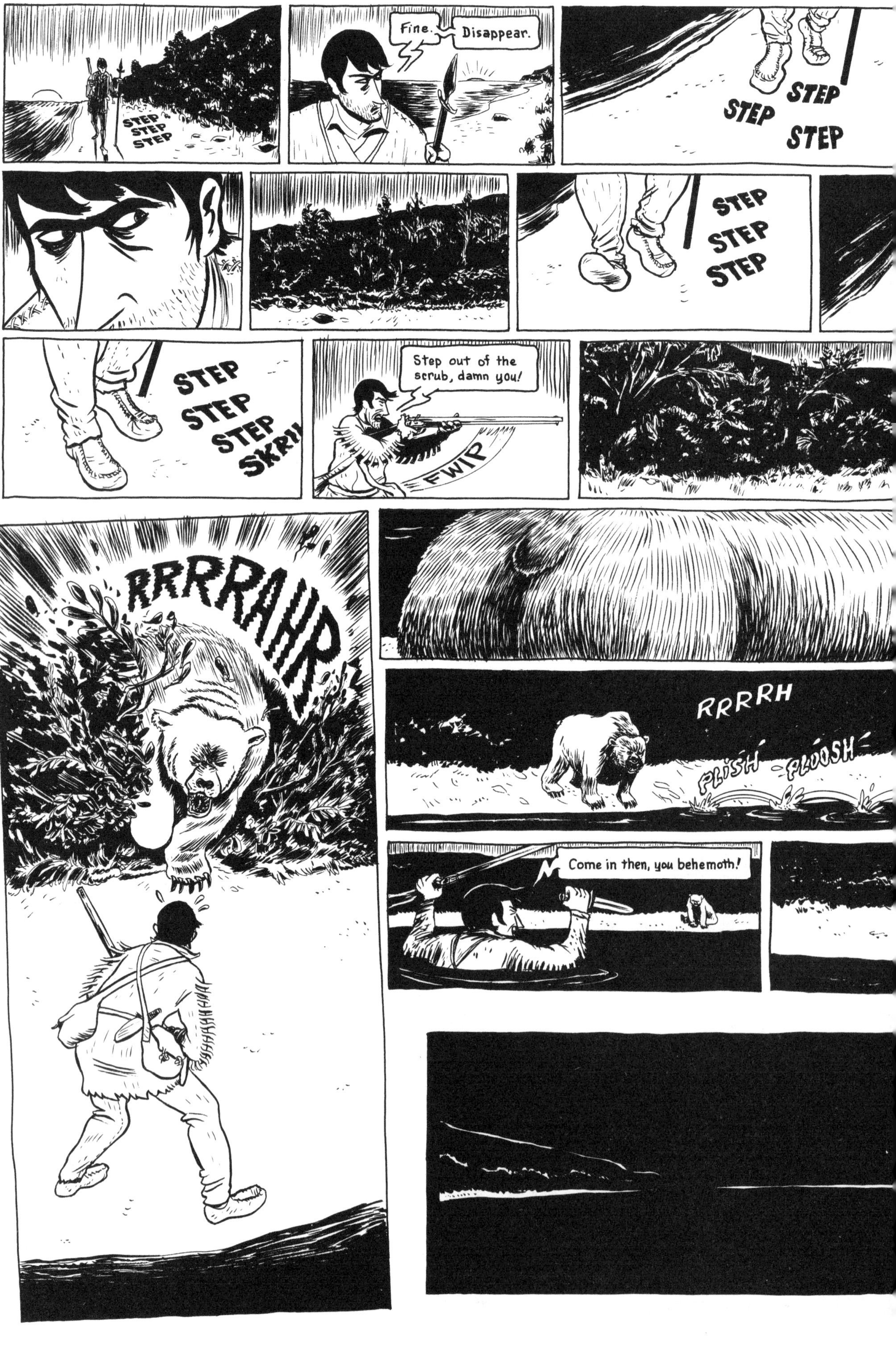
STEP STEP STEP
Fine.
Disappear.
STEP STEP STEP
STEP STEP STEP
STEP STEP STEP SKRI
Step out of the scrub, damn you!
FWIP
RRRRAHR
RRRRH
PLISH
PLOOSH
Come in then, you behemoth!

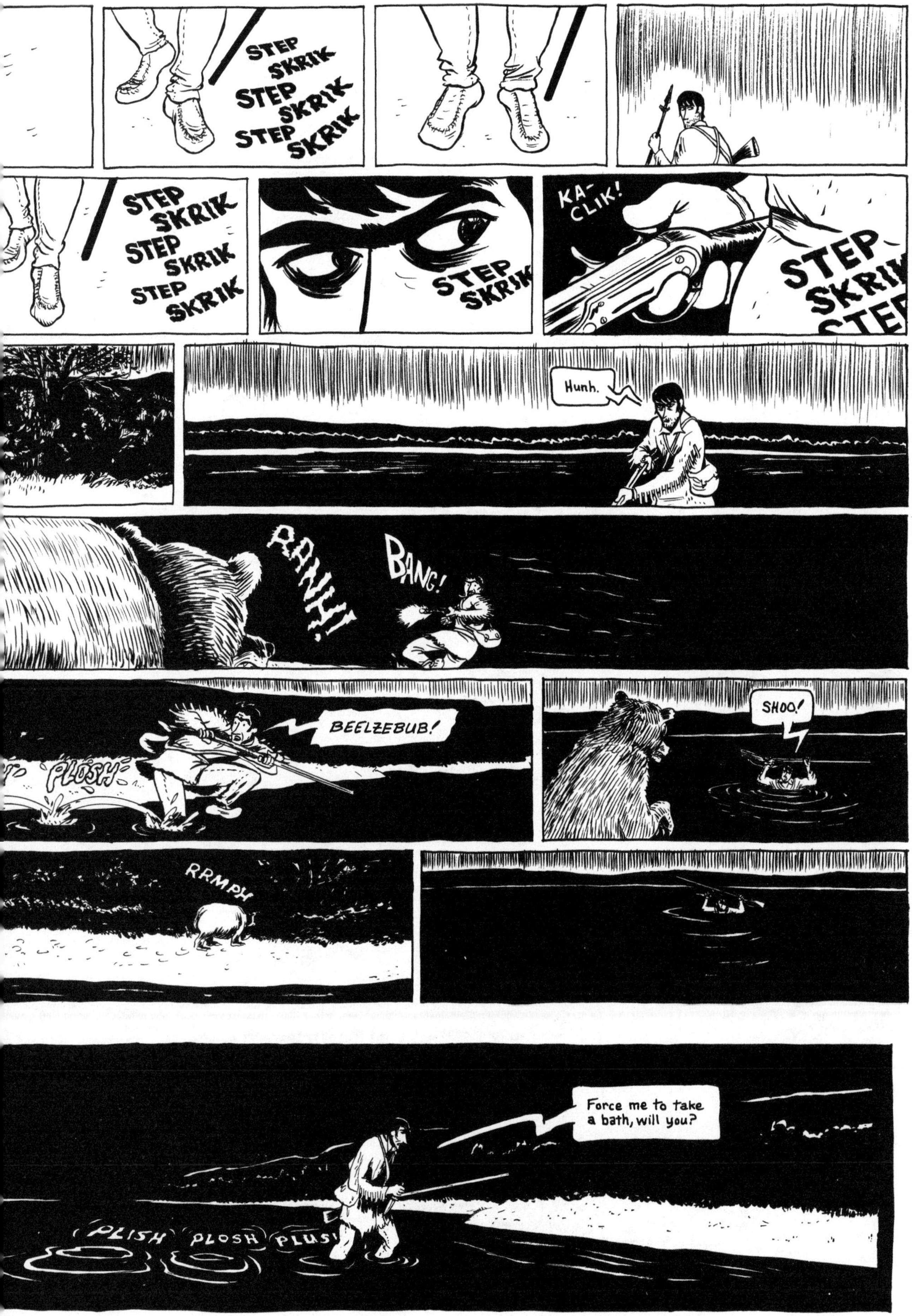
STEP
SKRIK
STEP
SKRIK
STEP
SKRIK
STEP
SKRIK
STEP
SKRIK
STEP
SKRIK
STEP
SKRIK
KA-CLIK!
STEP
SKRI
STE
Hunh.
RAWH!
BANG!
PLOSH
BEELZEBUB!
SHOO!
RRMPH
Force me to take a bath, will you?
PLISH
PLOSH
PLUS

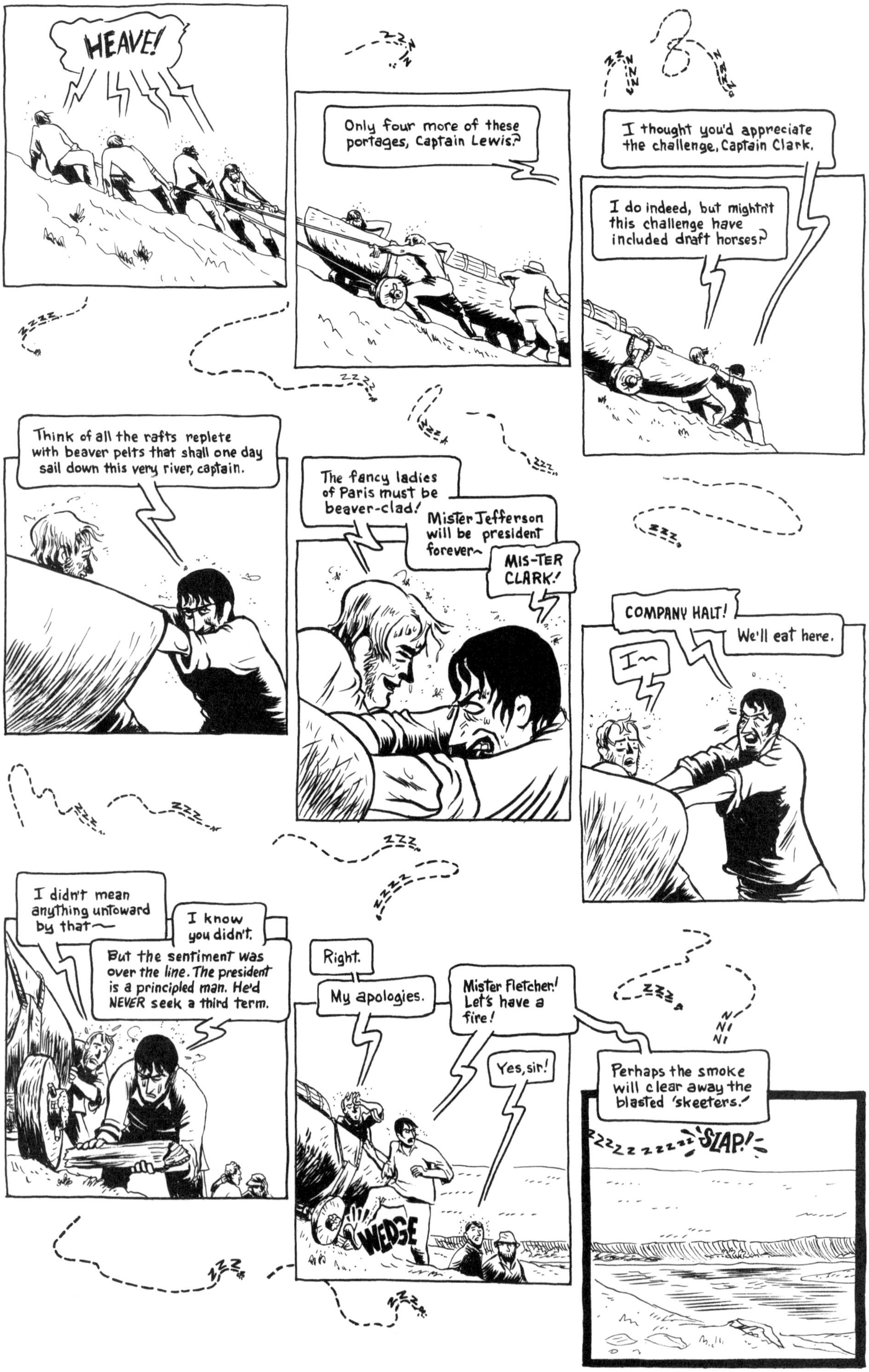
HEAVE!
Only four more of these portages, Captain Lewis?
I thought you'd appreciate the challenge, Captain Clark.
I do indeed, but mightn't this challenge have included draft horses?
Think of all the rafts replete with beaver pelts that shall one day sail down this very river, captain.
The fancy ladies of Paris must be beaver-clad!
Mister Jefferson will be president forever~
MIS-TER CLARK!
COMPANY HALT!
We'll eat here.
I~
I didn't mean anything untoward by that~
I know you didn't.
But the sentiment was over the line. The president is a principled man. He'd NEVER seek a third term.
Right.
My apologies.
Mister Fletcher! Let's have a fire!
Yes, sir!
Perhaps the smoke will clear away the blasted 'skeeters.
WEDGE
SLAP!

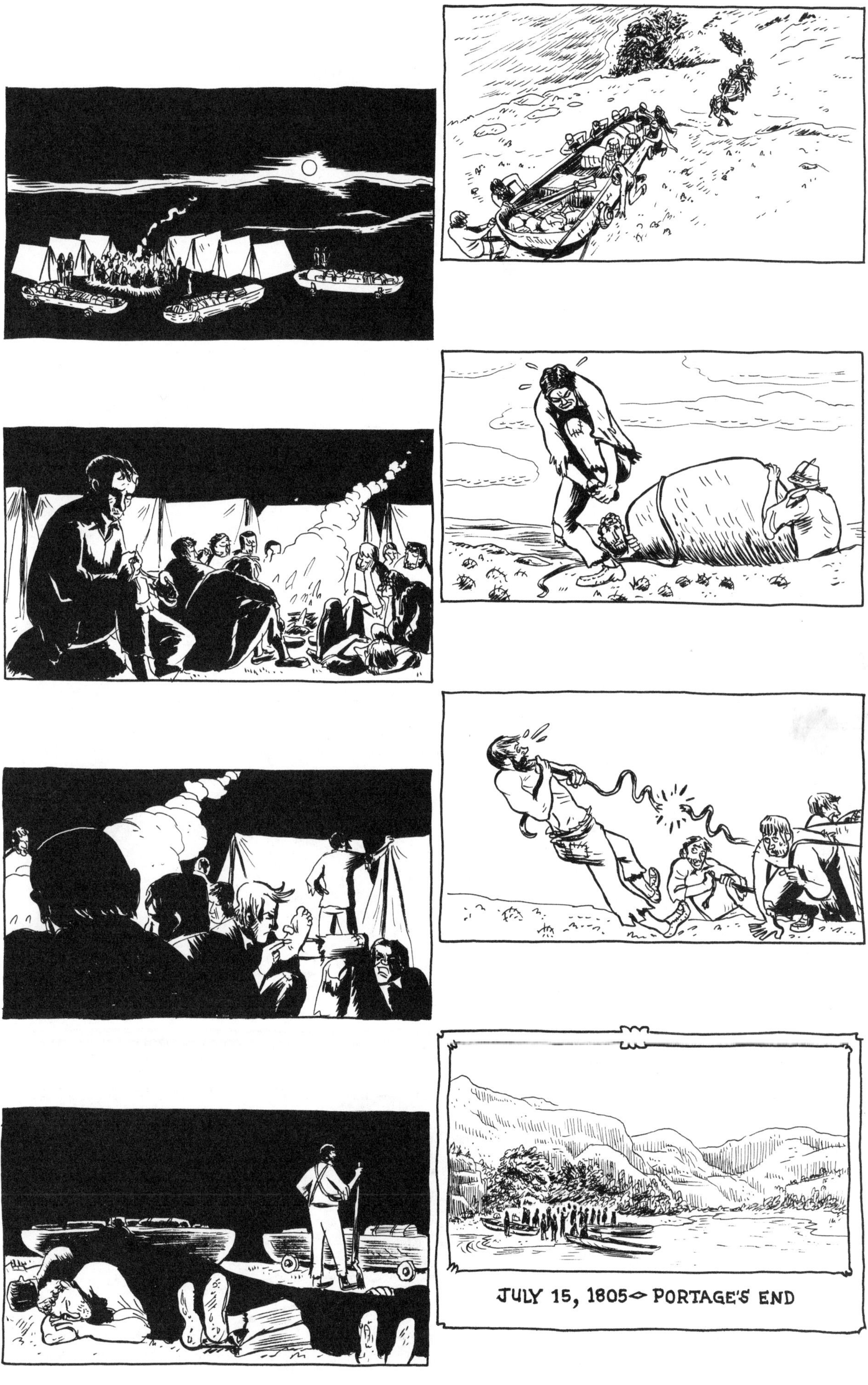
JULY 15, 1805 ◇ PORTAGE'S END

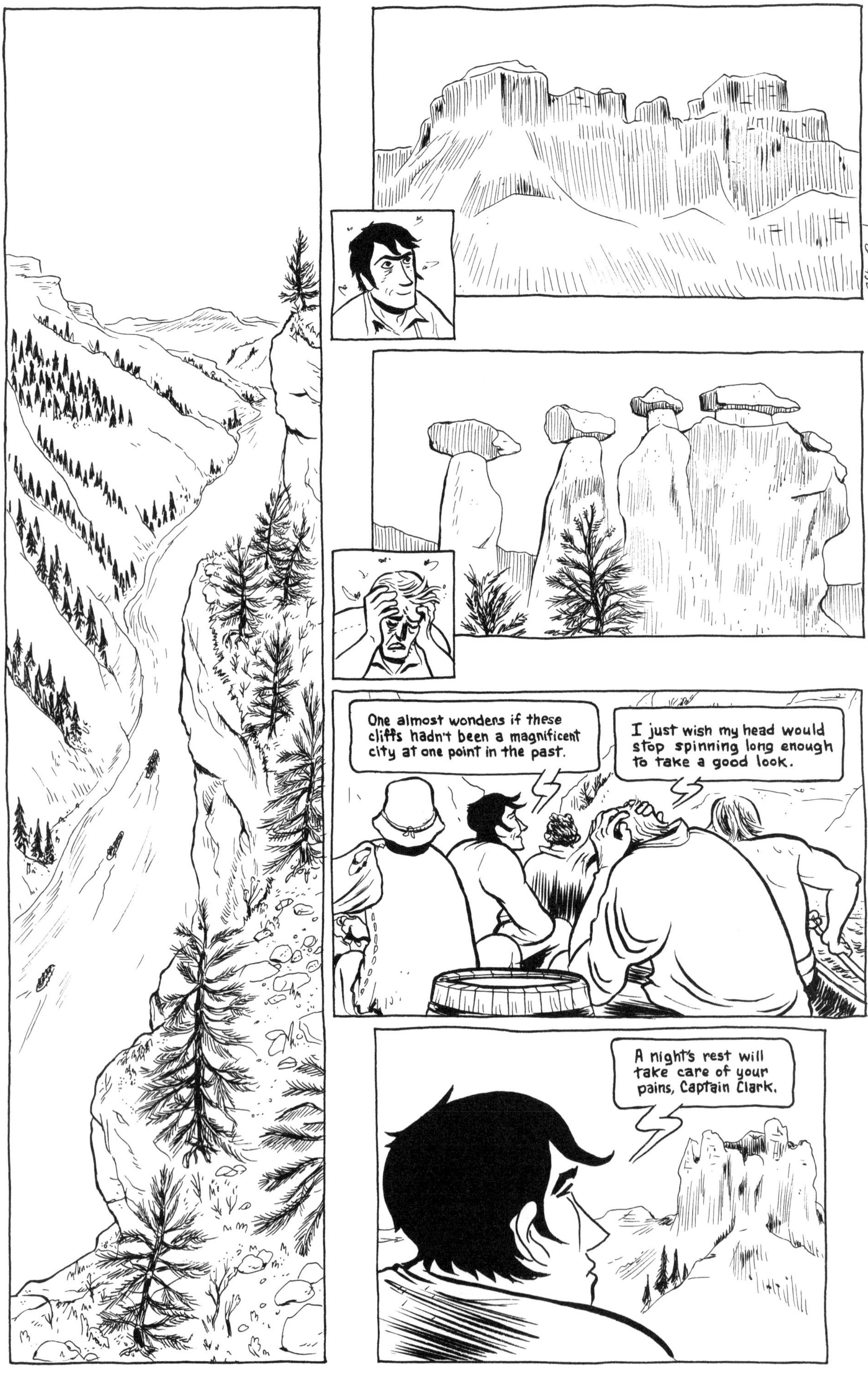

After Bodmer
One almost wonders if these cliffs hadn't been a magnificent city at one point in the past.
I just wish my head would stop spinning long enough to take a good look.
A night's rest will take care of your pains, Captain Clark.

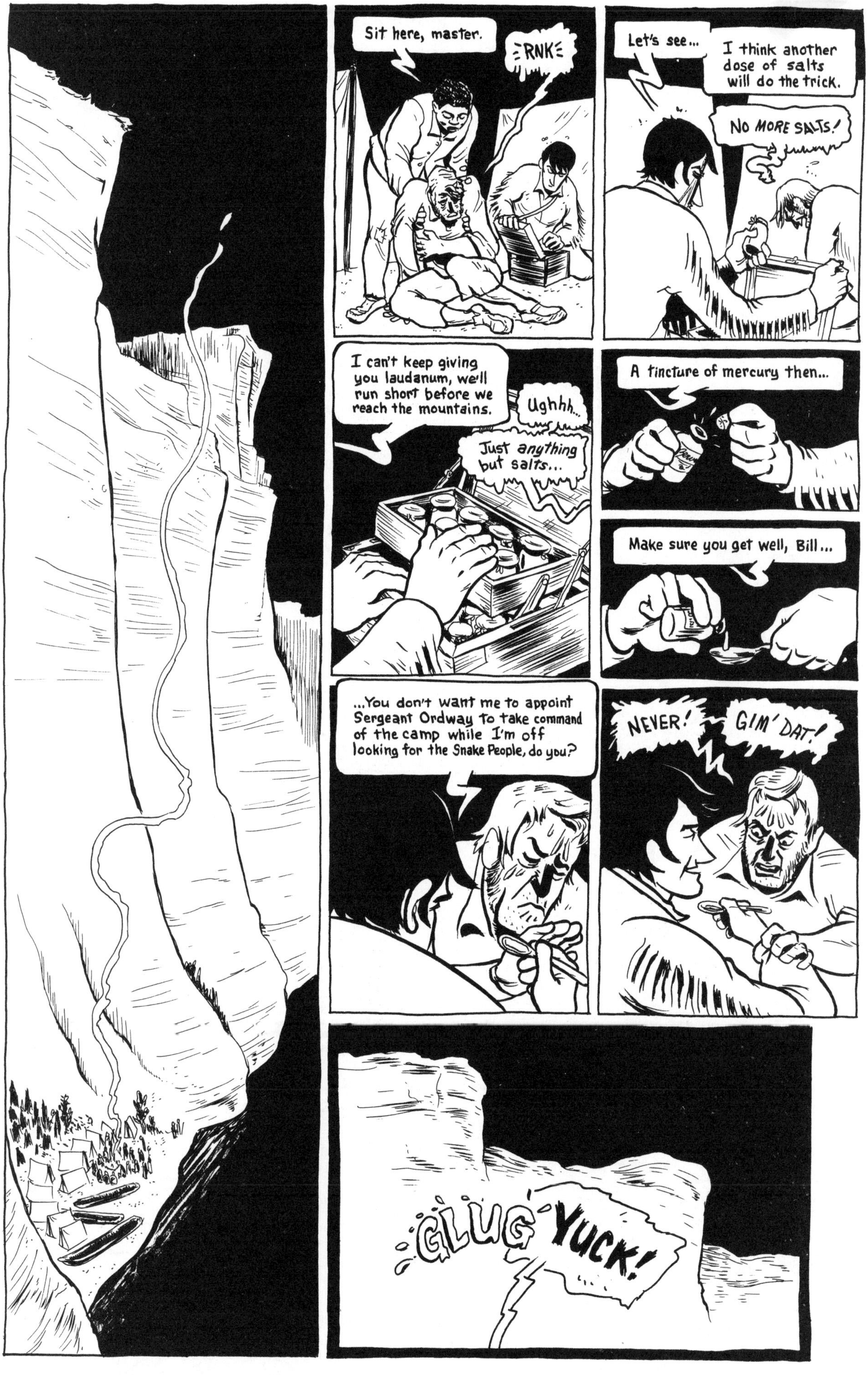
Sit here, master.
RNK
Let's see...
I think another dose of salts will do the trick.
NO MORE SALTS!
I can't keep giving you laudanum, we'll run short before we reach the mountains.
Ughhh...
Just anything but salts...
A tincture of mercury then...
Make sure you get well, Bill...
...You don't want me to appoint Sergeant Ordway to take command of the camp while I'm off looking for the Snake People, do you?
NEVER!
GIM' DAT!
GLUG
YUCK!

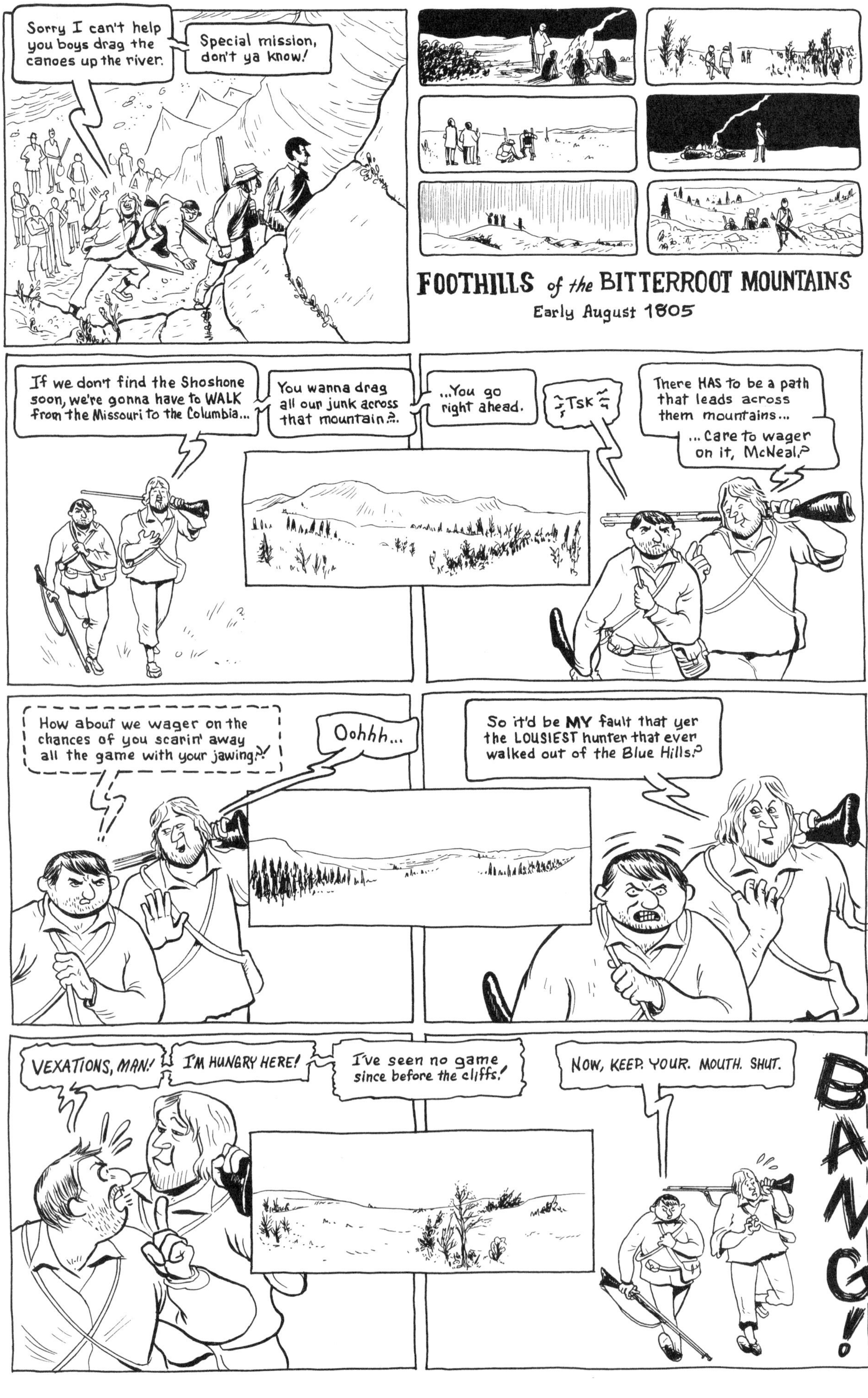

Sorry I can't help you boys drag the canoes up the river.
Special mission, don't ya know!
FOOTHILLS of the BITTERROOT MOUNTAINS
Early August 1805
If we don't find the Shoshone soon, we're gonna have to WALK from the Missouri to the Columbia...
You wanna drag all our junk across that mountain?
...You go right ahead.
Tsk
There HAS to be a path that leads across them mountains...
...Care to wager on it, McNeal?
How about we wager on the chances of you scarin' away all the game with your jawing?
Oohhh...
So it'd be MY fault that yer the LOUSIEST hunter that ever walked out of the Blue Hills?
VEXATIONS, MAN!
I'M HUNGRY HERE!
I've seen no game since before the cliffs!
NOW, KEEP. YOUR. MOUTH. SHUT.
BANG!

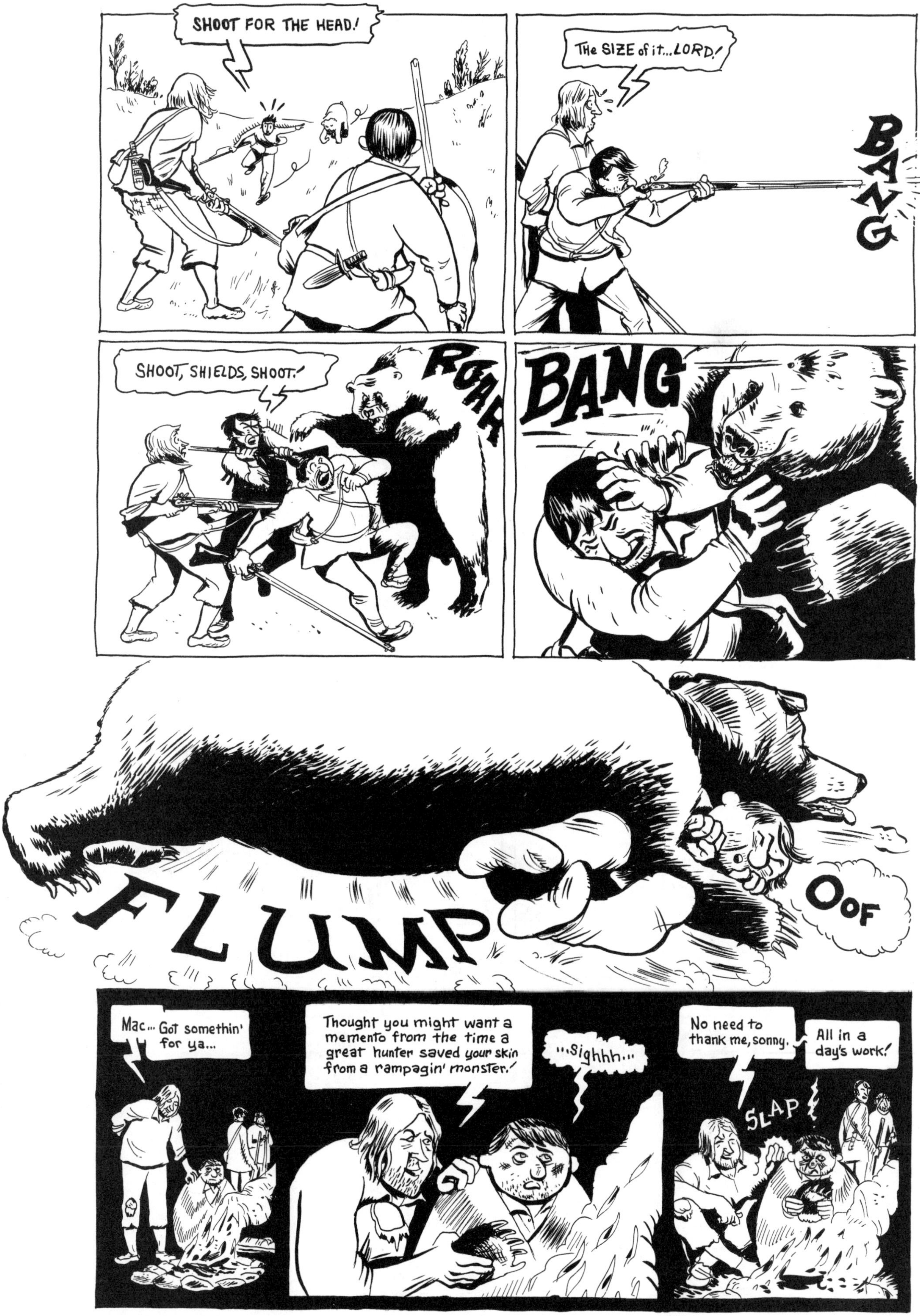

SHOOT FOR THE HEAD!
The SIZE of it... LORD!
BANG
SHOOT, SHIELDS, SHOOT!
ROAR
BANG
FLUMP
OOF
Mac... Got somethin' for ya...
Thought you might want a memento from the time a great hunter saved your skin from a rampagin' monster!
...Sighhh...
No need to thank me, sonny.
All in a day's work!
SLAP

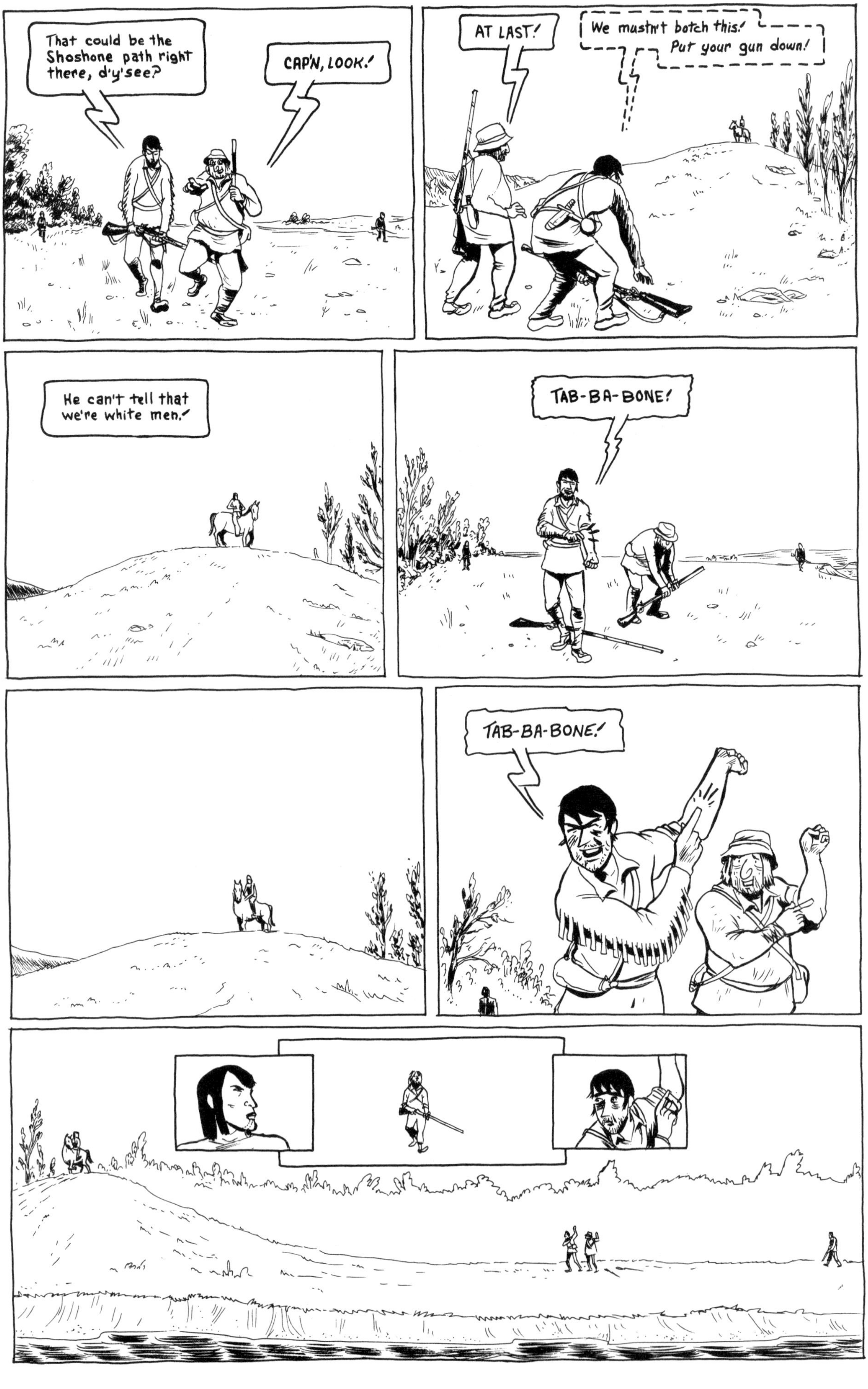
That could be the Shoshone path right there, d'y'see?
CAP'N, LOOK!
AT LAST!
We mustn't botch this! Put your gun down!
He can't tell that we're white men!
TAB-BA-BONE!
TAB-BA-BONE!

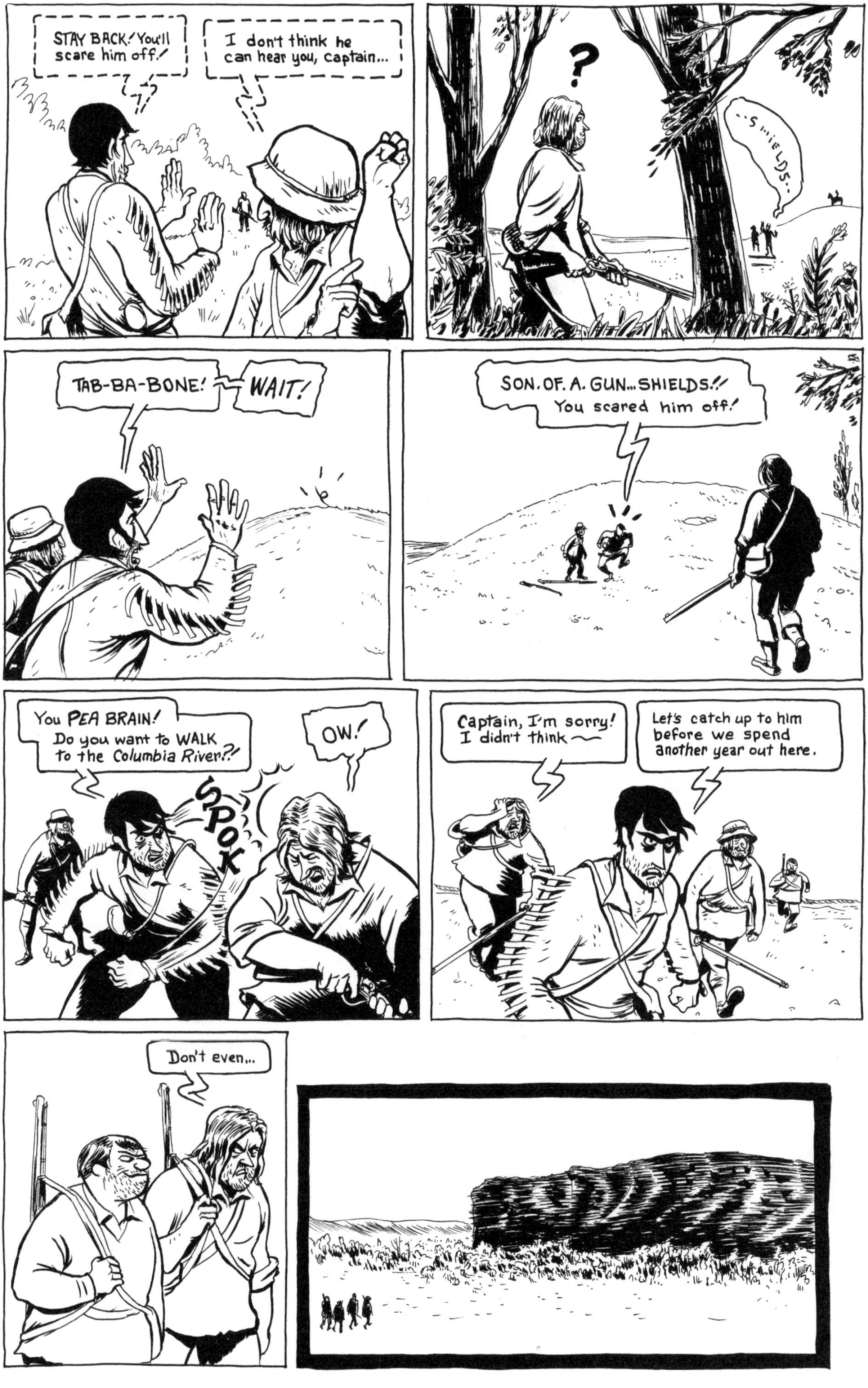
STAY BACK! You'll scare him off!
I don't think he can hear you, captain...
?
...SHIELDS...
TAB-BA-BONE!
WAIT!
SON.OF.A.GUN...SHIELDS!!
You scared him off!
You PEA BRAIN! Do you want to WALK to the Columbia River?!
SPOK
OW!
Captain, I'm sorry! I didn't think ~
Let's catch up to him before we spend another year out here.
Don't even...

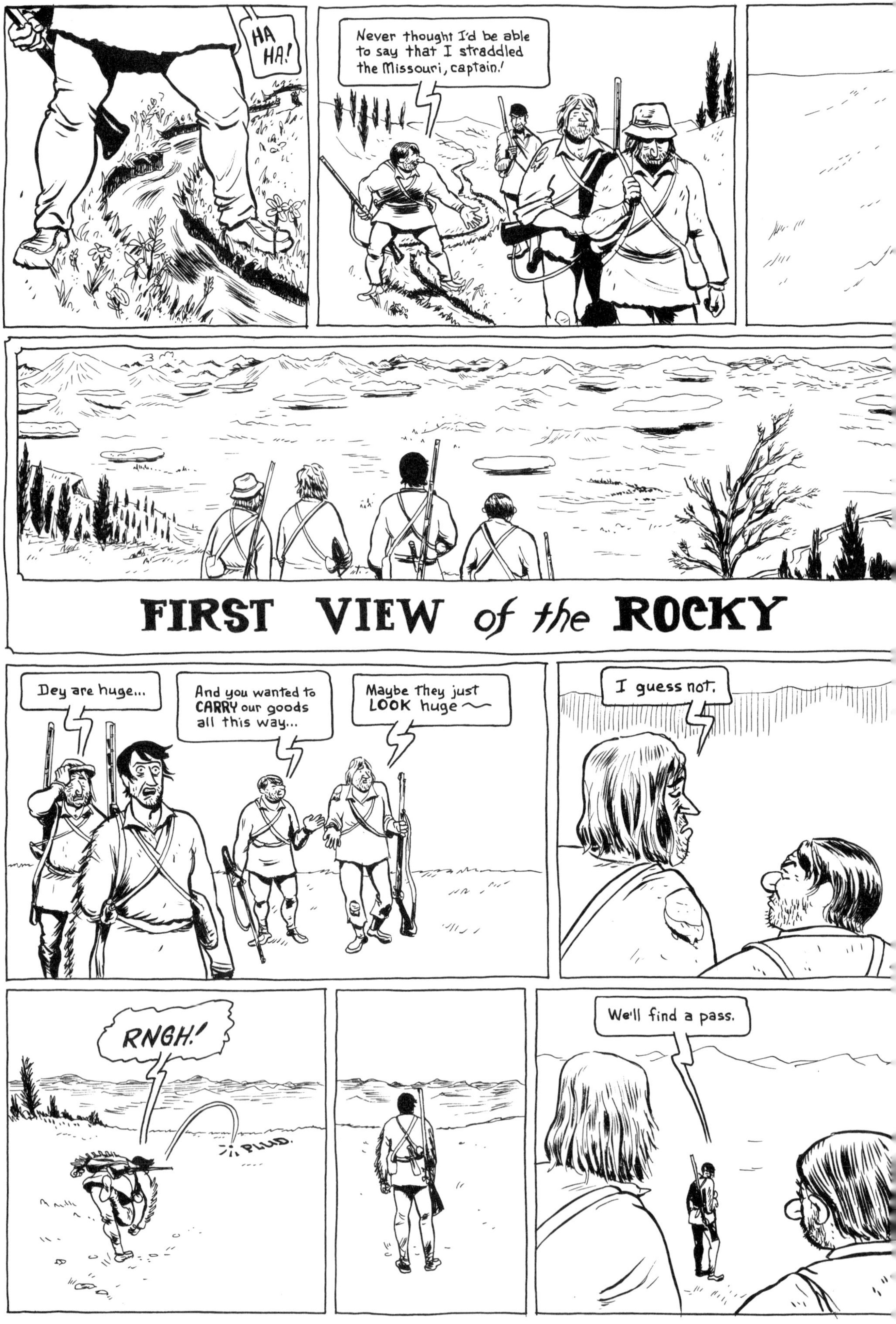
HA HA!
Never thought I'd be able to say that I straddled the Missouri, captain!
FIRST VIEW of the ROCKY
Dey are huge...
And you wanted to CARRY our goods all this way...
Maybe they just LOOK huge~
I guess not.
RNGH!
PLUD
We'll find a pass.

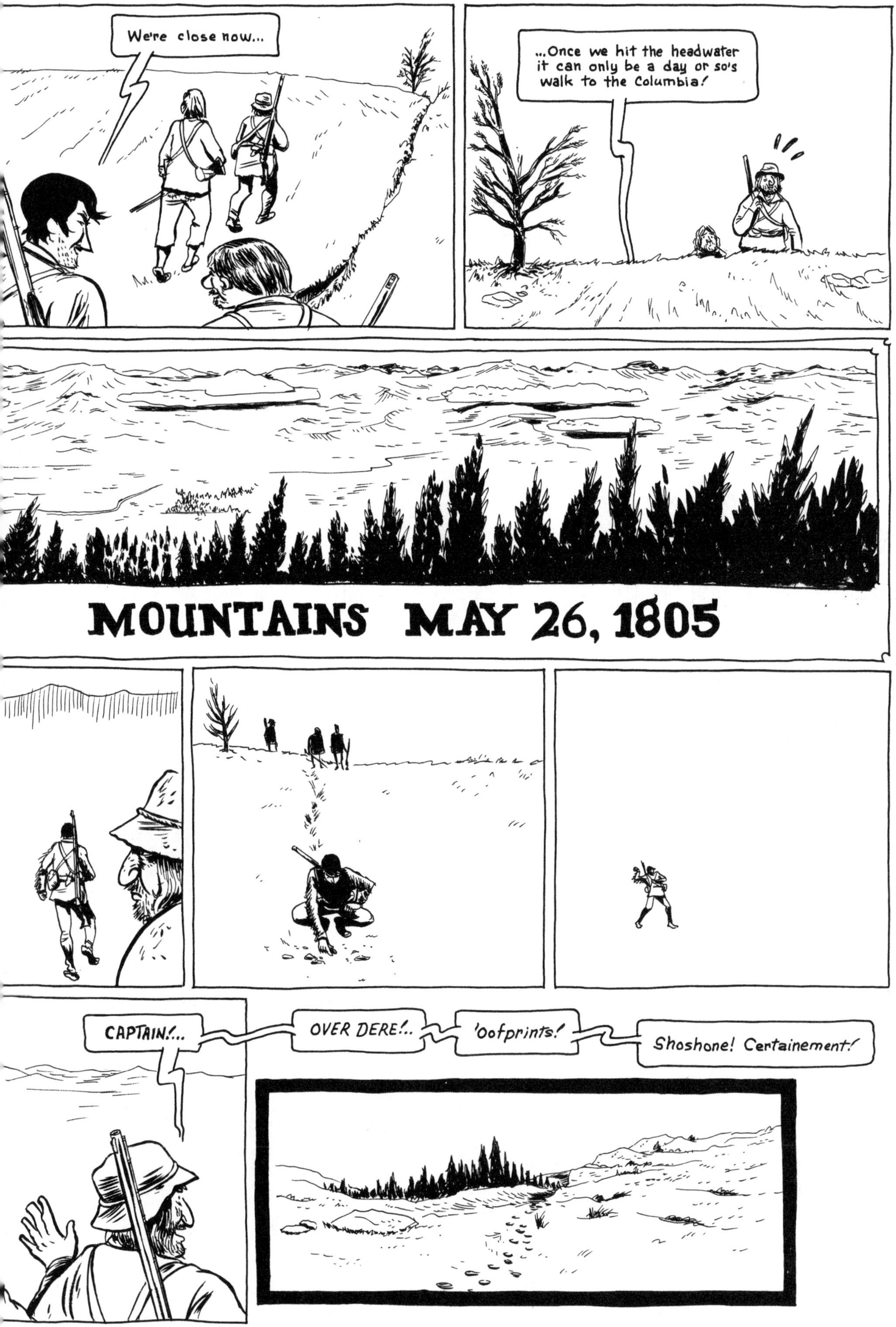
We're close now...
...Once we hit the headwater it can only be a day or so's walk to the Columbia!
MOUNTAINS MAY 26, 1805
CAPTAIN!...
OVER DERE!..
'oofprints!
Shoshone! Certainement!

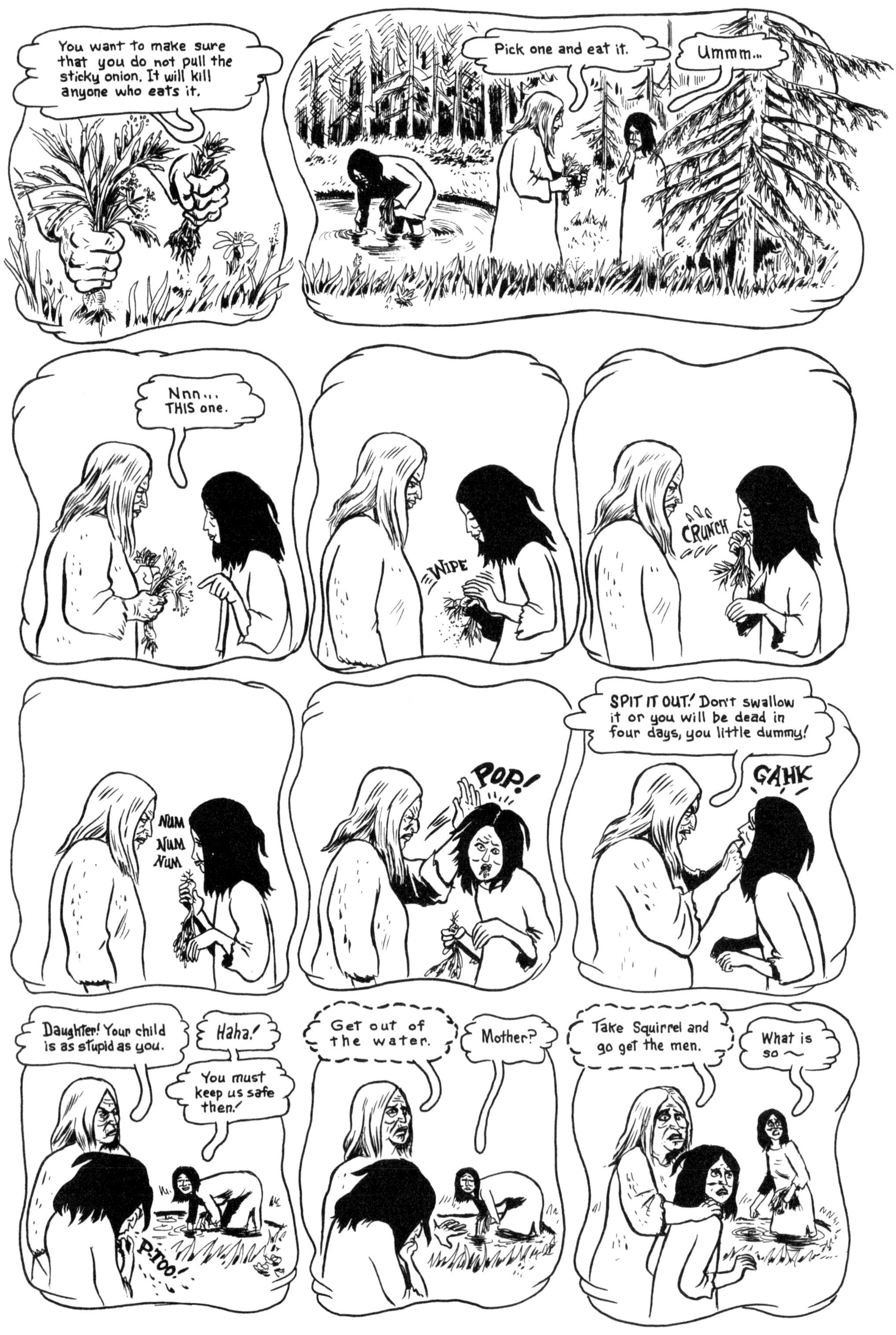
You want to make sure that you do not pull the sticky onion. It will kill anyone who eats it.
Pick one and eat it.
Ummm...
Nnn... THIS one.
WIPE
CRUNCH
NUM NUM NUM
POP!
SPIT IT OUT! Don't swallow it or you will be dead in four days, you little dummy!
GAHK
Daughter! Your child is as stupid as you.
Haha!
You must keep us safe then!
P-TOO!
Get out of the water.
Mother?
Take Squirrel and go get the men.
What is so ~

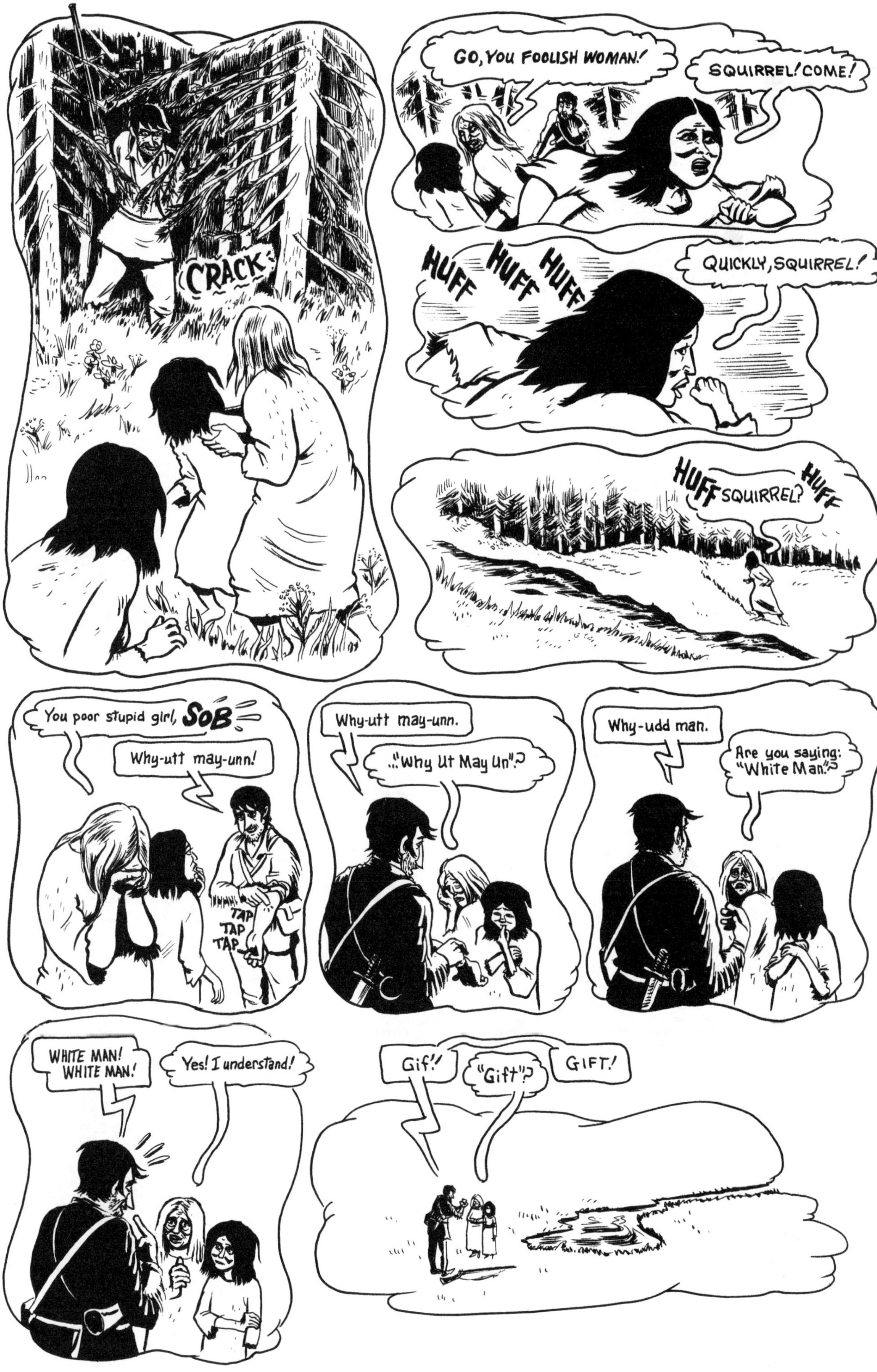
CRACK
GO, YOU FOOLISH WOMAN!
SQUIRREL! COME!
HUFF HUFF HUFF
QUICKLY, SQUIRREL!
HUFF SQUIRREL? HUFF
You poor stupid girl, SOB
Why-utt may-unn!
TAP TAP TAP
Why-utt may-unn.
..."Why Ut May Un"?
Why-udd man.
Are you saying: "White Man."?
WHITE MAN! WHITE MAN!
Yes! I understand!
Gif!
"Gift"?
GIFT!

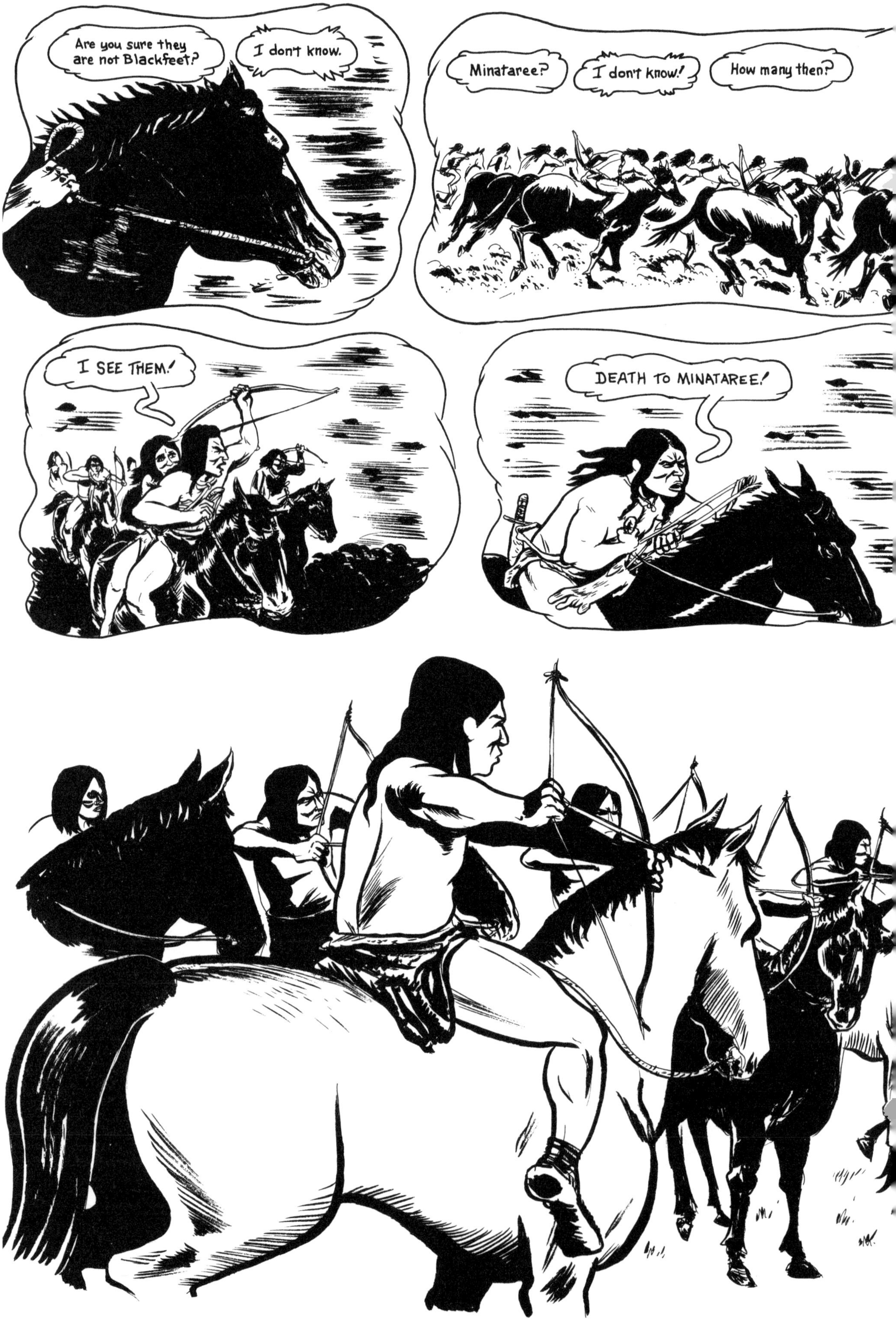
Are you sure they are not Blackfeet?
I don't know.
Minataree?
I don't know!
How many then?
I SEE THEM!
DEATH TO MINATAREE!

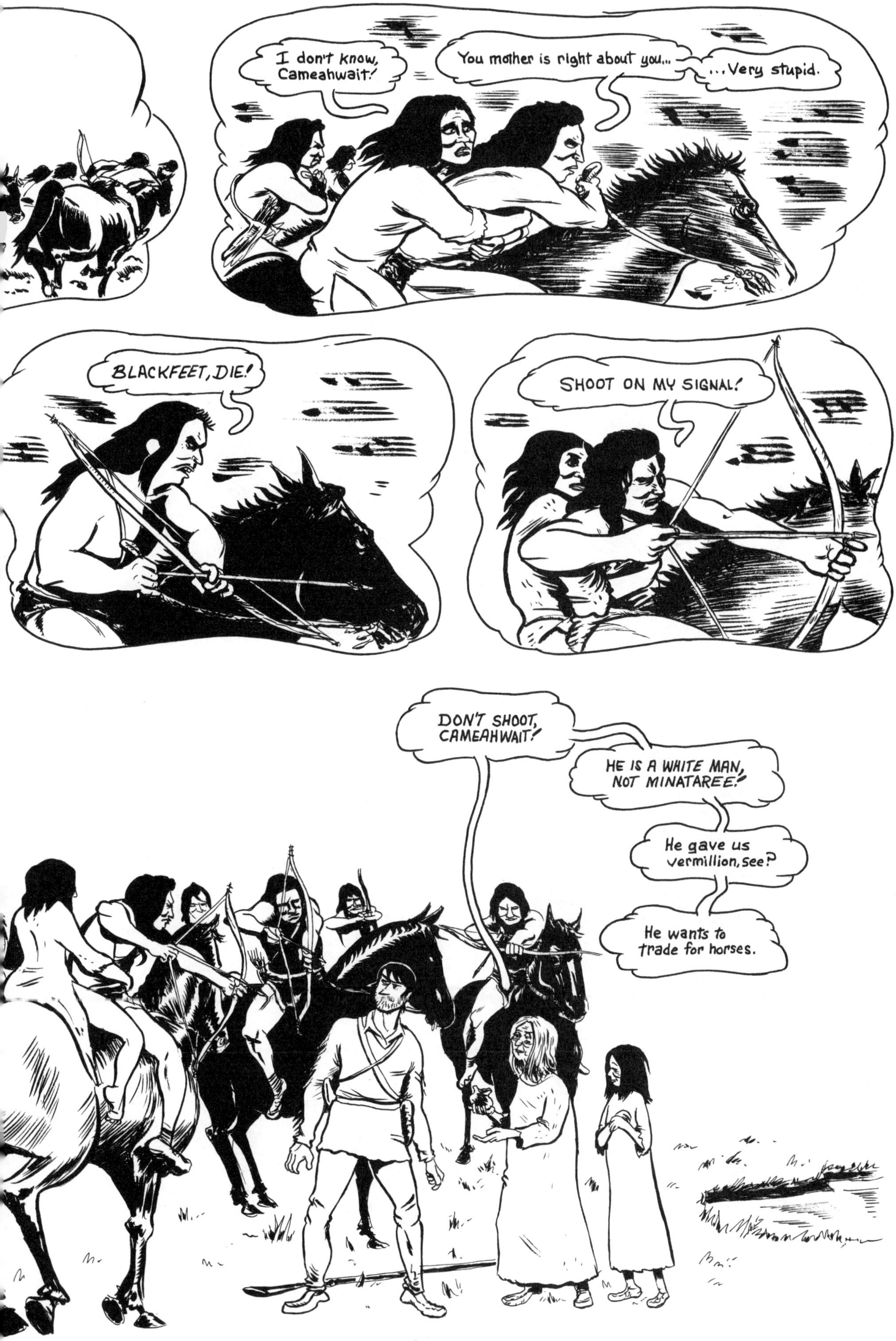
I don't know, Cameahwait!
You mother is right about you...
...Very stupid.
BLACKFEET, DIE!
SHOOT ON MY SIGNAL!
DON'T SHOOT, CAMEAHWAIT!
HE IS A WHITE MAN, NOT MINATAREE!
He gave us vermillion, see?
He wants to trade for horses.

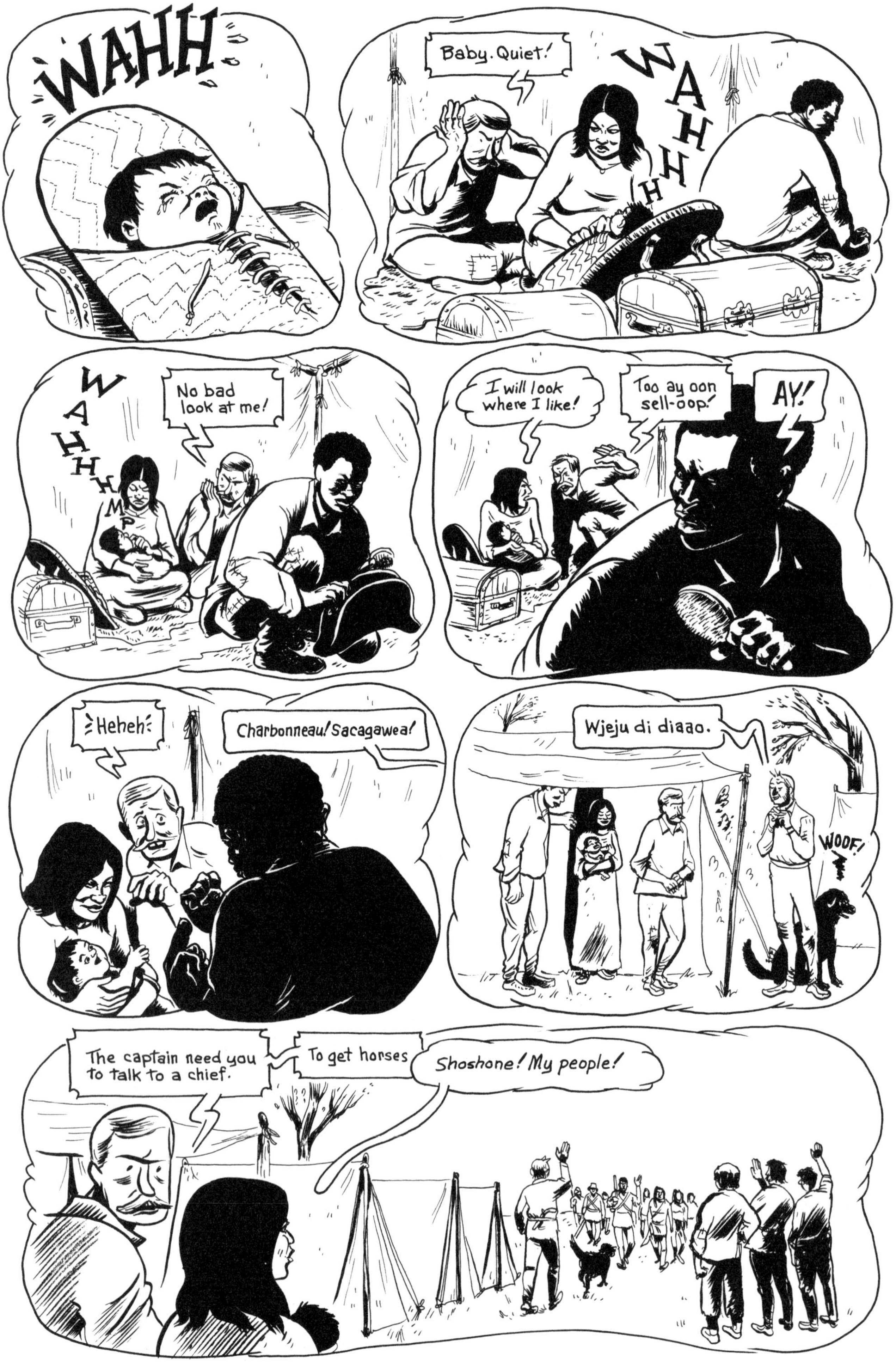
WAHH
Baby. Quiet!
WAHHH
WAHHHMP
No bad look at me!
I will look where I like!
Too ay oon sell-oop!
AY!
Heheh
Charbonneau! Sacagawea!
Wjeju di diaao.
WOOF!
The captain need you to talk to a chief.
To get horses
Shoshone! My people!

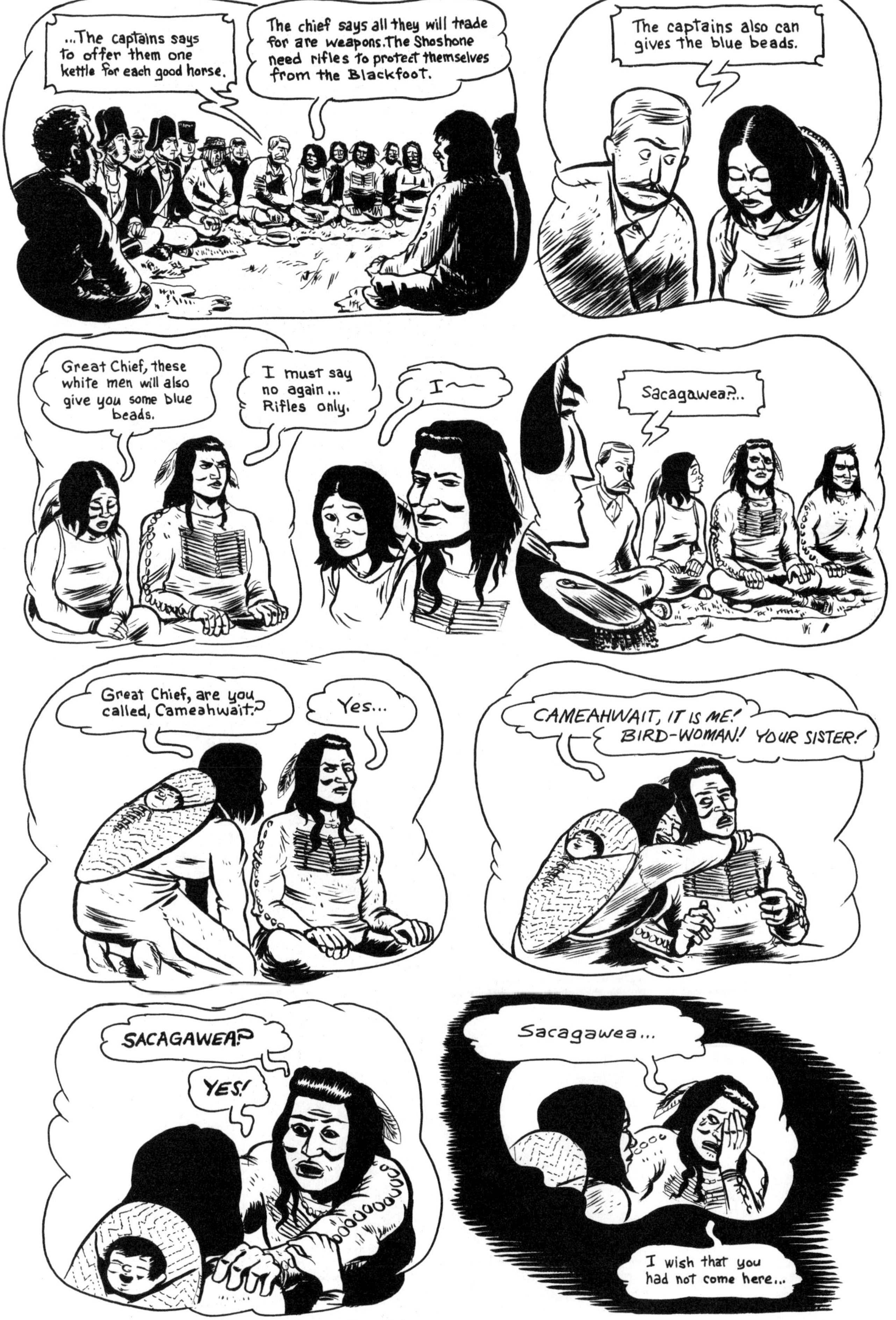
...The captains says to offer them one kettle for each good horse.
The chief says all they will trade for are weapons. The Shoshone need rifles to protect themselves from the Blackfoot.
The captains also can gives the blue beads.
Great Chief, these white men will also give you some blue beads.
I must say no again... Rifles only.
I~~
Sacagawea?..
Great Chief, are you called, Cameahwait?
Yes...
CAMEAHWAIT, IT IS ME! BIRD-WOMAN! YOUR SISTER!
SACAGAWEA?
YES!
Sacagawea...
I wish that you had not come here...

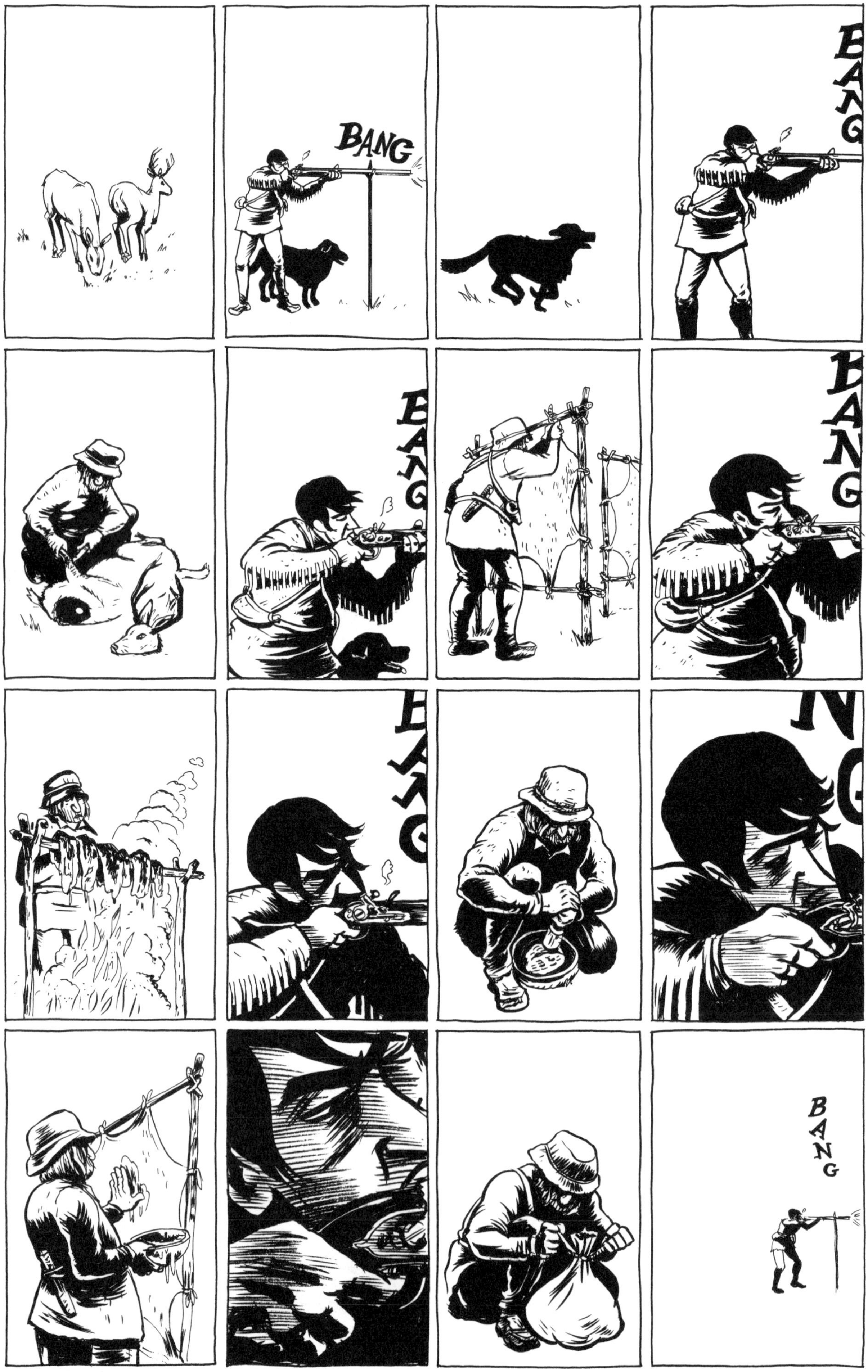
BANG
BANG
BANG
BANG
BANG
NG
BANG

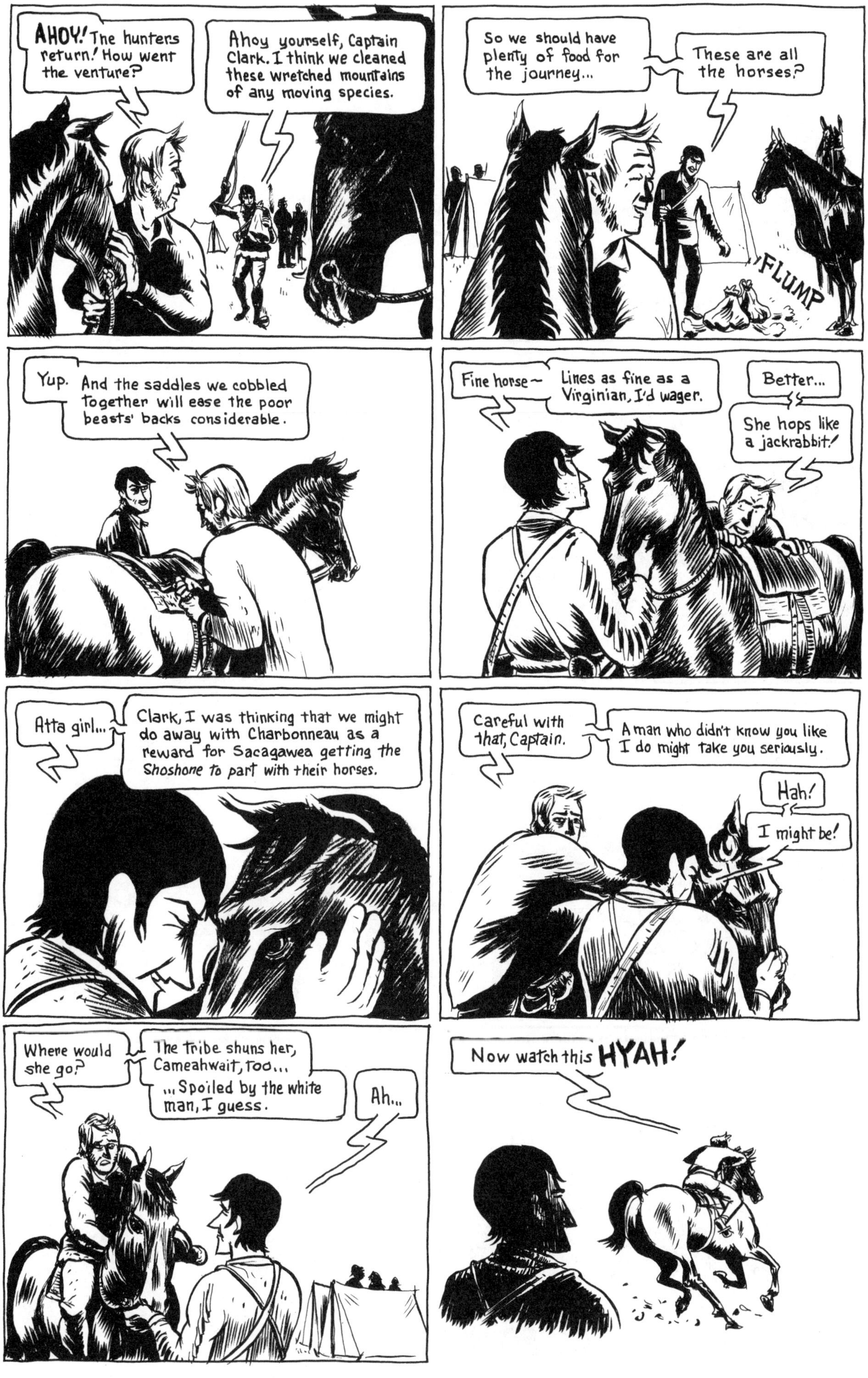
AHOY! The hunters return! How went the venture?
Ahoy yourself, Captain Clark. I think we cleaned these wretched mountains of any moving species.
So we should have plenty of food for the journey...
These are all the horses?
FLUMP
Yup.
And the saddles we cobbled together will ease the poor beasts' backs considerable.
Fine horse~
Lines as fine as a Virginian, I'd wager.
Better...
She hops like a jackrabbit!
Atta girl...
Clark, I was thinking that we might do away with Charbonneau as a reward for Sacagawea getting the Shoshone to part with their horses.
Careful with that, Captain.
A man who didn't know you like I do might take you seriously.
Hah!
I might be!
Where would she go?
The tribe shuns her, Cameahwait, too...
...Spoiled by the white man, I guess.
Ah...
Now watch this HYAH!

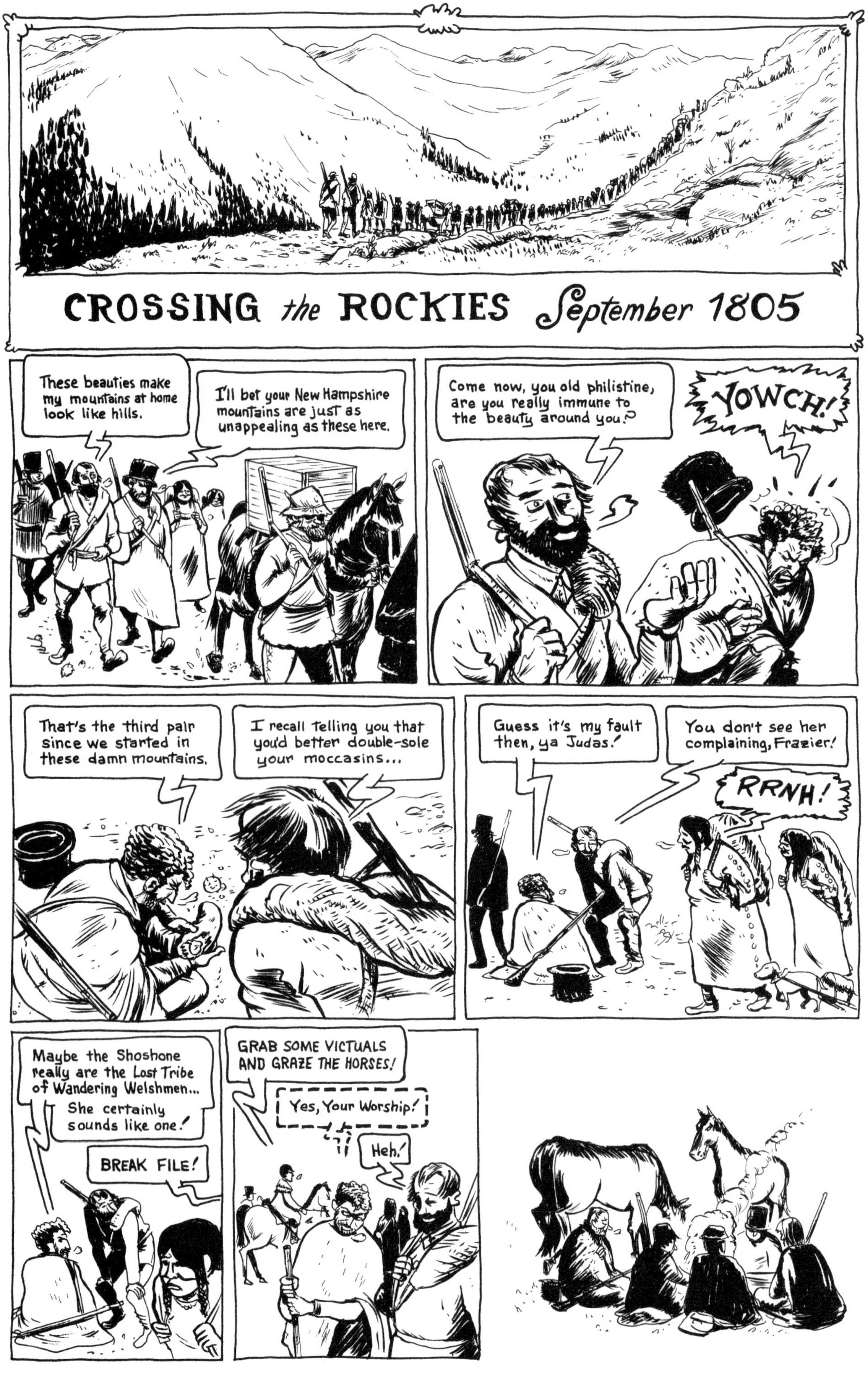
CROSSING the ROCKIES September 1805
These beauties make my mountains at home look like hills.
I'll bet your New Hampshire mountains are just as unappealing as these here.
Come now, you old philistine, are you really immune to the beauty around you?
YOWCH!
That's the third pair since we started in these damn mountains.
I recall telling you that you'd better double-sole your moccasins...
Guess it's my fault then, ya Judas!
You don't see her complaining, Frazier!
RRNH!
Maybe the Shoshone really are the Lost Tribe of Wandering Welshmen...
She certainly sounds like one!
BREAK FILE!
GRAB SOME VICTUALS AND GRAZE THE HORSES!
Yes, Your Worship!
Heh!

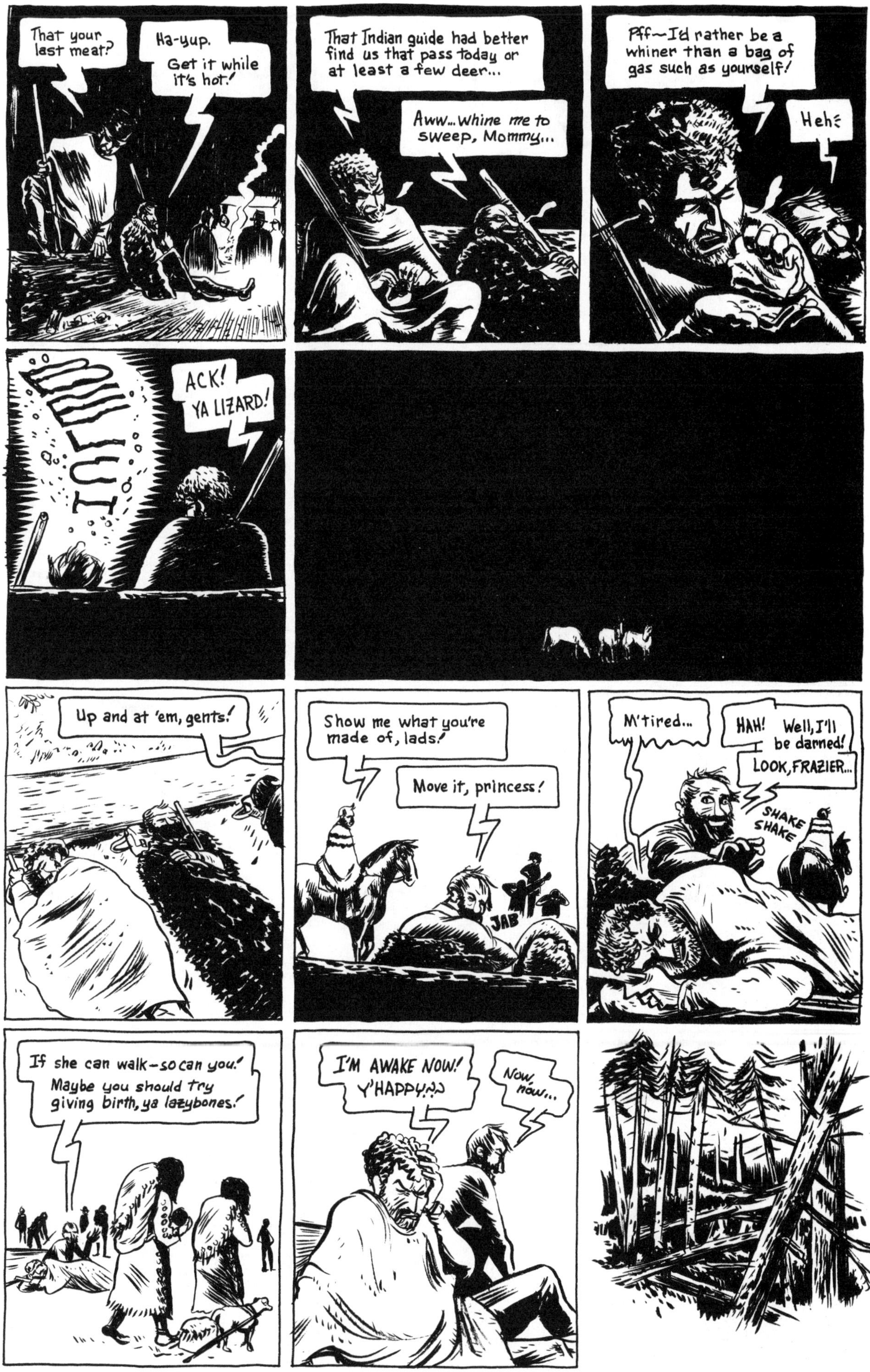
That your last meat?
Ha-yup.
Get it while it's hot!
That Indian guide had better find us that pass today or at least a few deer...
Aww... whine me to sweep, Mommy...
Pff—I'd rather be a whiner than a bag of gas such as yourself!
Heh
BELCH
ACK! YA LIZARD!
Up and at 'em, gents!
Show me what you're made of, lads!
Move it, princess!
JAB
M'tired...
HAH!
Well, I'll be darned!
LOOK, FRAZIER...
SHAKE SHAKE
If she can walk—so can you!
Maybe you should try giving birth, ya lazybones!
I'M AWAKE NOW! Y'HAPPY?!?
Now, now...

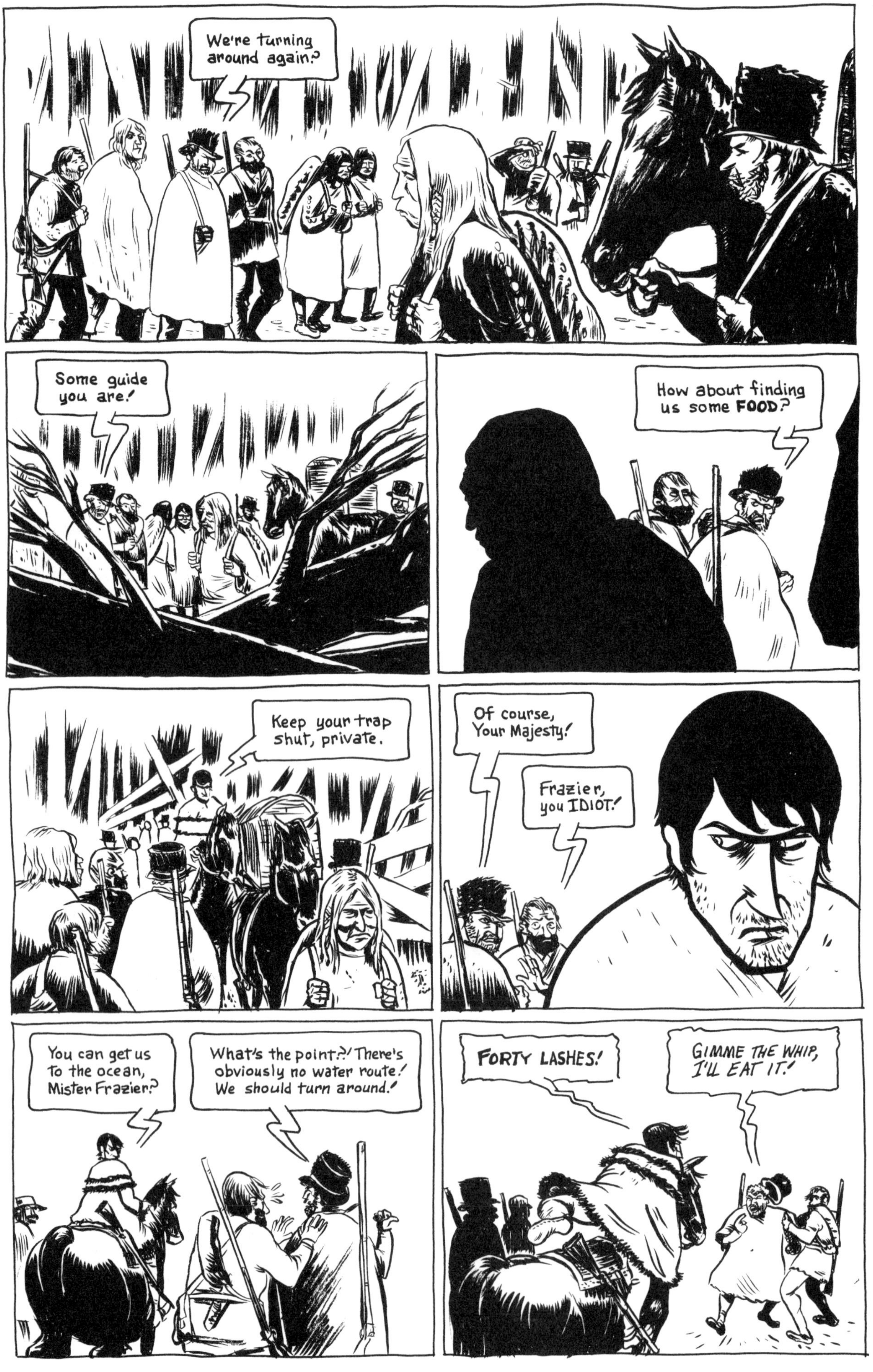

We're turning around again?
Some guide you are!
How about finding us some **FOOD**?
Keep your trap shut, private.
Of course, Your Majesty!
Frazier, you IDIOT!
You can get us to the ocean, Mister Frazier?
What's the point?! There's obviously no water route! We should turn around!
FORTY LASHES!
GIMME THE WHIP, I'LL EAT IT!

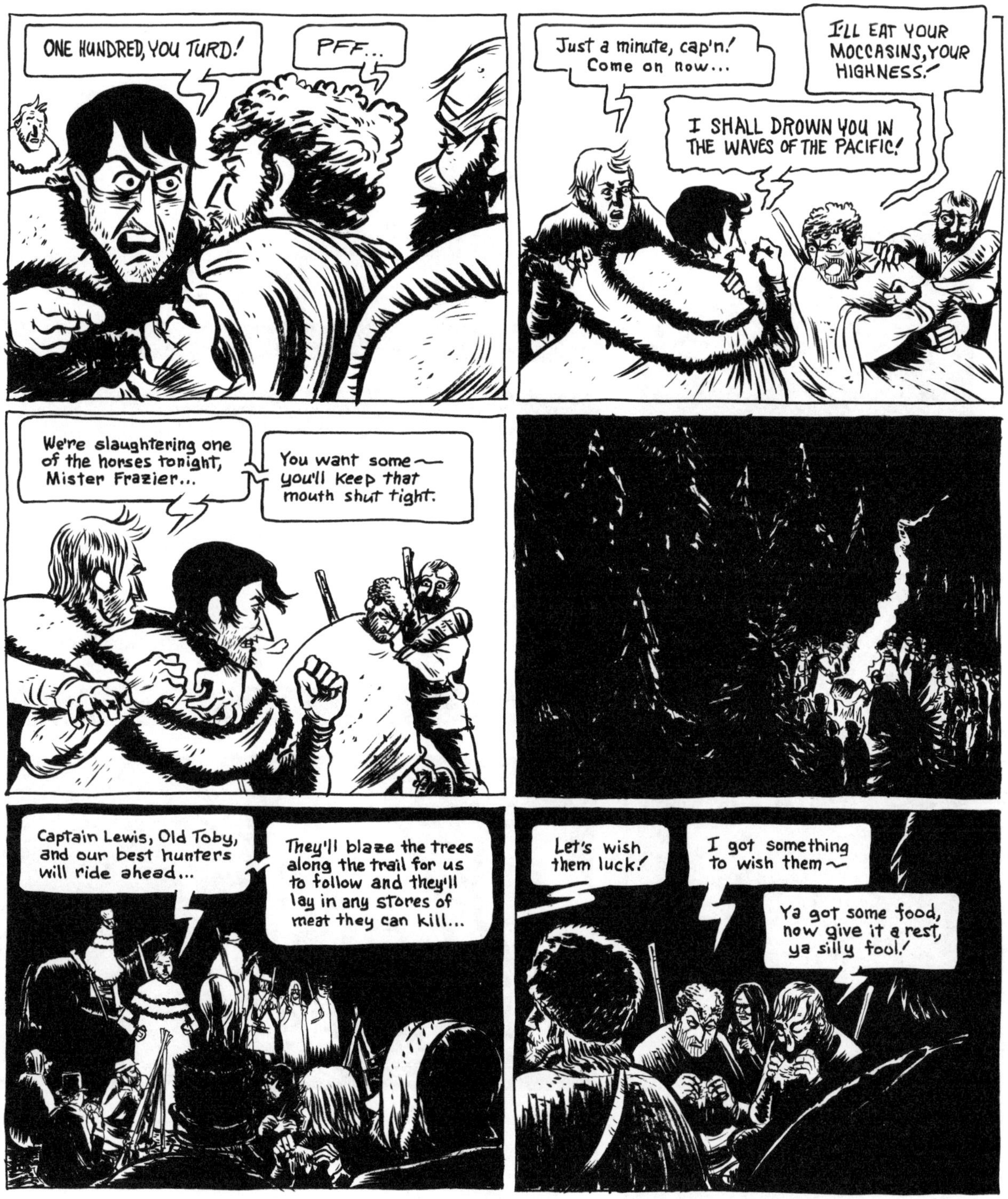
ONE HUNDRED, YOU TURD!
PFF...
Just a minute, cap'n! Come on now...
I'LL EAT YOUR MOCCASINS, YOUR HIGHNESS!
I SHALL DROWN YOU IN THE WAVES OF THE PACIFIC!
We're slaughtering one of the horses tonight, Mister Frazier...
You want some — you'll keep that mouth shut tight.
Captain Lewis, Old Toby, and our best hunters will ride ahead...
They'll blaze the trees along the trail for us to follow and they'll lay in any stores of meat they can kill...
Let's wish them luck!
I got something to wish them —
Ya got some food, now give it a rest, ya silly fool!

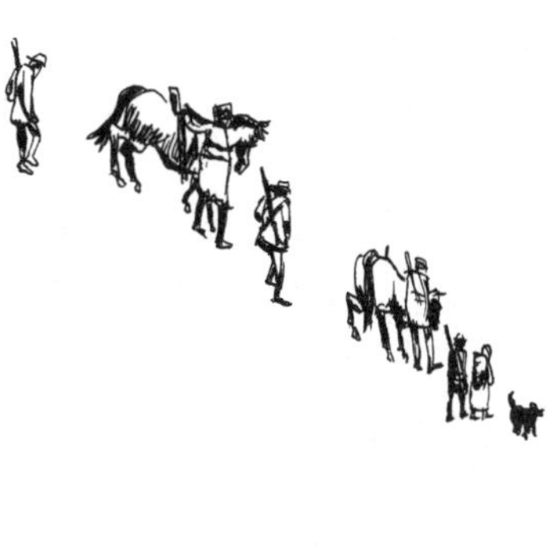

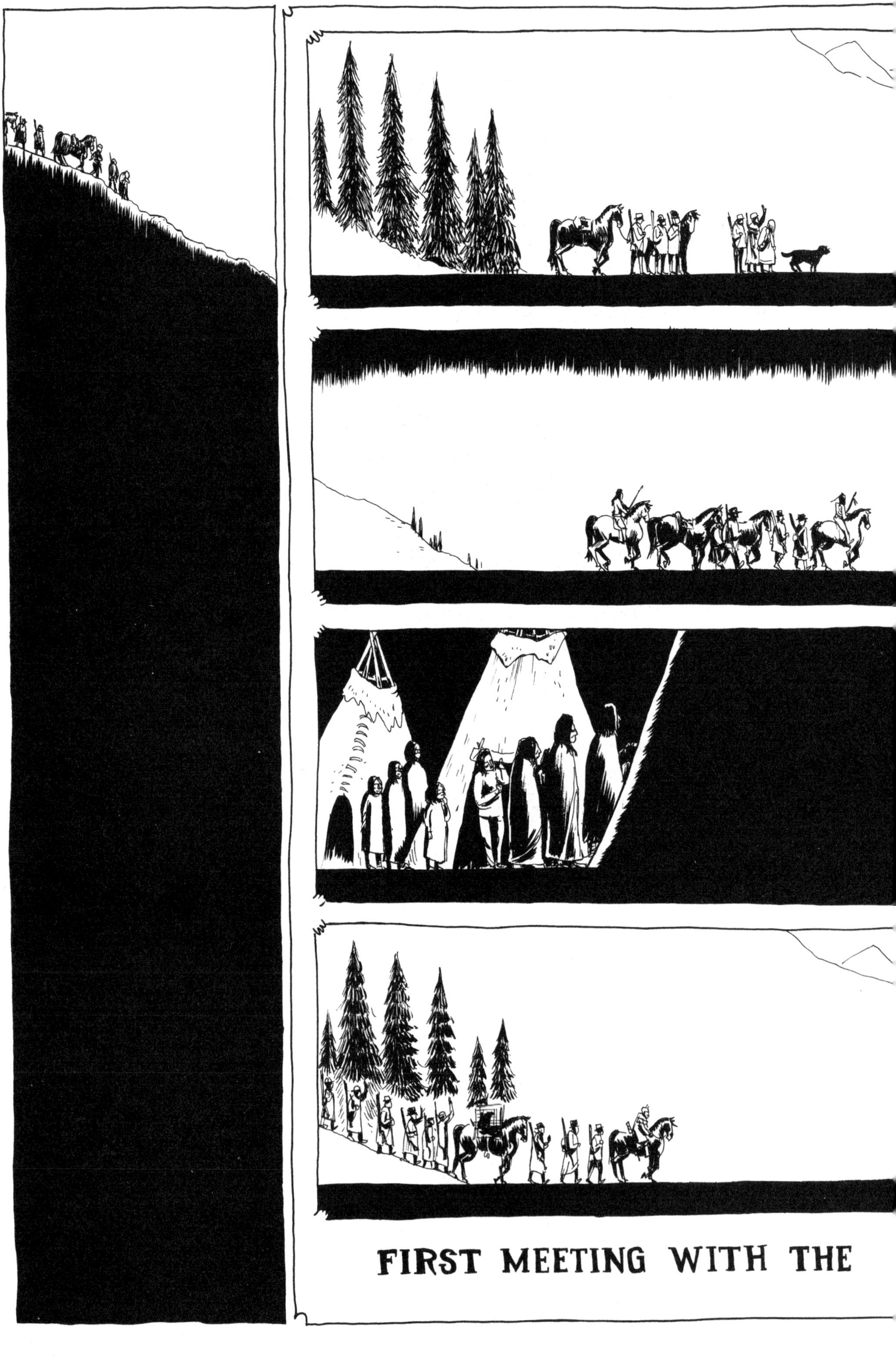
FIRST MEETING WITH THE

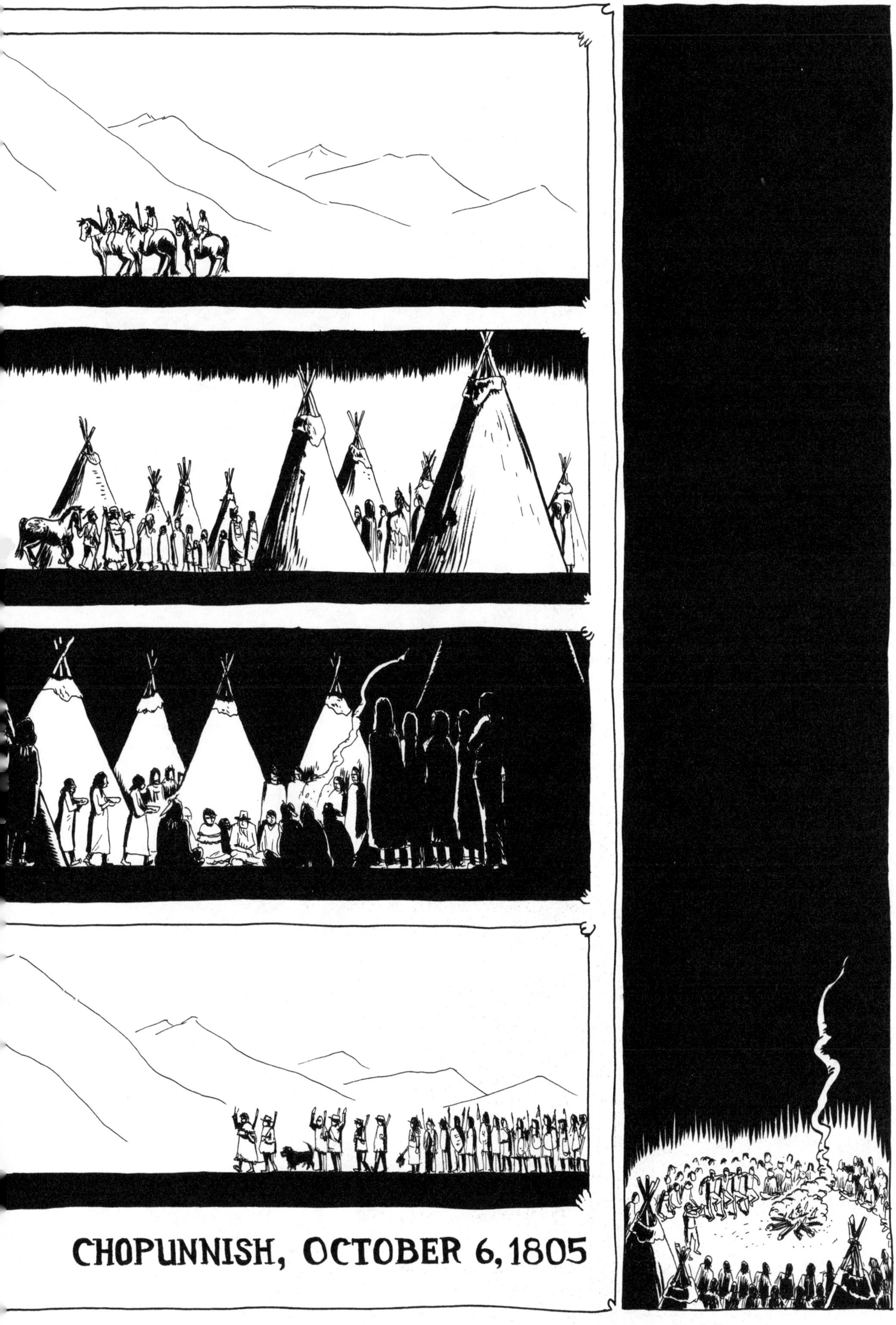
CHOPUNNISH, OCTOBER 6, 1805

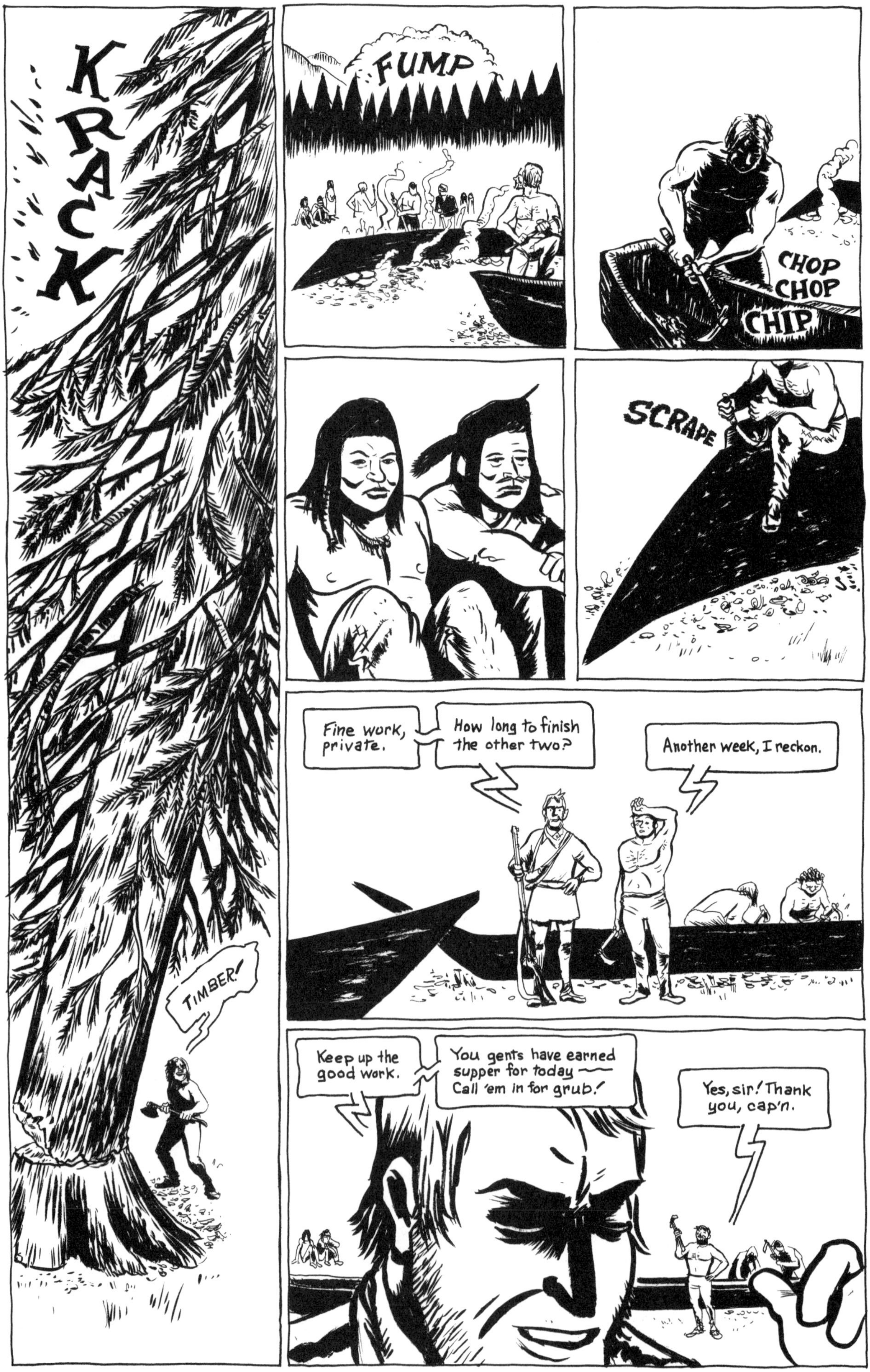
KRACK
TIMBER!
FUMP
CHOP
CHOP
CHIP
SCRAPE
Fine work, private.
How long to finish the other two?
Another week, I reckon.
Keep up the good work.
You gents have earned supper for today — Call 'em in for grub!
Yes, sir! Thank you, cap'n.

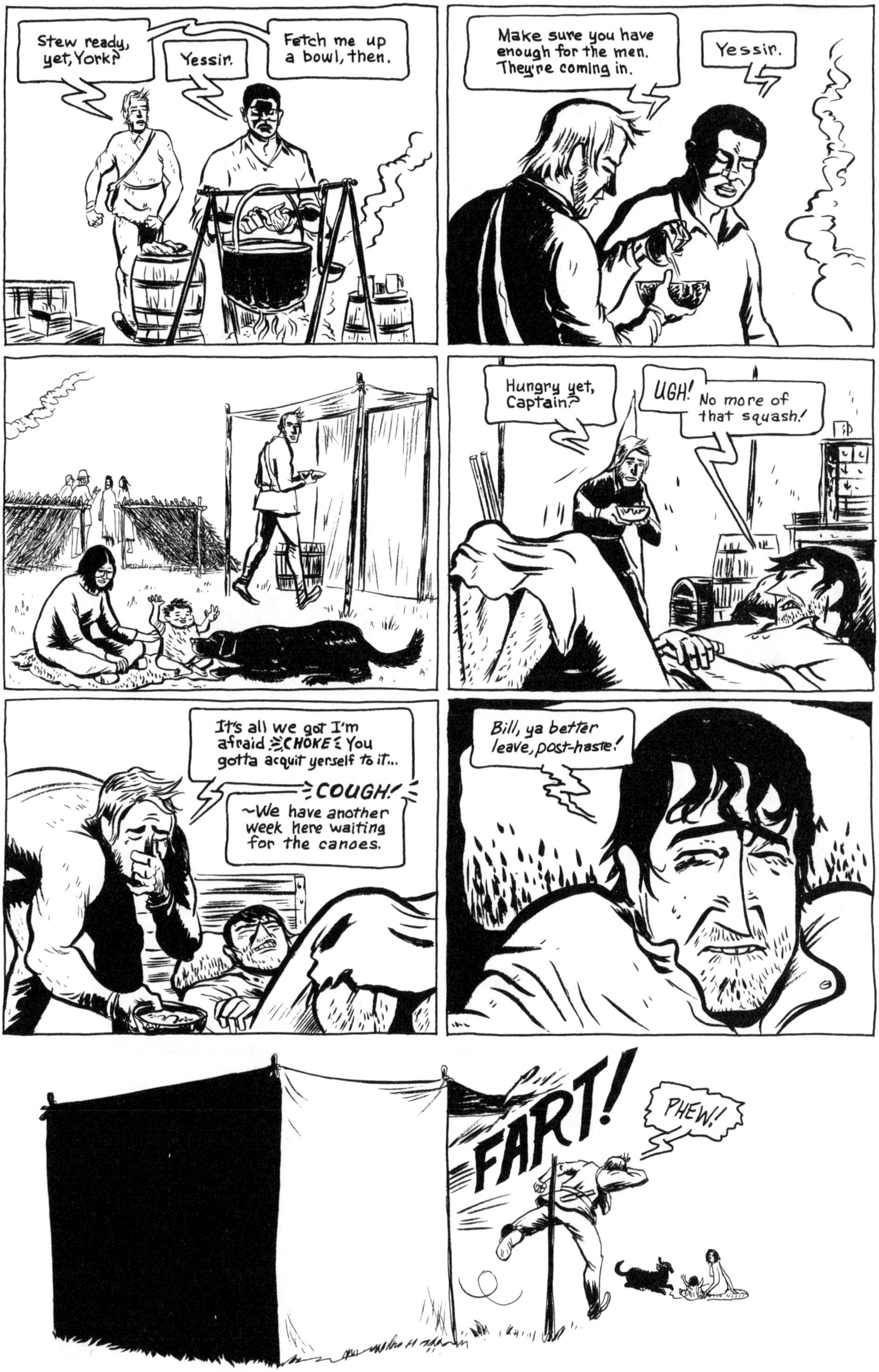
Stew ready, yet, York?
Yessir.
Fetch me up a bowl, then.
Make sure you have enough for the men. They're coming in.
Yessir.
Hungry yet, Captain?
UGH!
No more of that squash!
It's all we got I'm afraid CHOKE You gotta acquit yerself to it...
COUGH!
~We have another week here waiting for the canoes.
Bill, ya better leave, post-haste!
FART!
PHEW!

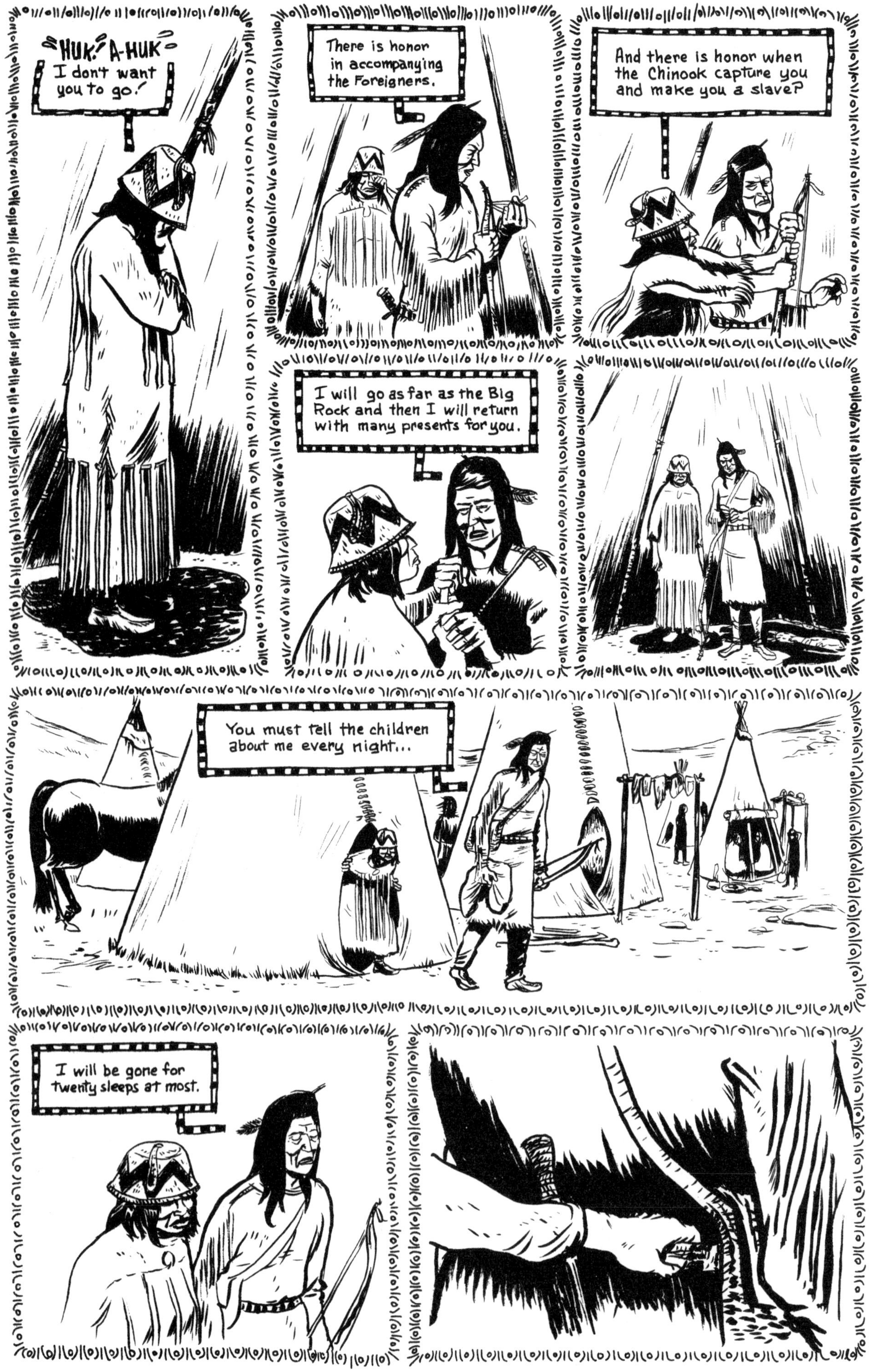
HUK! A-HUK
I don't want you to go!
There is honor in accompanying the Foreigners.
And there is honor when the Chinook capture you and make you a slave?
I will go as far as the Big Rock and then I will return with many presents for you.
You must tell the children about me every night...
I will be gone for twenty sleeps at most.

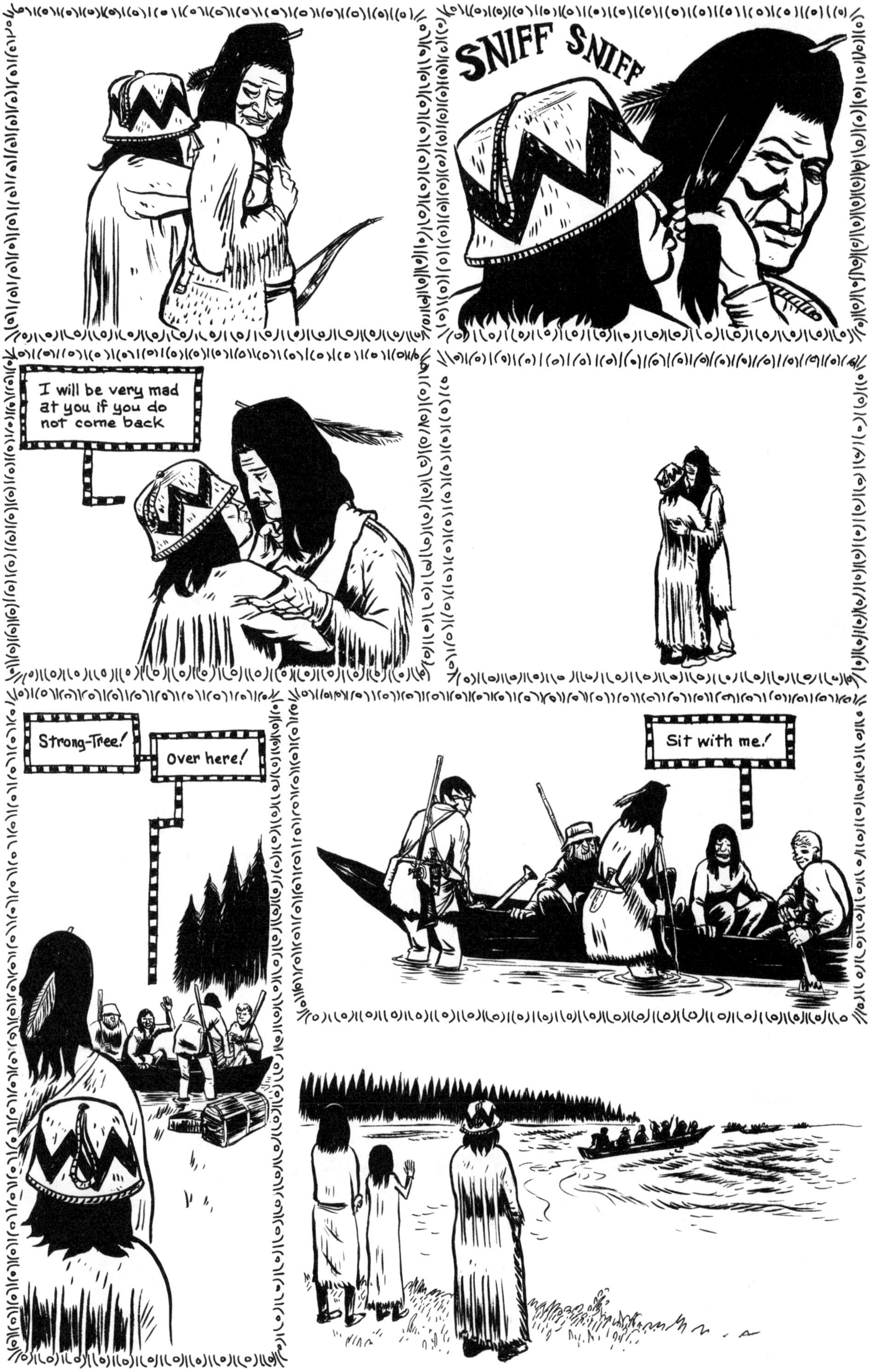
SNIFF SNIFF
I will be very mad at you if you do not come back
Strong-Tree!
Over here!
Sit with me!

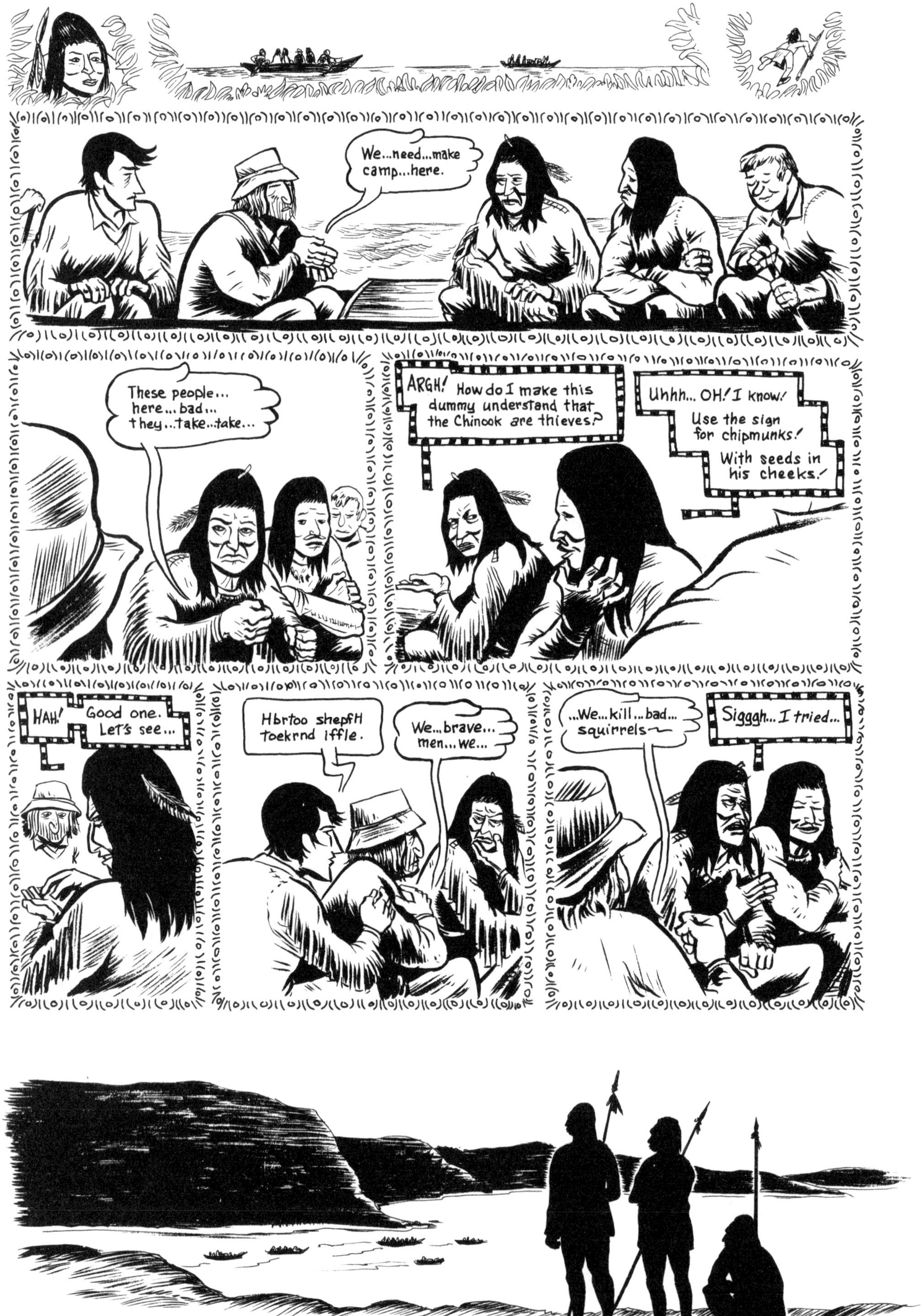
We...need...make camp...here.
These people... here...bad... they...take...take...
ARGH! How do I make this dummy understand that the Chinook are thieves?
Uhhh... OH! I know! Use the sign for chipmunks! With seeds in his cheeks!
HAH! Good one. Let's see...
Hbrtoo shepfH toekrnd iffle.
We...brave... men...we...
...We...kill...bad... squirrels~
Sigggh... I tried...

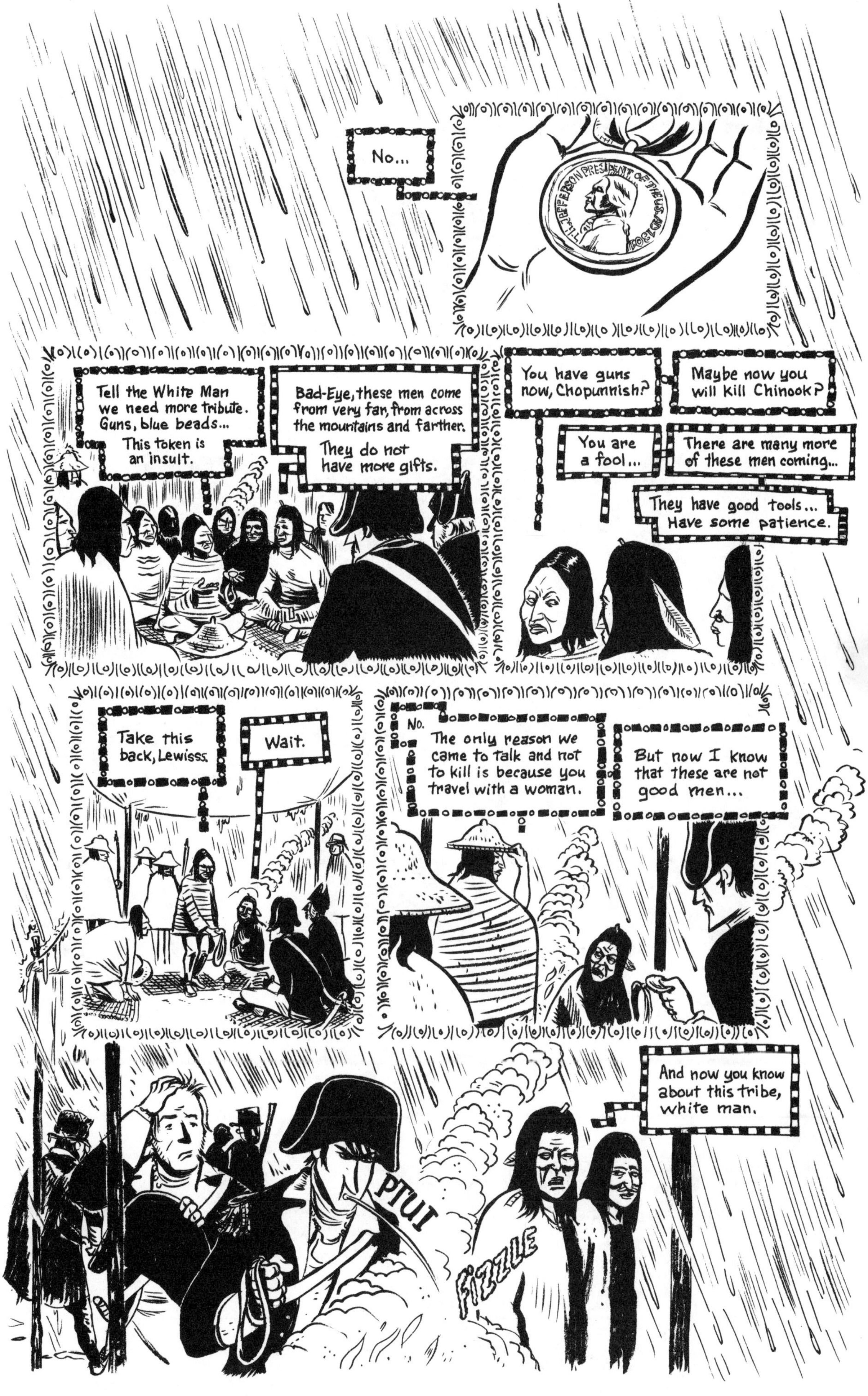
No...
TH: JEFFERSON PRESIDENT OF THE U.S. 1801
Tell the White Man we need more tribute. Guns, blue beads...
This token is an insult.
Bad-Eye, these men come from very far, from across the mountains and farther.
They do not have more gifts.
You have guns now, Chopunnish?
Maybe now you will kill Chinook?
You are a fool...
There are many more of these men coming...
They have good tools... Have some patience.
Take this back, Lewiss.
Wait.
No.
The only reason we came to talk and not to kill is because you travel with a woman.
But now I know that these are not good men...
And now you know about this tribe, white man.
PTUI
FIZZLE

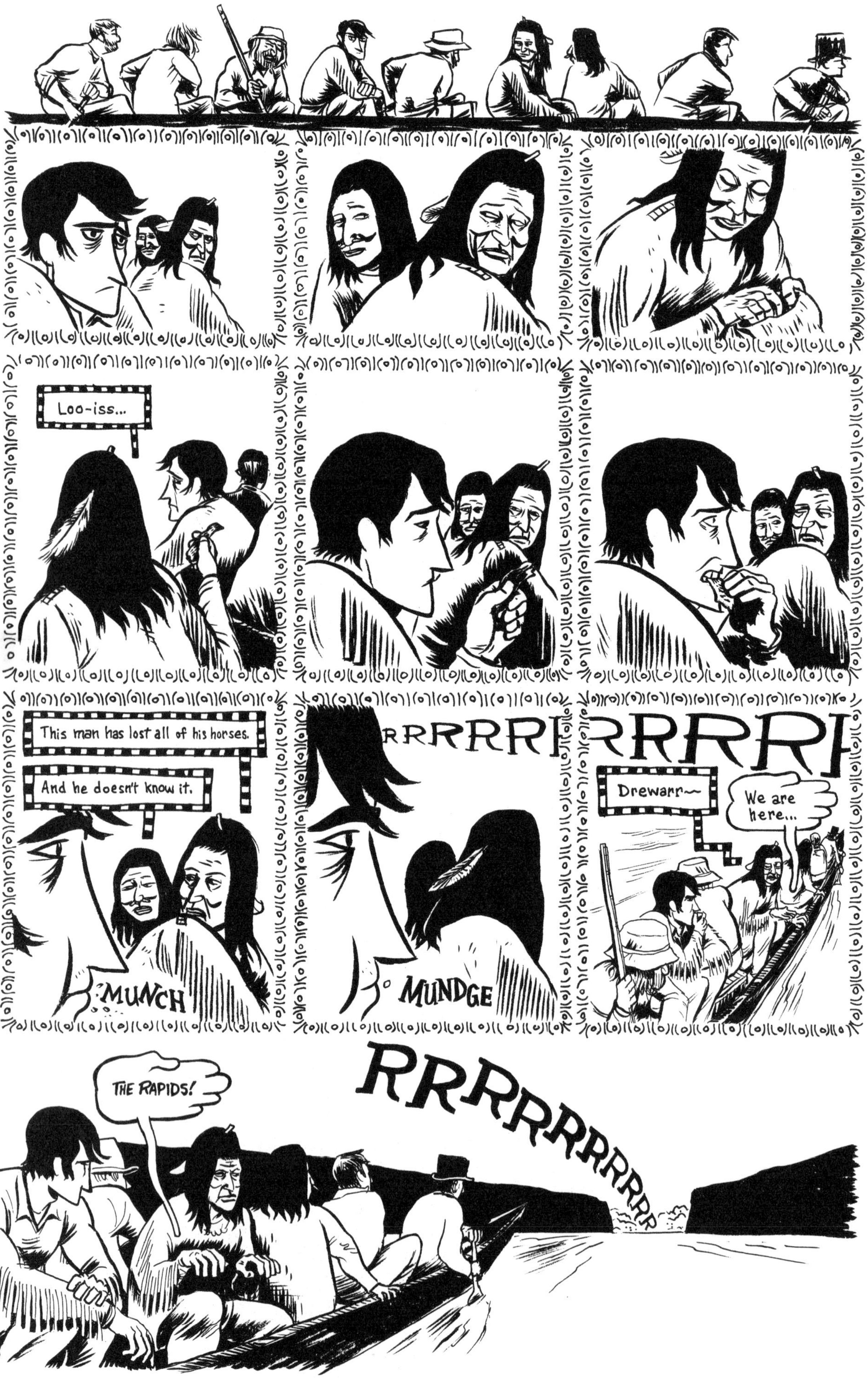
Loo-iss...
This man has lost all of his horses.
And he doesn't know it.
MUNCH
RRRRRR
MUNDGE
RRRRR
Drewarr~
We are here...
THE RAPIDS!
RRRRRRRRRRRRR

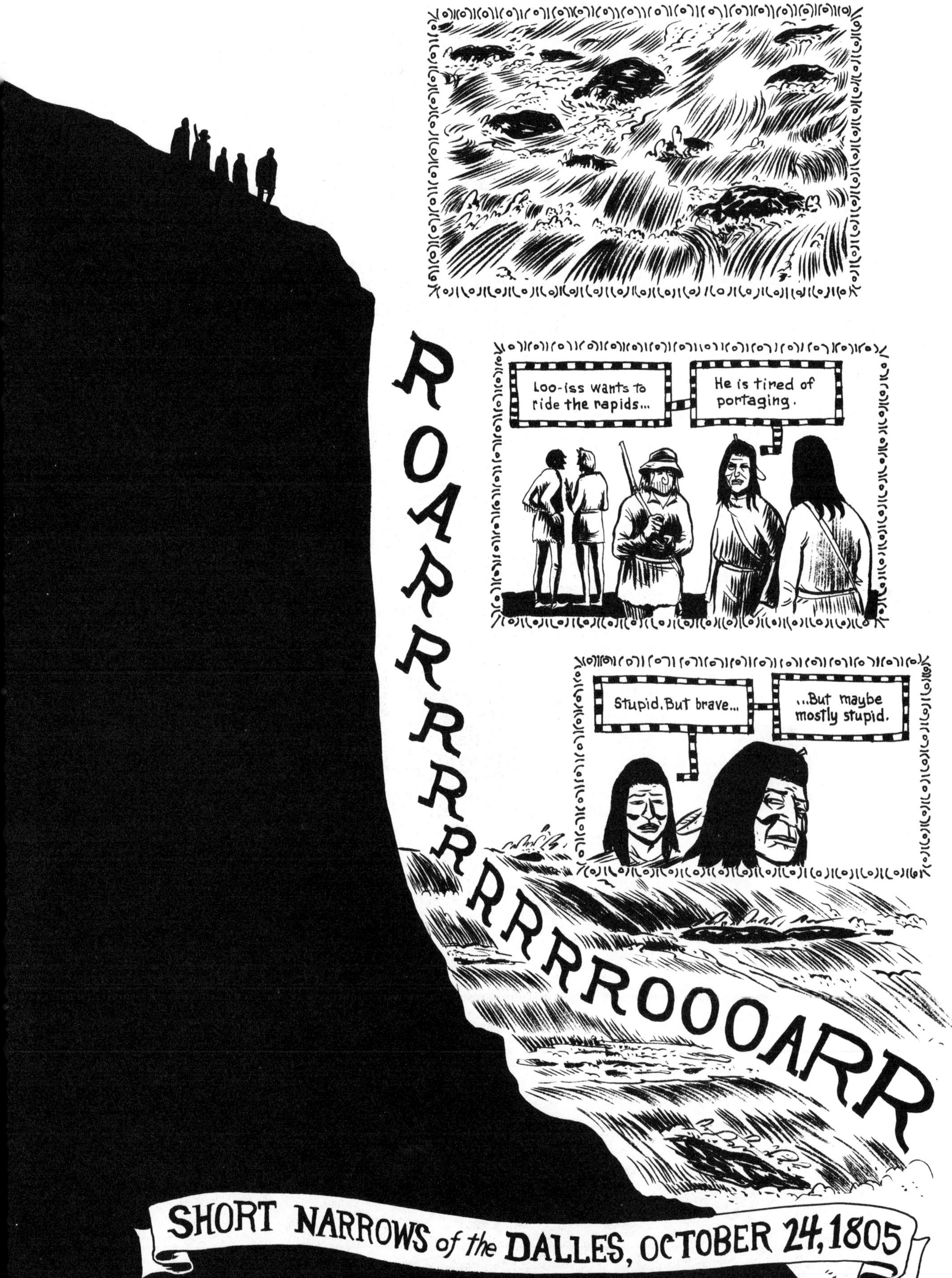

Loo-iss wants to ride the rapids...
He is tired of portaging.
Stupid. But brave...
...But maybe mostly stupid.
ROARRRRRRRRRRRROOOOARR
SHORT NARROWS of the DALLES, OCTOBER 24, 1805

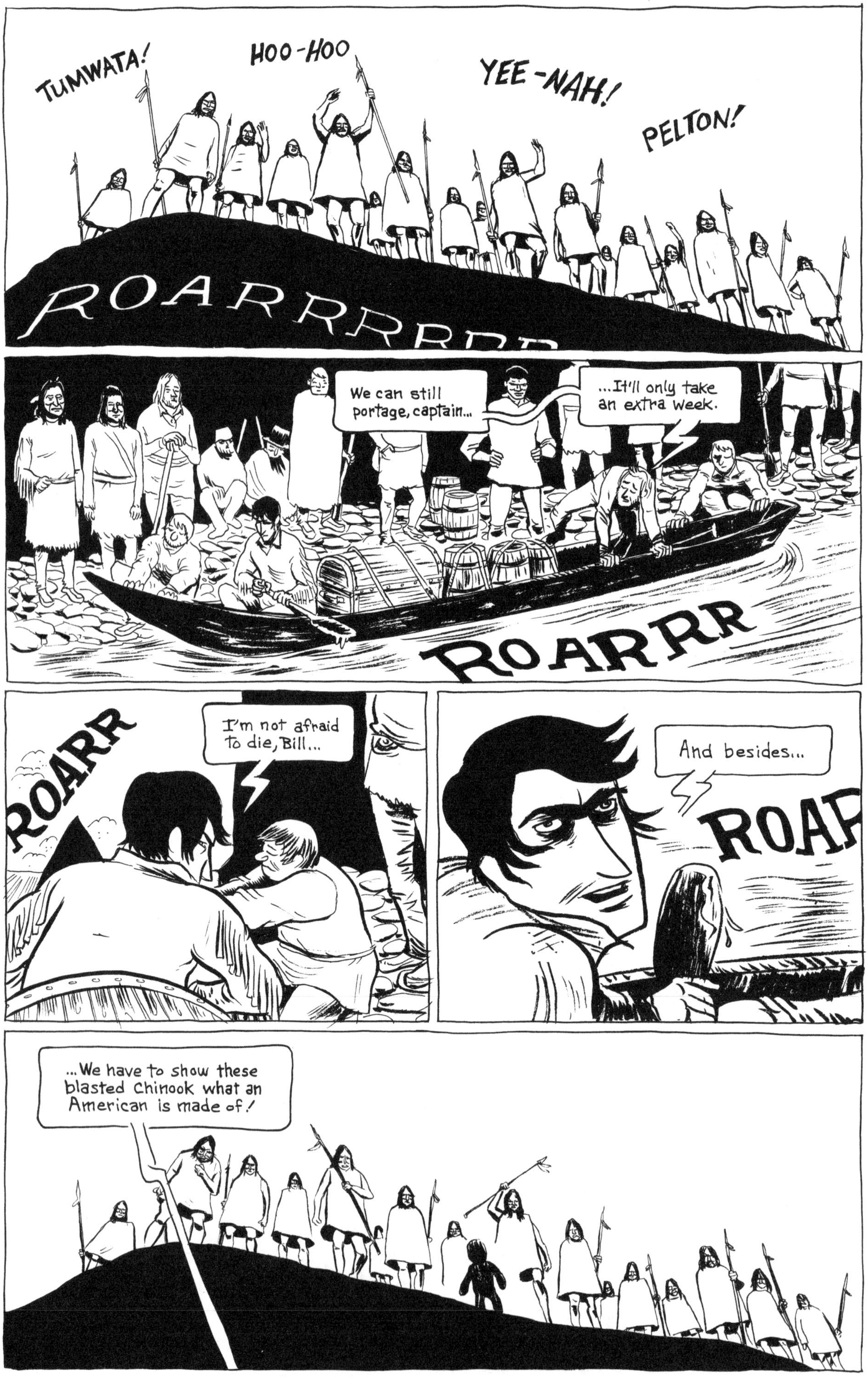
TUMWATA!
HOO-HOO
YEE-NAH!
PELTON!
ROARRRRRR
We can still portage, captain...
...It'll only take an extra week.
ROARRR
ROARR
I'm not afraid to die, Bill...
And besides...
ROAR
...We have to show these blasted Chinook what an American is made of!

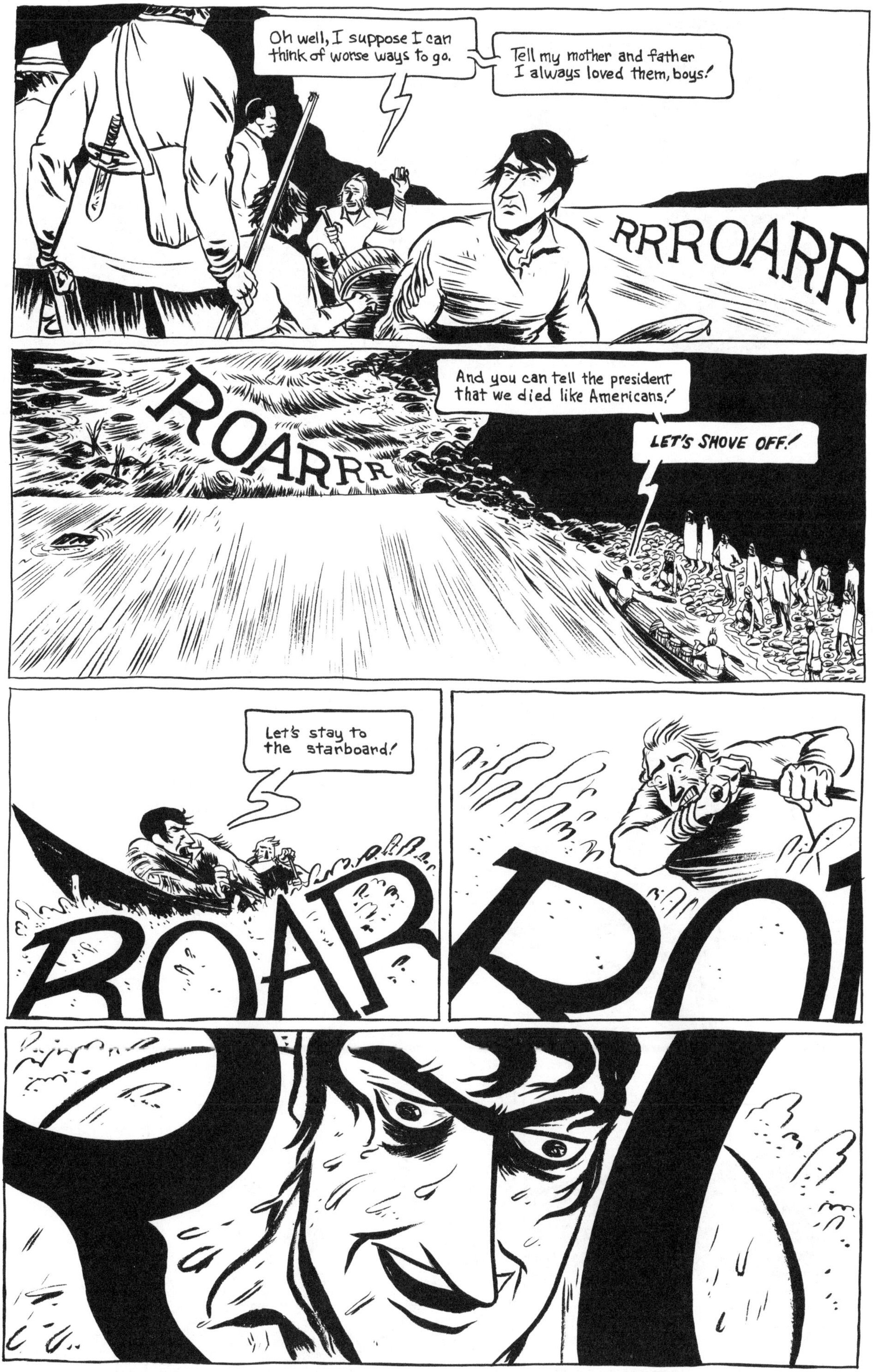
Oh well, I suppose I can think of worse ways to go.
Tell my mother and father I always loved them, boys!
RRROARR
ROARRR
And you can tell the president that we died like Americans!
LET'S SHOVE OFF!
Let's stay to the starboard!
ROAR

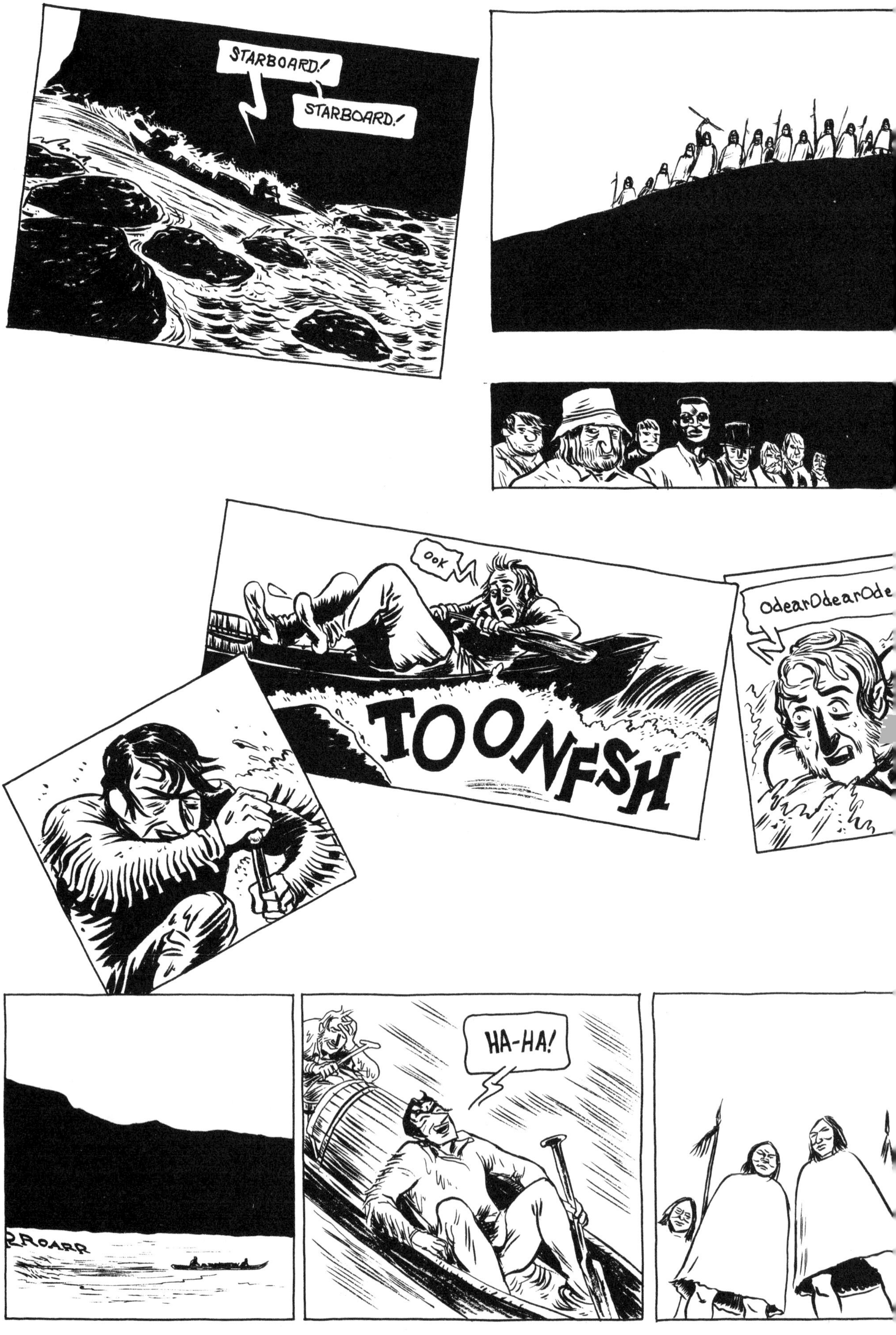
STARBOARD!
STARBOARD!
OOK
TOONFSH
OdearOdearOde
RROARR
HA-HA!

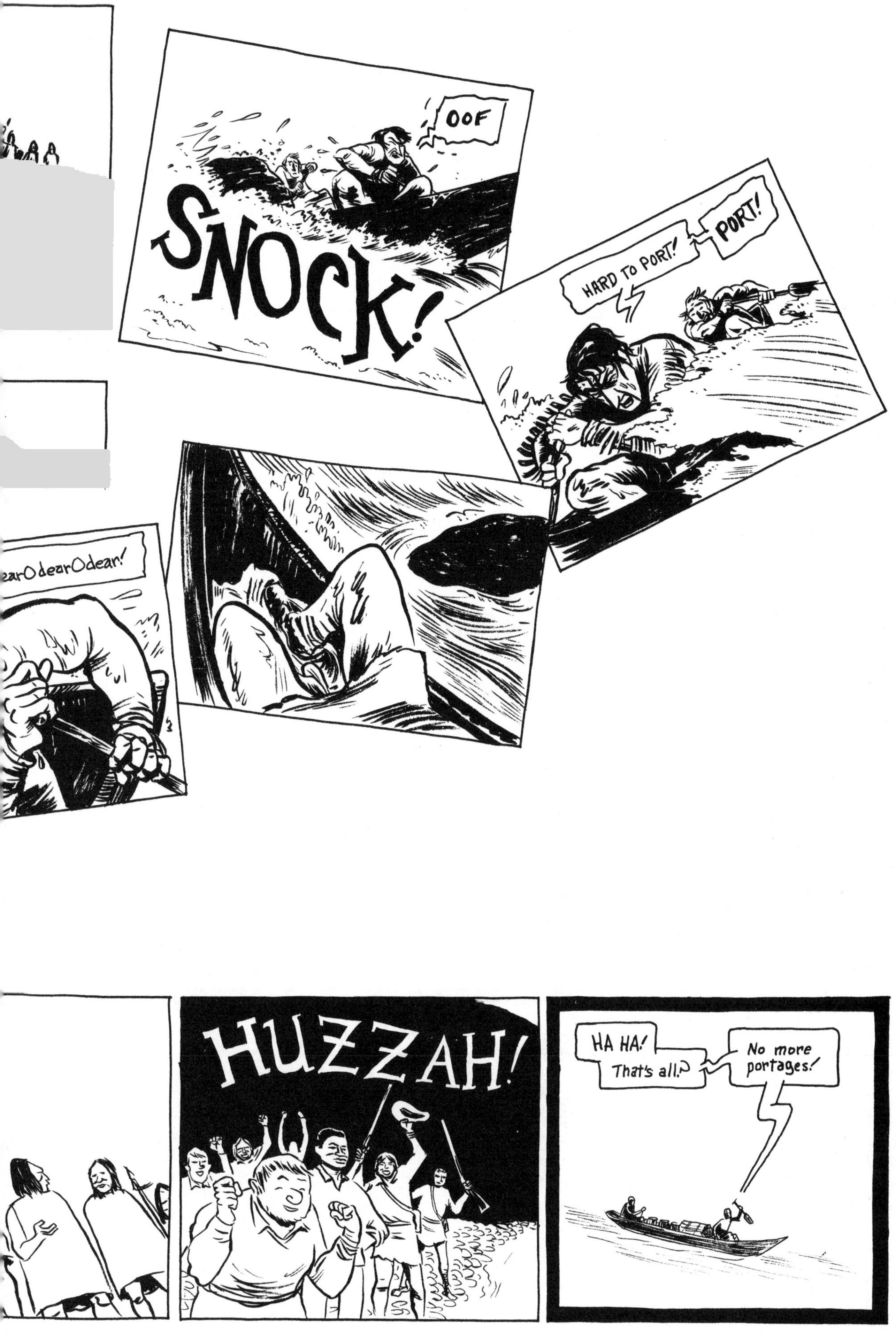

OOF
SNOCK!
HARD TO PORT!
PORT!
earOdearOdearOdear!
HUZZAH!
HA HA! That's all.?
No more portages!

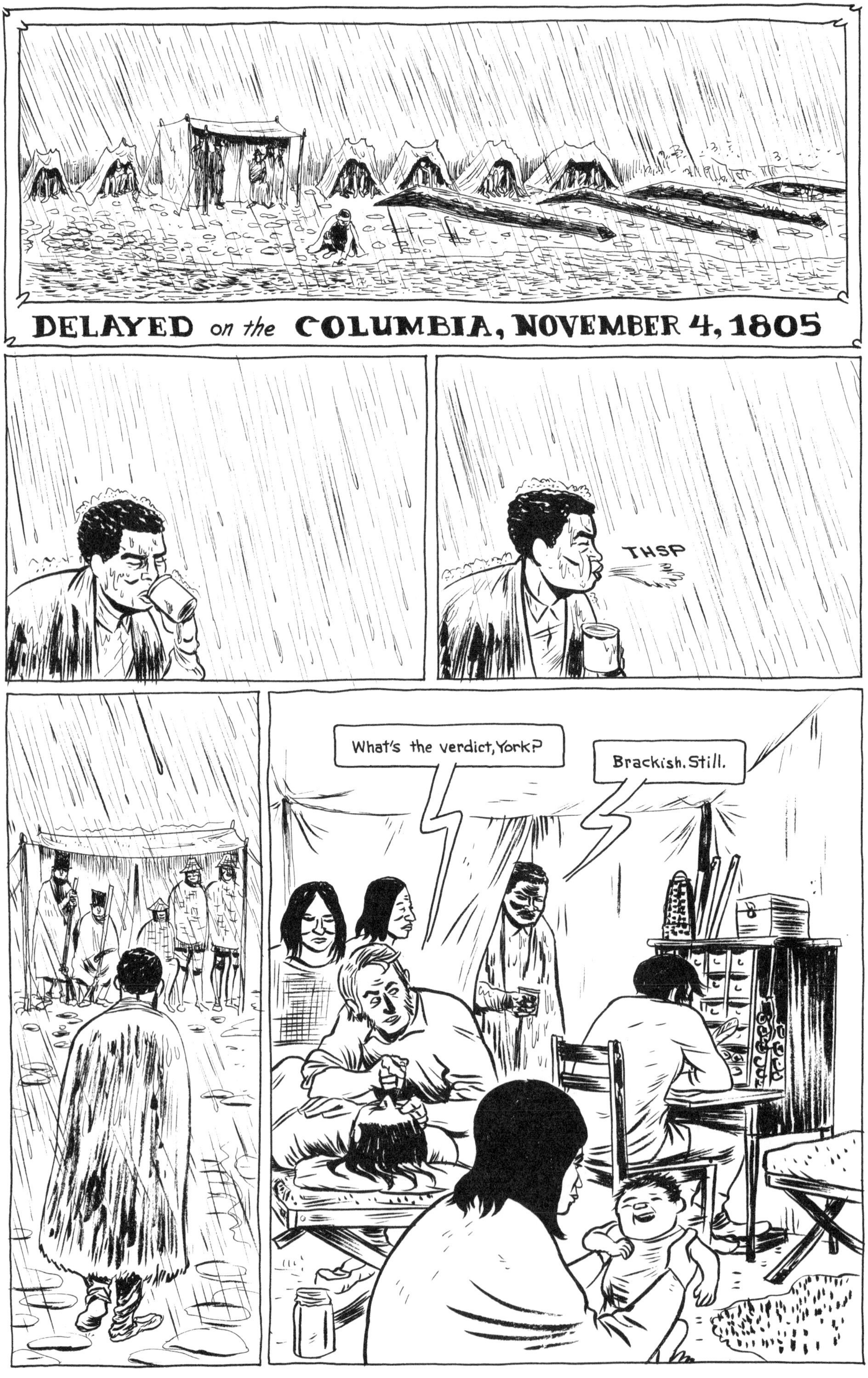
DELAYED on the COLUMBIA, NOVEMBER 4, 1805
THSP
What's the verdict, York?
Brackish. Still.

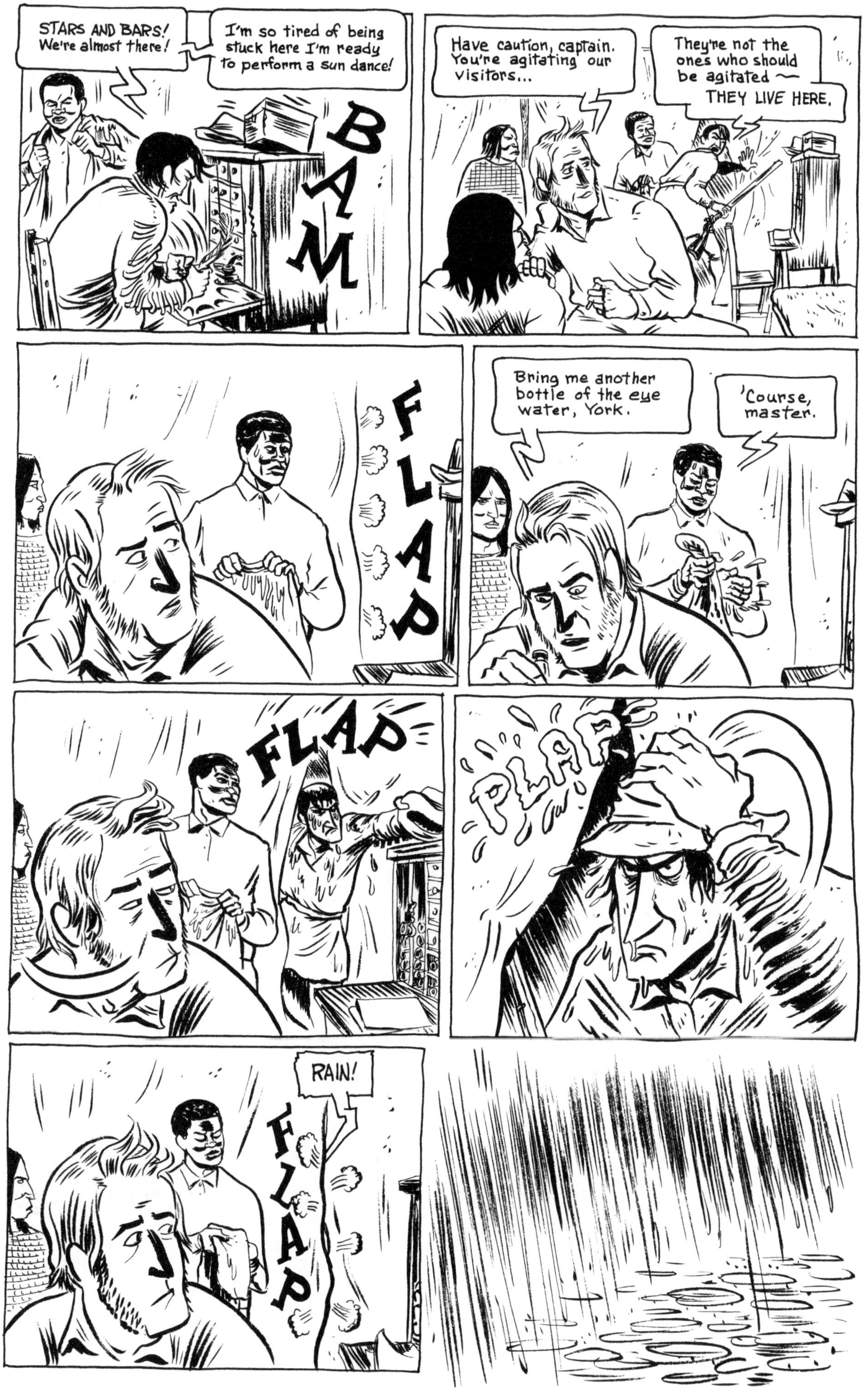
STARS AND BARS! We're almost there!
I'm so tired of being stuck here I'm ready to perform a sun dance!
BAM
Have caution, captain. You're agitating our visitors...
They're not the ones who should be agitated ~ THEY LIVE HERE.
FLAP
Bring me another bottle of the eye water, York.
'Course, master.
FLAP
PLAP
RAIN!
FLAP

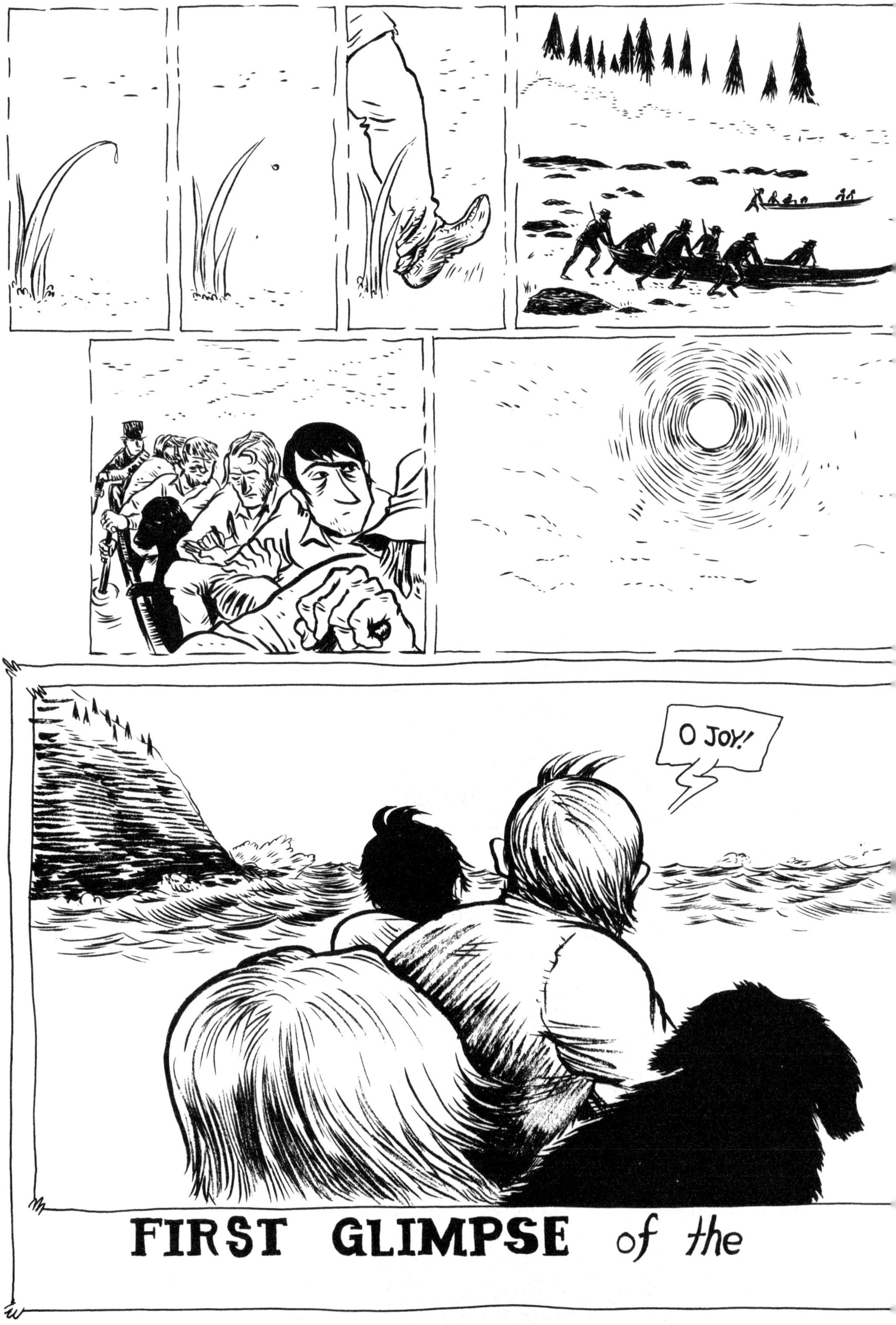
O JOY!
FIRST GLIMPSE of the

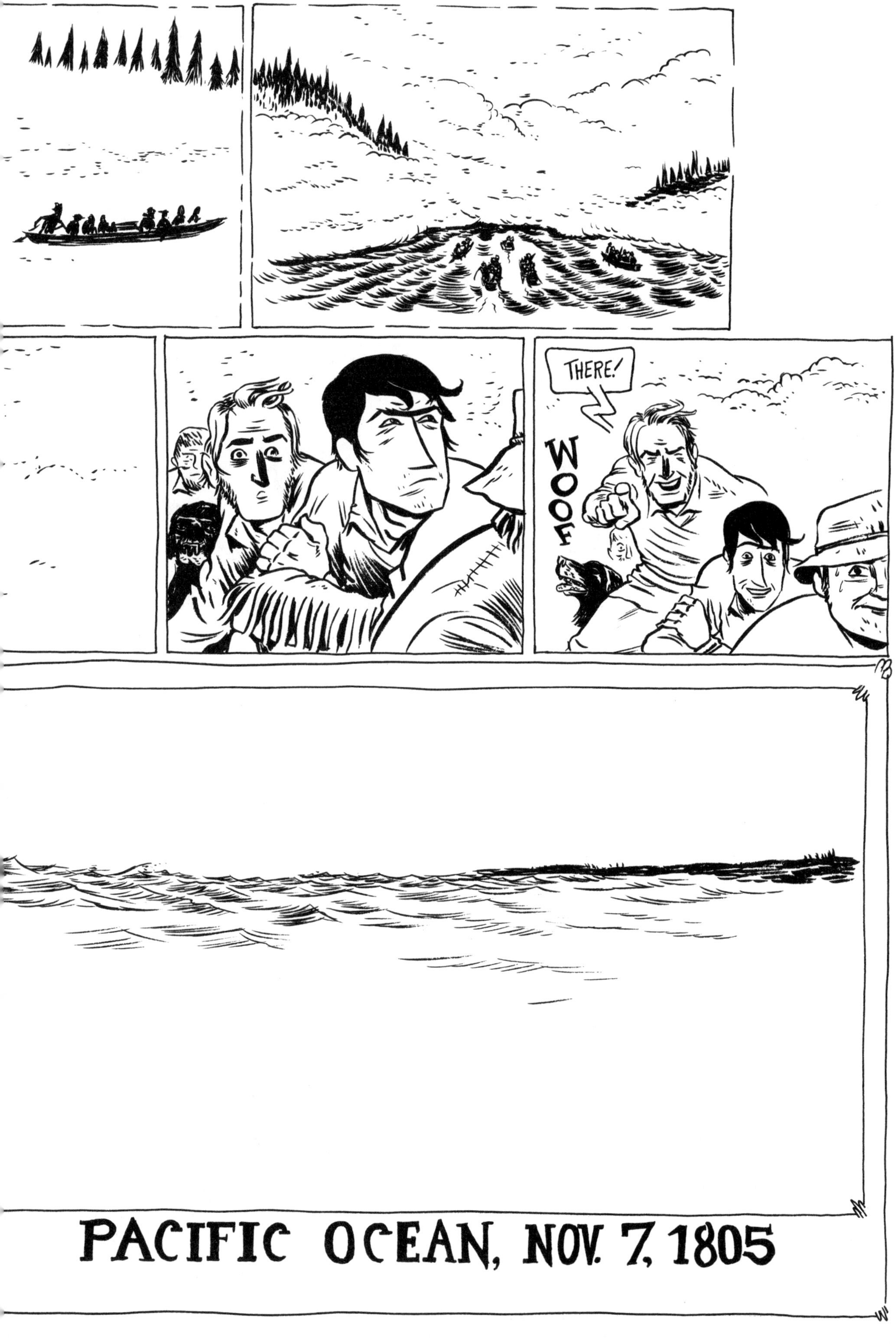
THERE!
WOOF
PACIFIC OCEAN, NOV. 7, 1805

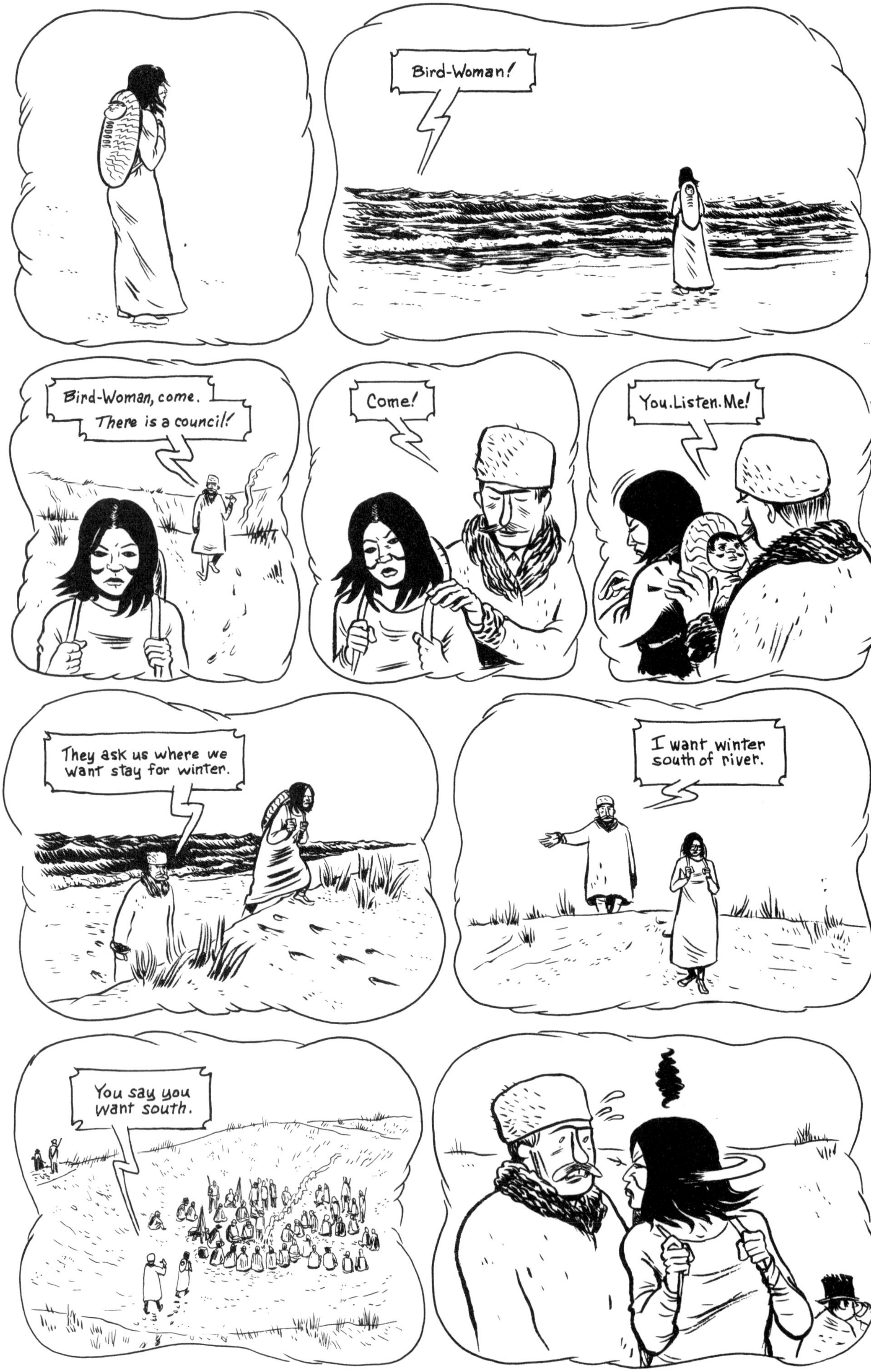
Bird-Woman!
Bird-Woman, come. There is a council!
Come!
You. Listen. Me!
They ask us where we want stay for winter.
I want winter south of river.
You say you want south.

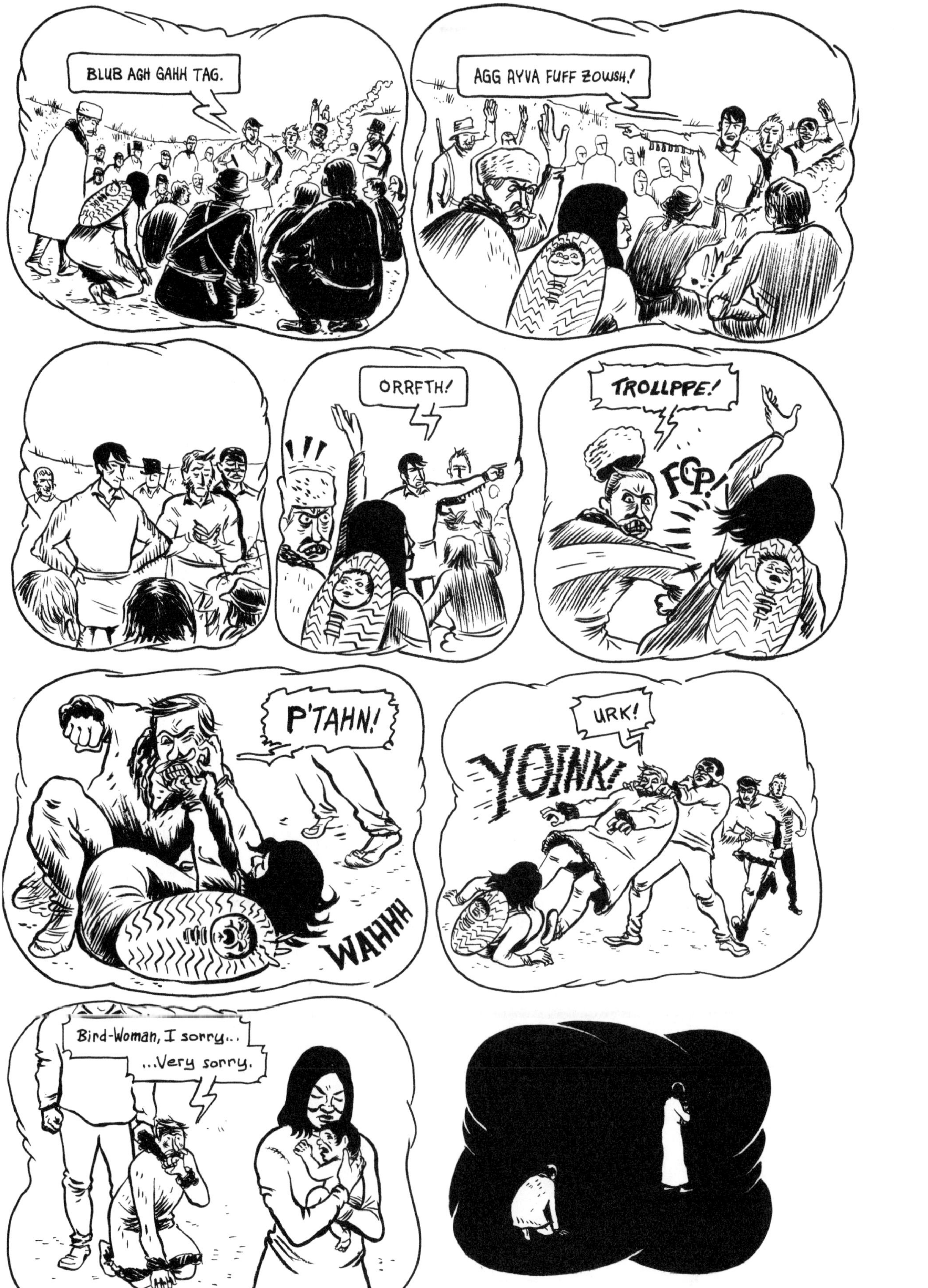
BLUB AGH GAHH TAG.
AGG AYVA FUFF ZOWSH!
ORRFTH!
TROLLPPE!
FCP!
P'TAHN!
WAHHH
URK!
YOINK!
Bird-Woman, I sorry...
...Very sorry.

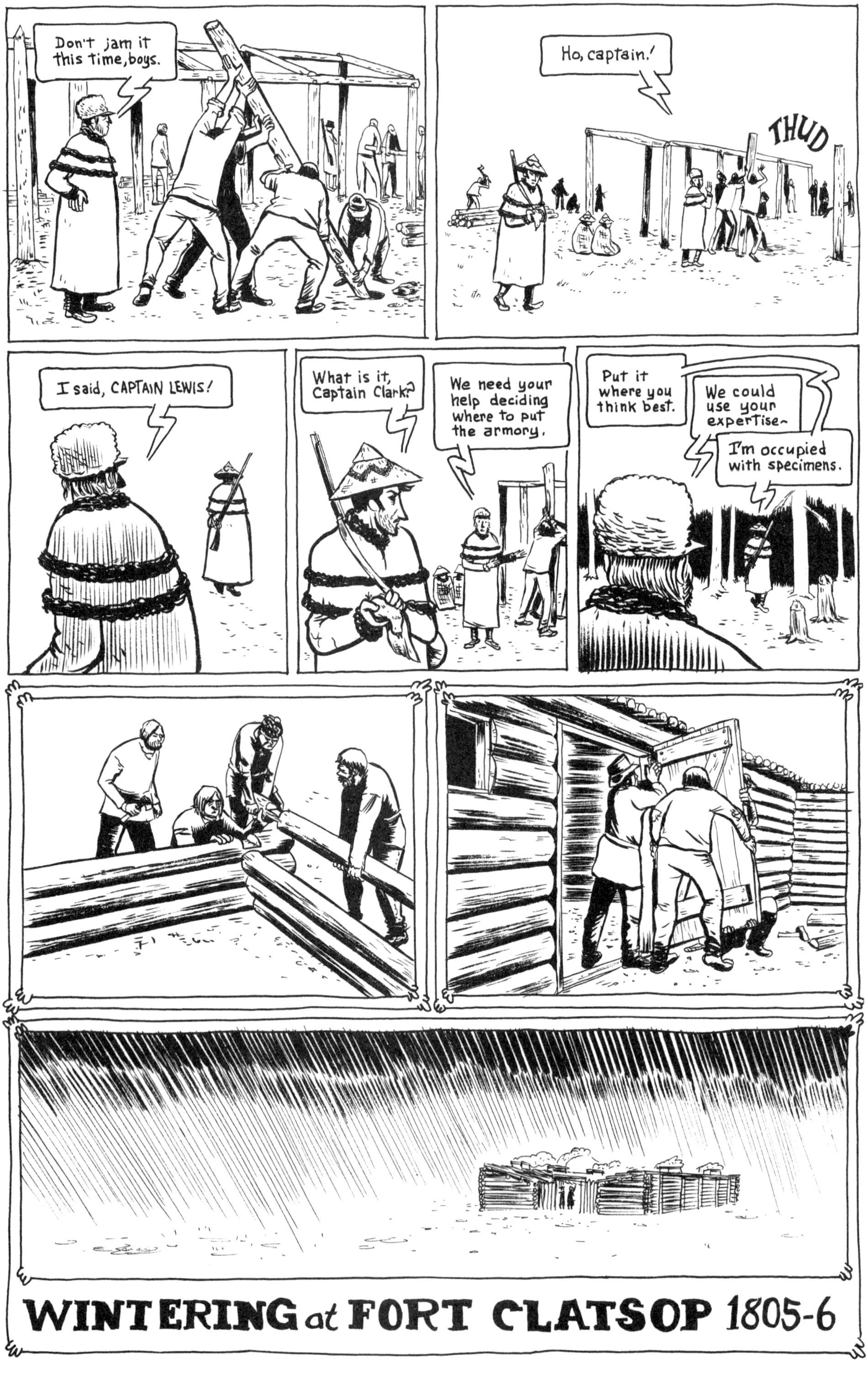
Don't jam it this time, boys.
Ho, captain!
THUD
I said, CAPTAIN LEWIS!
What is it, Captain Clark?
We need your help deciding where to put the armory.
Put it where you think best.
We could use your expertise~
I'm occupied with specimens.
WINTERING at FORT CLATSOP 1805-6

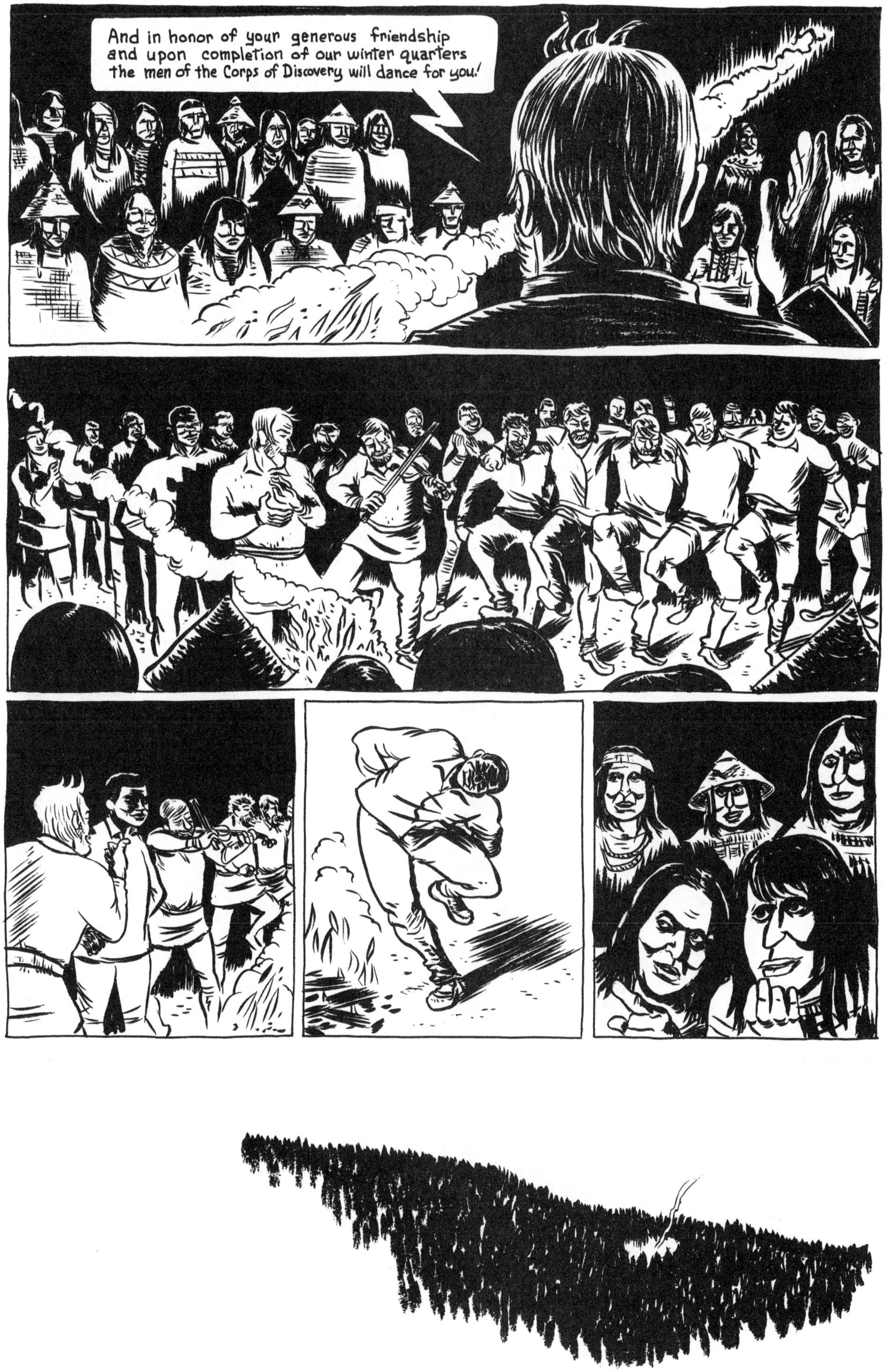
And in honor of your generous friendship and upon completion of our winter quarters the men of the Corps of Discovery will dance for you!

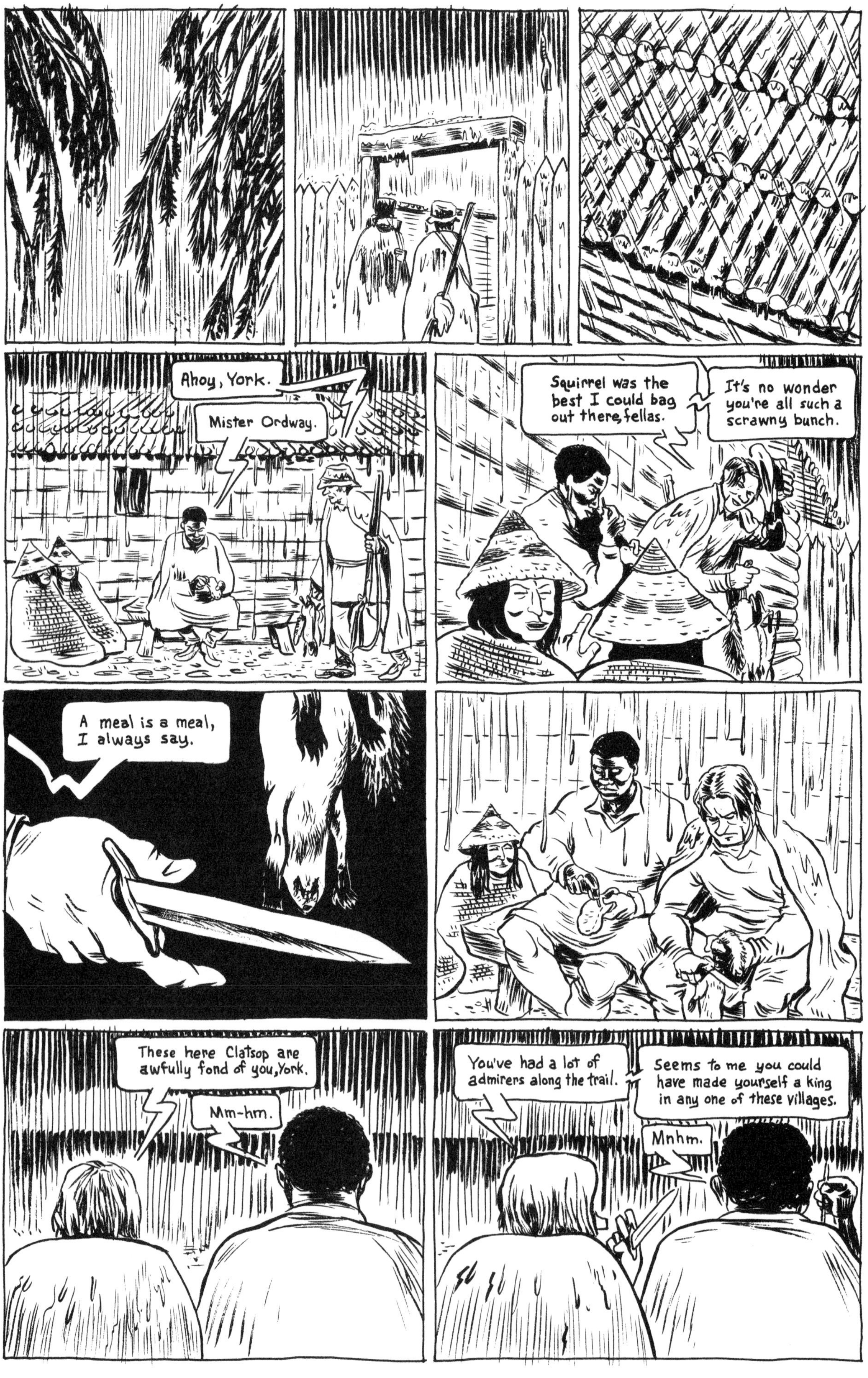

Ahoy, York.
Mister Ordway.
Squirrel was the best I could bag out there, fellas.
It's no wonder you're all such a scrawny bunch.
A meal is a meal, I always say.
These here Clatsop are awfully fond of you, York.
Mm-hm.
You've had a lot of admirers along the trail.
Seems to me you could have made yourself a king in any one of these villages.
Mnhm.

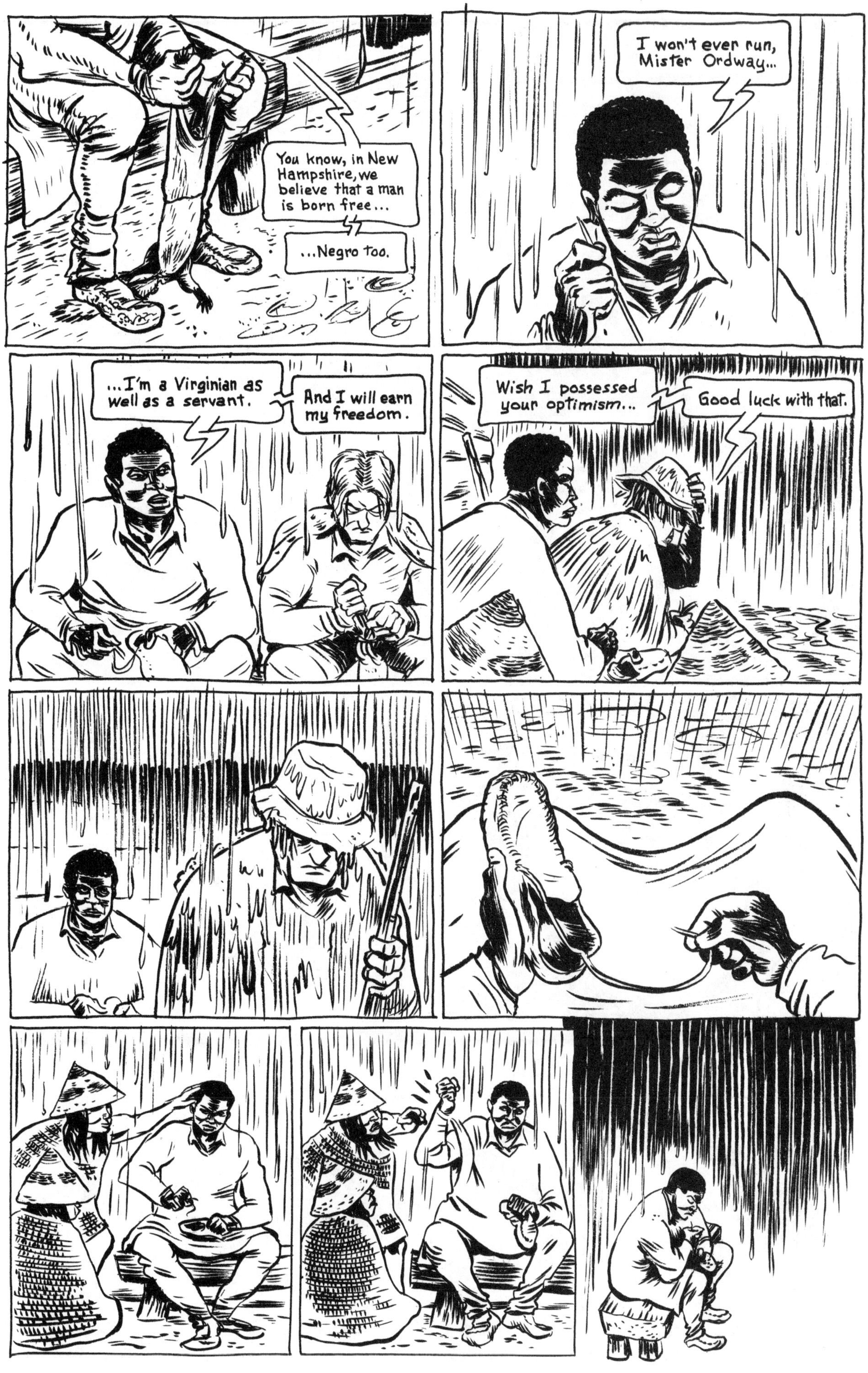
You know, in New Hampshire, we believe that a man is born free...
...Negro too.
I won't ever run, Mister Ordway...
...I'm a Virginian as well as a servant.
And I will earn my freedom.
Wish I possessed your optimism...
Good luck with that.

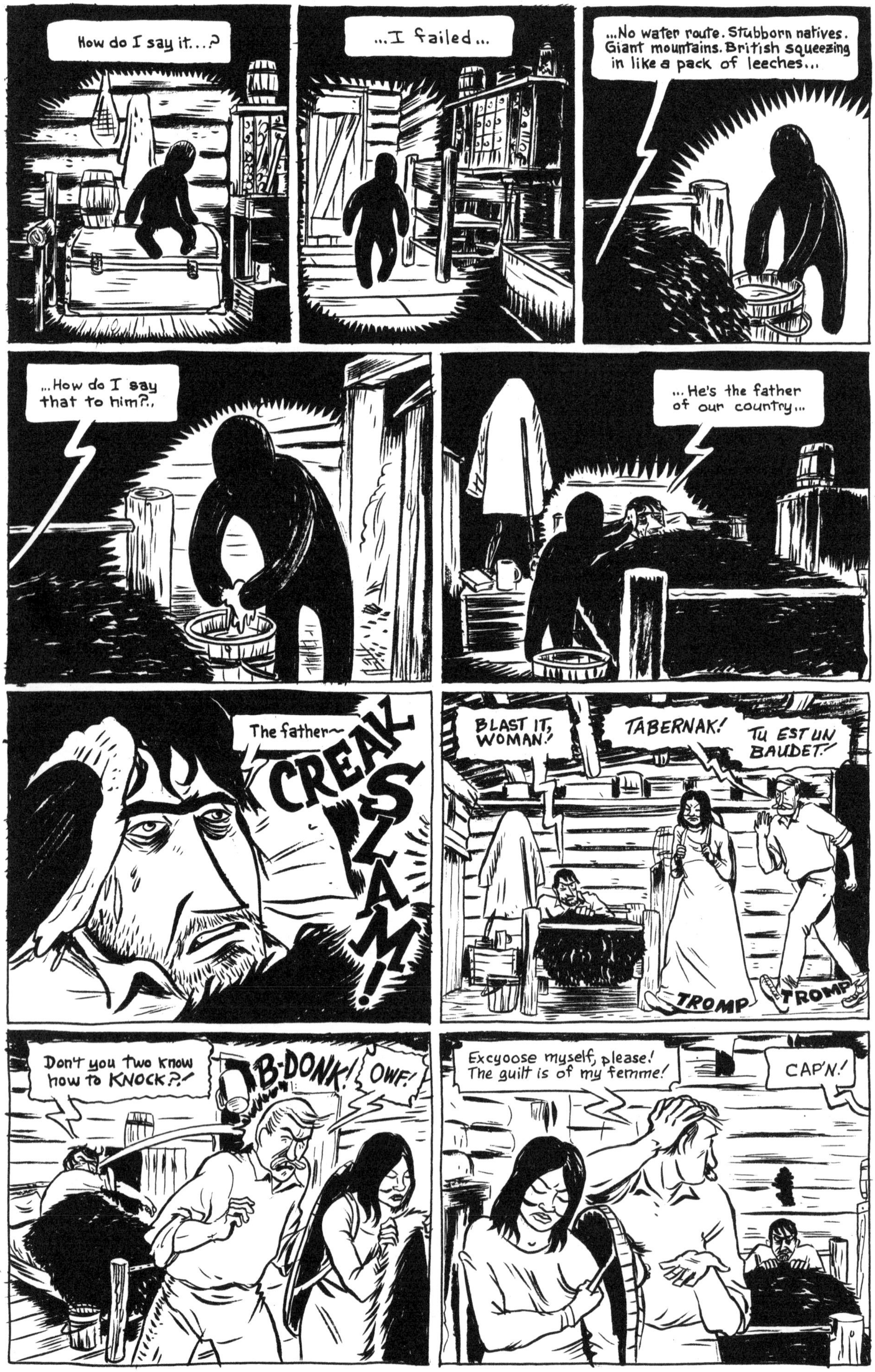
How do I say it...?
...I failed...
...No water route. Stubborn natives. Giant mountains. British squeezing in like a pack of leeches...
...How do I say that to him?..
...He's the father of our country...
The father~
CREAK
SLAM!
BLAST IT, WOMAN!
TABERNAK!
TU EST UN BAUDET!
TROMP
TROMP
Don't you two know how to KNOCK?!
B-DONK!
OWF!
Excyoose myself, please! The guilt is of my femme!
CAP'N!

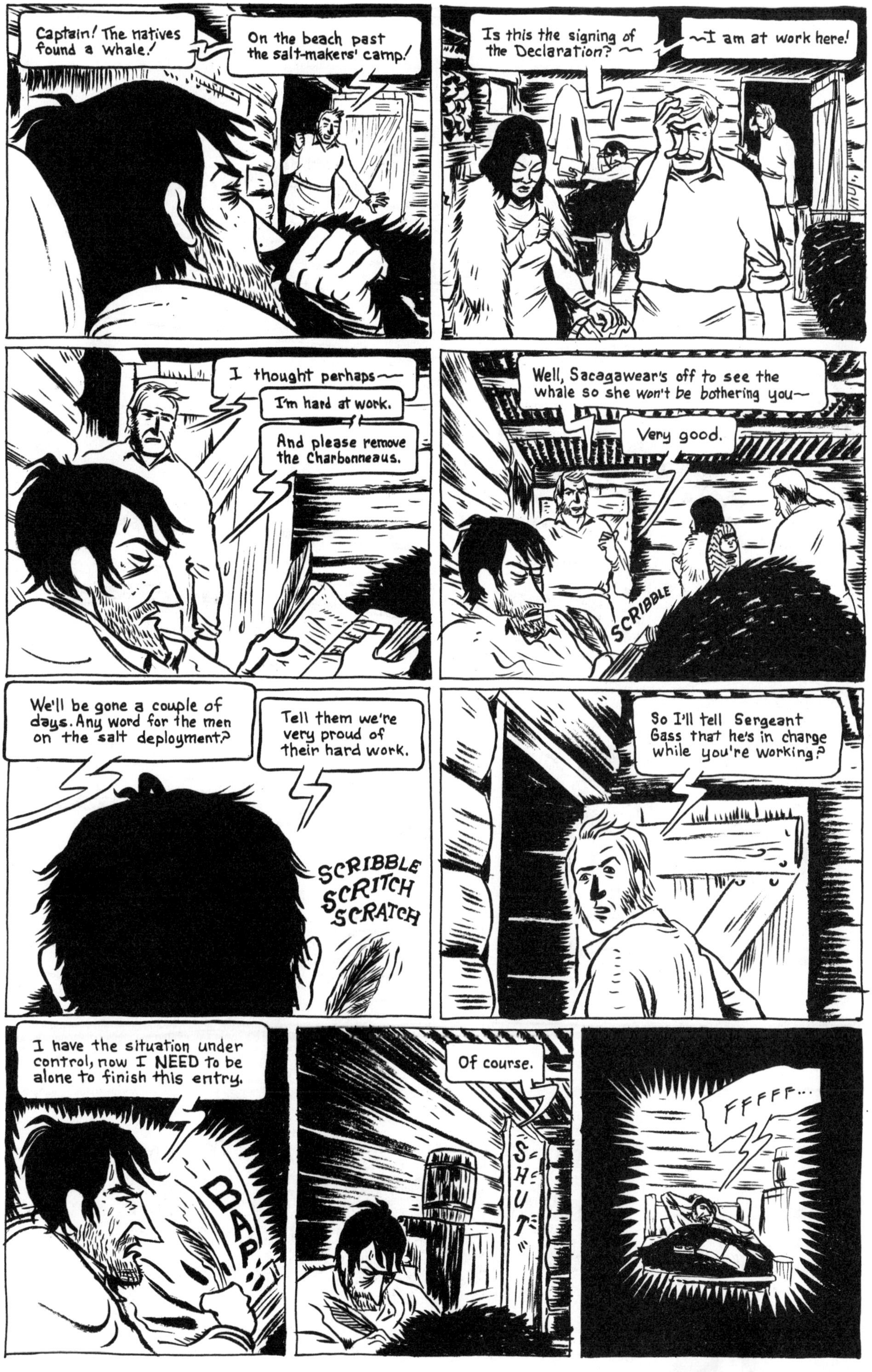
Captain! The natives found a whale!
On the beach past the salt-makers' camp!
Is this the signing of the Declaration?~
~I am at work here!
I thought perhaps~
I'm hard at work.
And please remove the Charbonneaus.
Well, Sacagawear's off to see the whale so she won't be bothering you~
Very good.
SCRIBBLE
We'll be gone a couple of days. Any word for the men on the salt deployment?
Tell them we're very proud of their hard work.
SCRIBBLE
SCRITCH
SCRATCH
So I'll tell Sergeant Gass that he's in charge while you're working?
I have the situation under control, now I NEED to be alone to finish this entry.
BAP!
Of course.
SHUT
FFFFF...

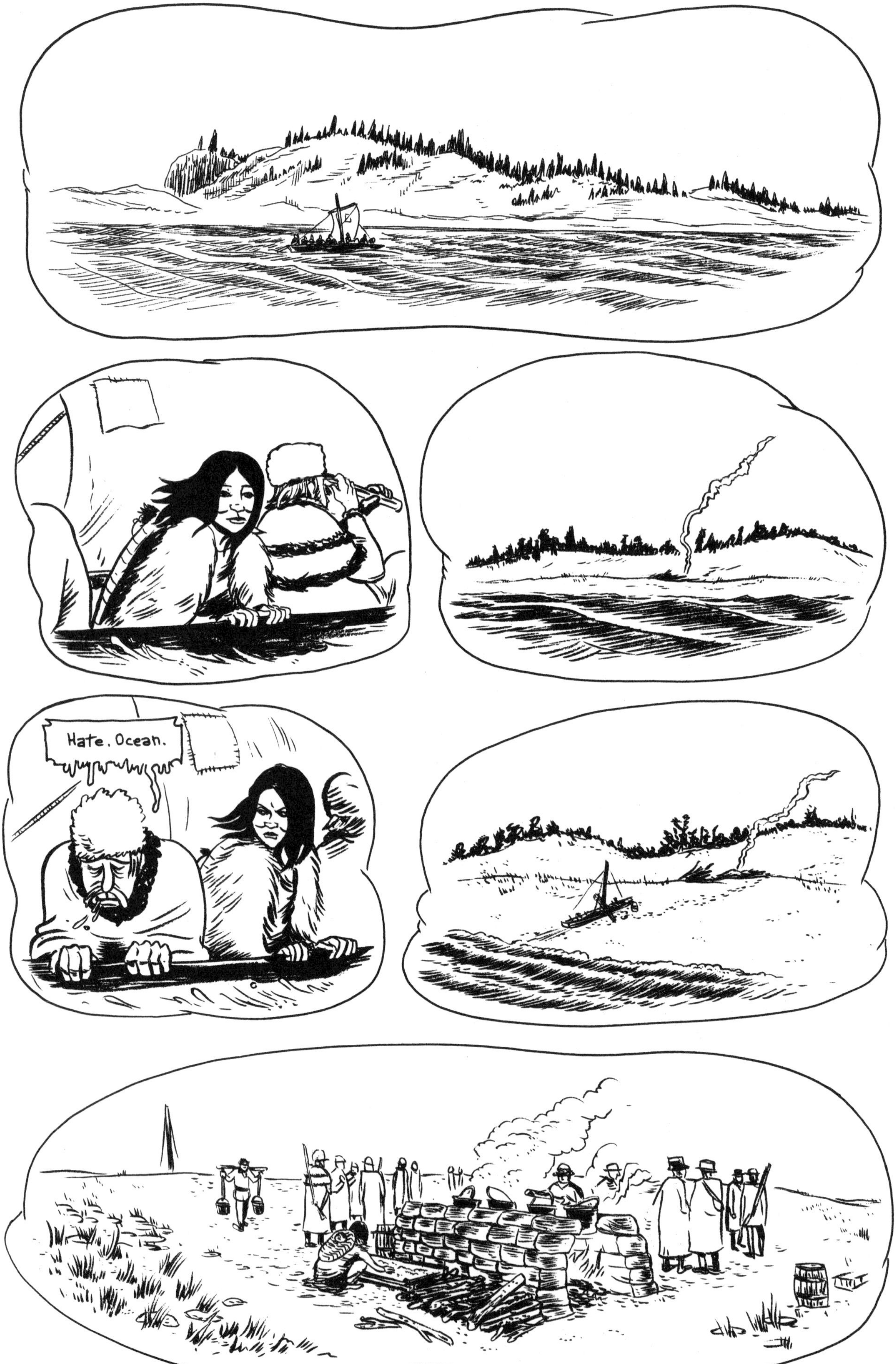
Hate. Ocean.

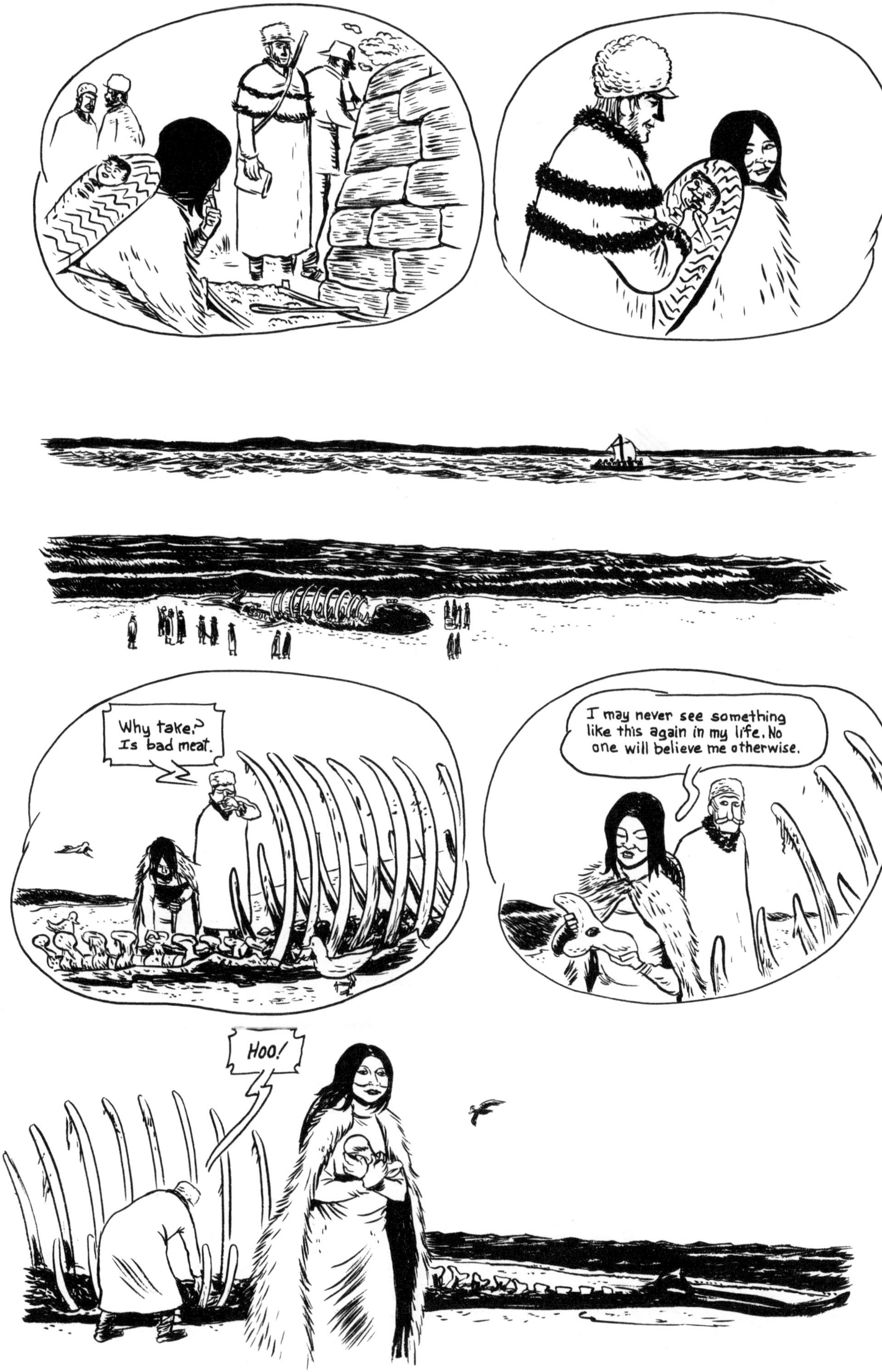
Why take?
Is bad meat.
I may never see something like this again in my life. No one will believe me otherwise.
Hoo!

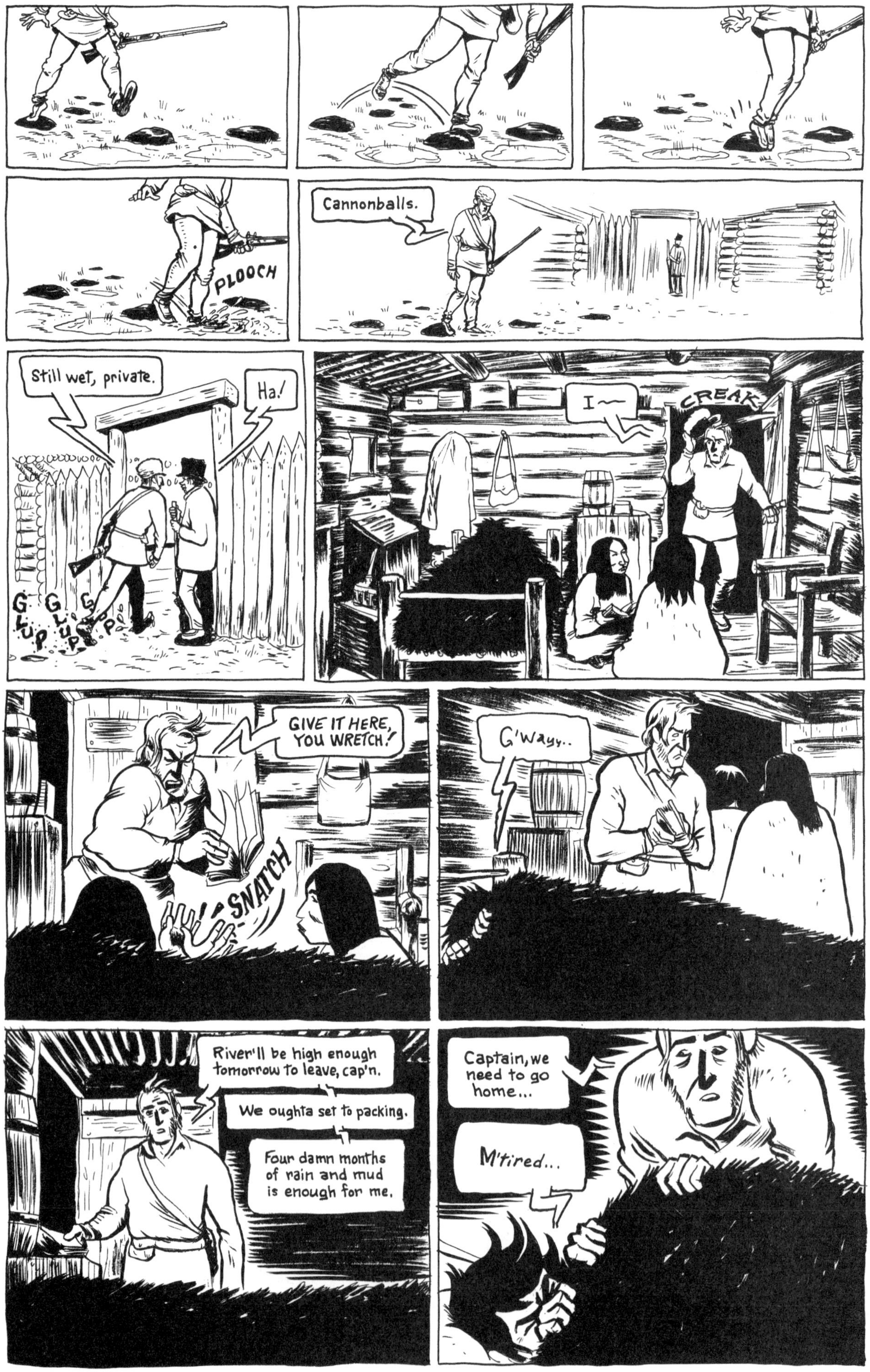
PLOOCH
Cannonballs.
Still wet, private.
Ha!
GLUP GLUP GLUP
I~~
CREAK
GIVE IT HERE, YOU WRETCH!
SNATCH
G'wayy..
River'll be high enough tomorrow to leave, cap'n.
We oughta set to packing.
Four damn months of rain and mud is enough for me.
Captain, we need to go home...
M'tired...

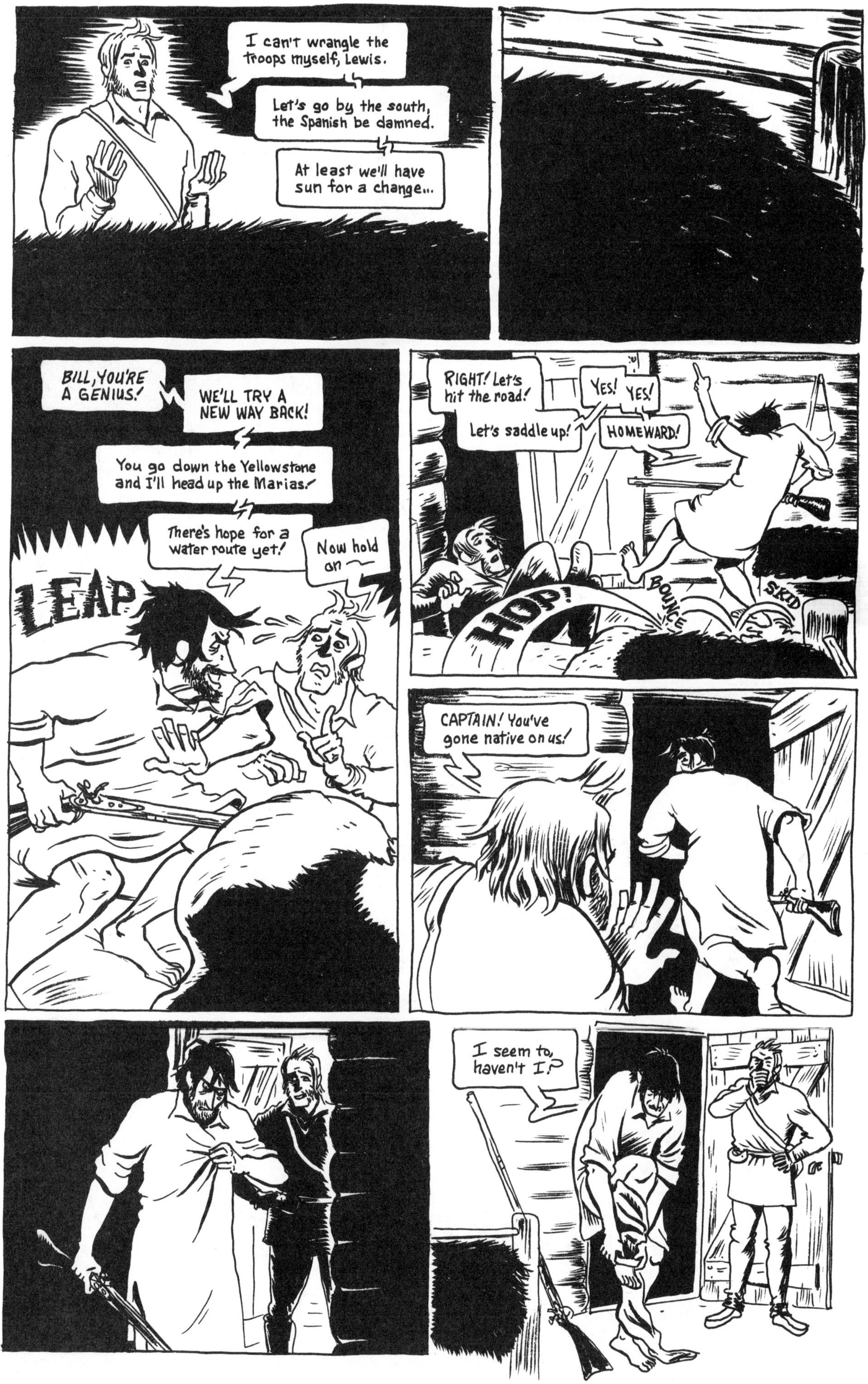
I can't wrangle the troops myself, Lewis.
Let's go by the south, the Spanish be damned.
At least we'll have sun for a change...
BILL, YOU'RE A GENIUS!
WE'LL TRY A NEW WAY BACK!
You go down the Yellowstone and I'll head up the Marias!
There's hope for a water route yet!
Now hold on—
LEAP
RIGHT! Let's hit the road!
YES!
YES!
Let's saddle up!
HOMEWARD!
HOP!
BOUNCE
SKID
CAPTAIN! You've gone native on us!
I seem to, haven't I?

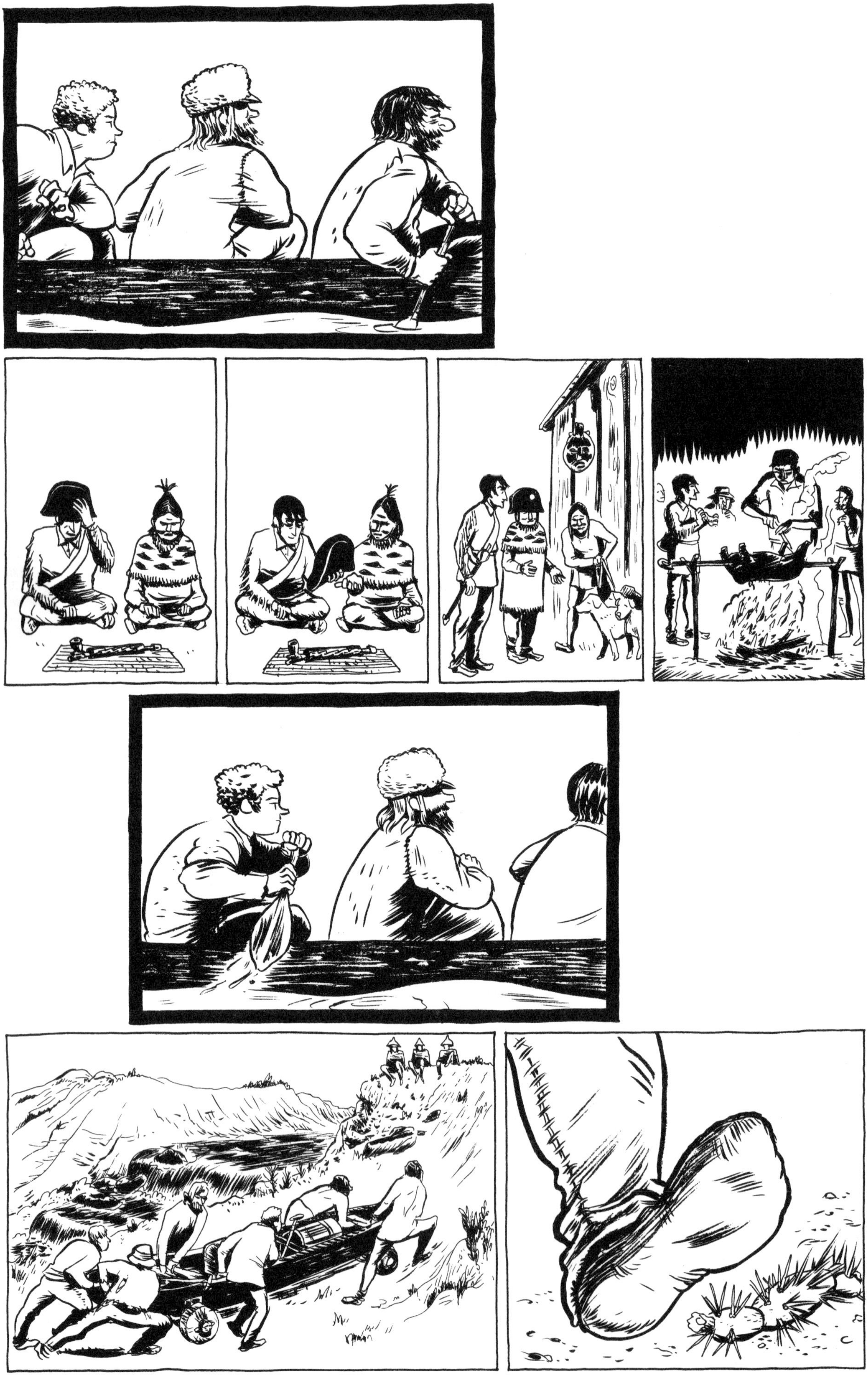

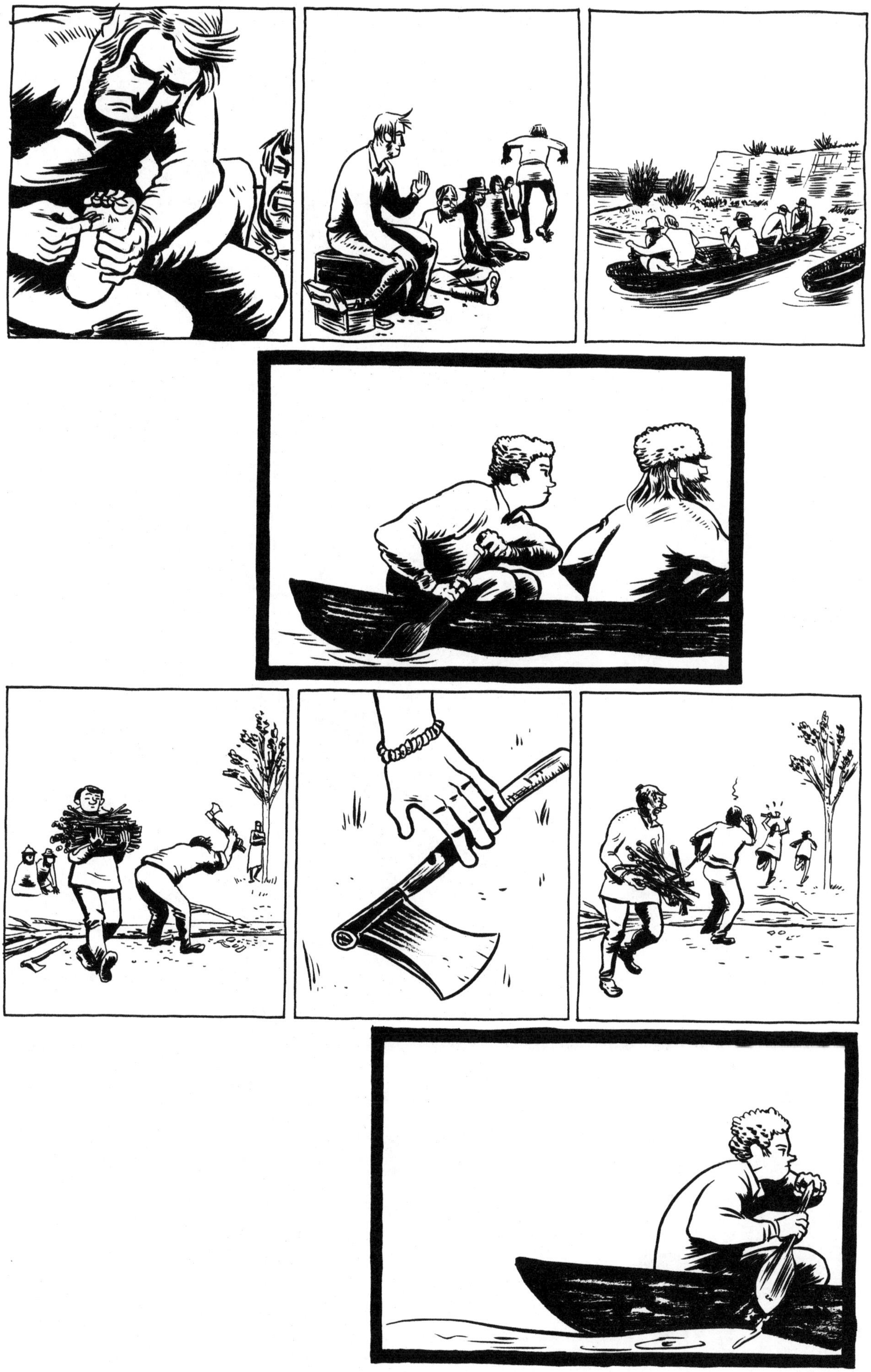

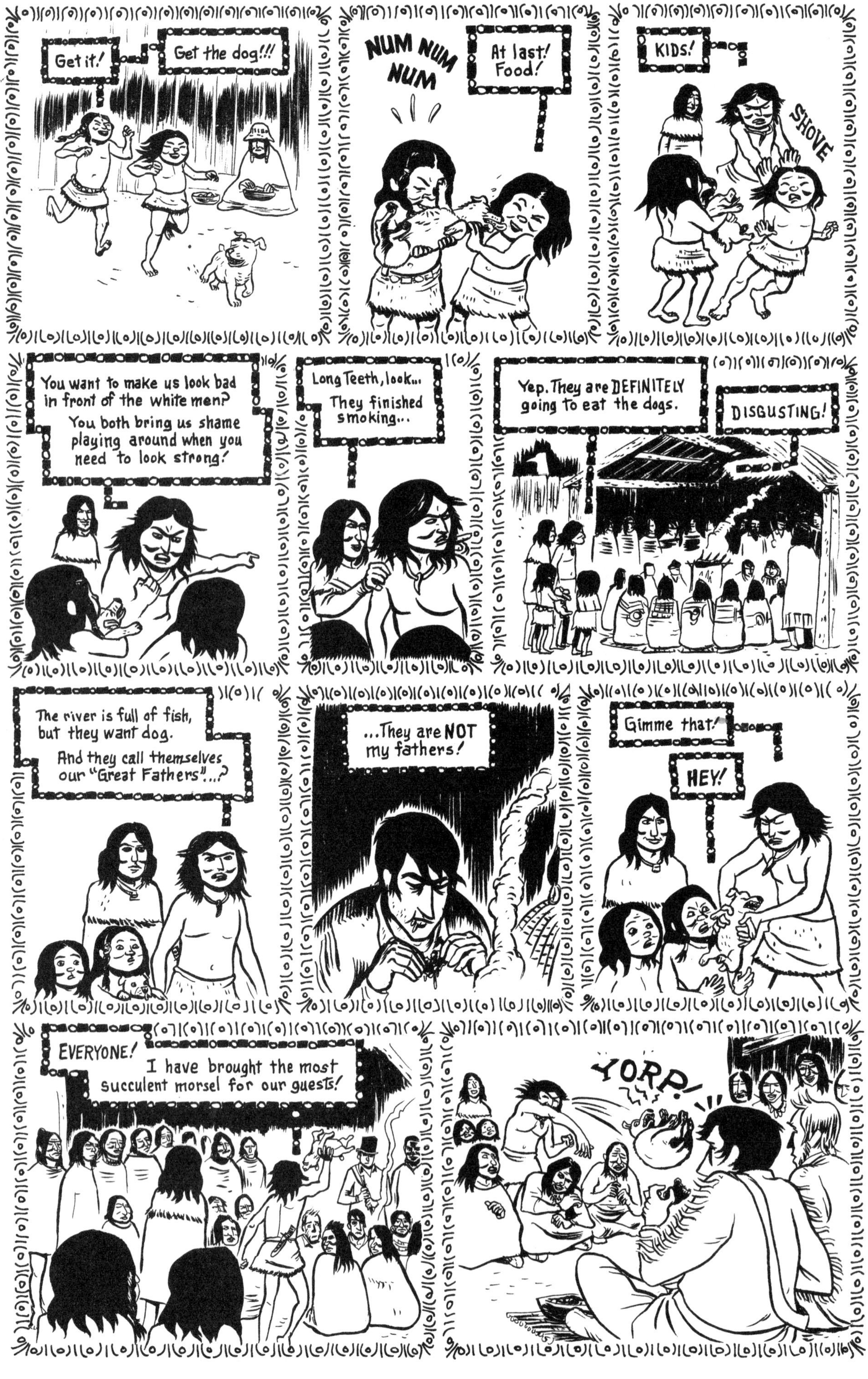

Get it!
Get the dog!!!
NUM NUM NUM
At last! Food!
KIDS!
SHOVE
You want to make us look bad in front of the white men? You both bring us shame playing around when you need to look strong!
Long Teeth, look... They finished smoking...
Yep. They are DEFINITELY going to eat the dogs.
DISGUSTING!
The river is full of fish, but they want dog. And they call themselves our "Great Fathers"...?
...They are NOT my fathers!
Gimme that!
HEY!
EVERYONE! I have brought the most succulent morsel for our guests!
YORP!

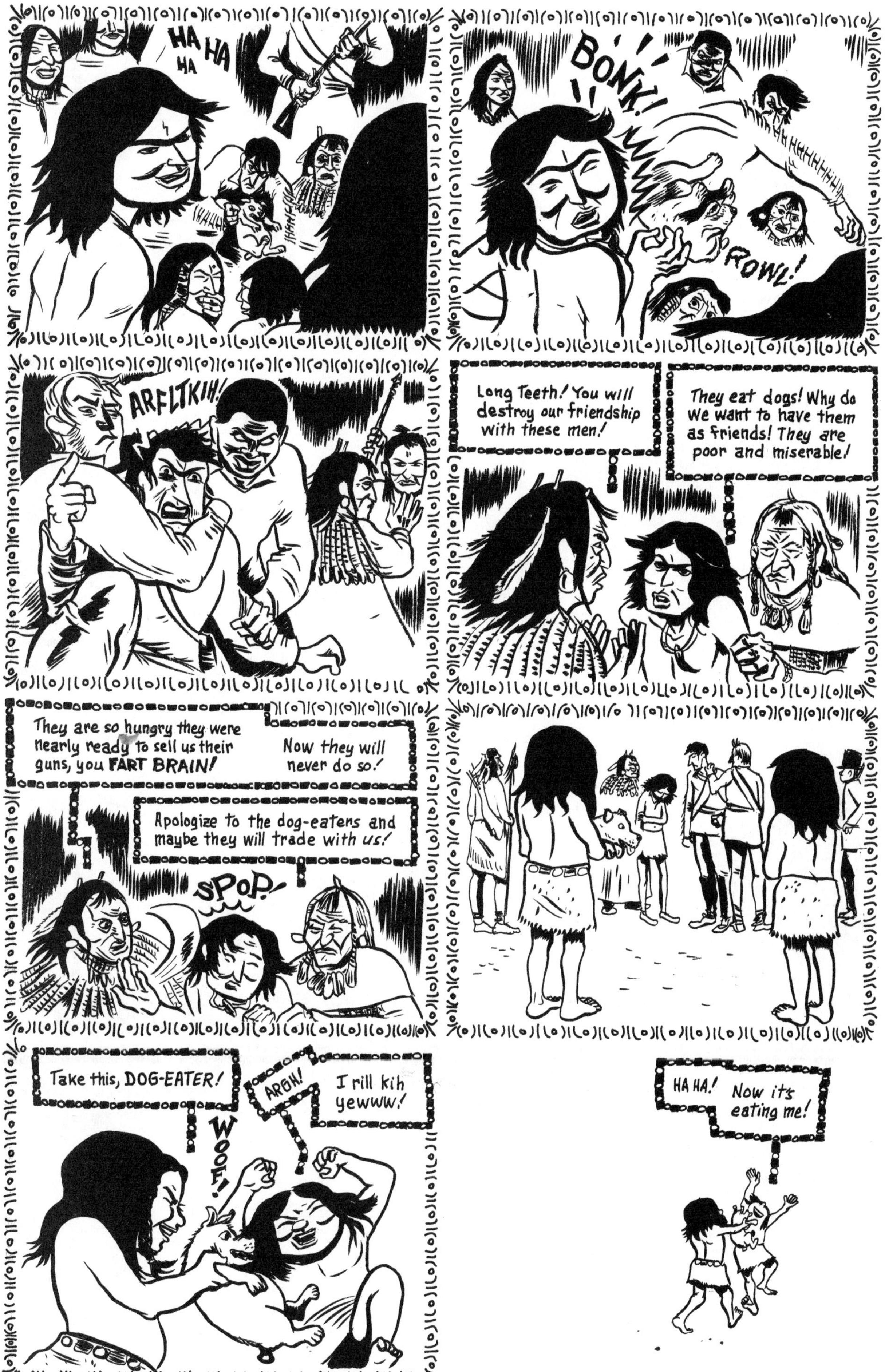

HA HA HA
HA HA
BONK!
ROWL!
ARFLTKIH!
Long Teeth! You will destroy our friendship with these men!
They eat dogs! Why do we want to have them as friends! They are poor and miserable!
They are so hungry they were nearly ready to sell us their guns, you FART BRAIN!
Now they will never do so!
Apologize to the dog-eaters and maybe they will trade with us!
SPOP!
Take this, DOG-EATER!
WOOF!
ARGH!
I rill kih yewww!
HA HA!
Now it's eating me!

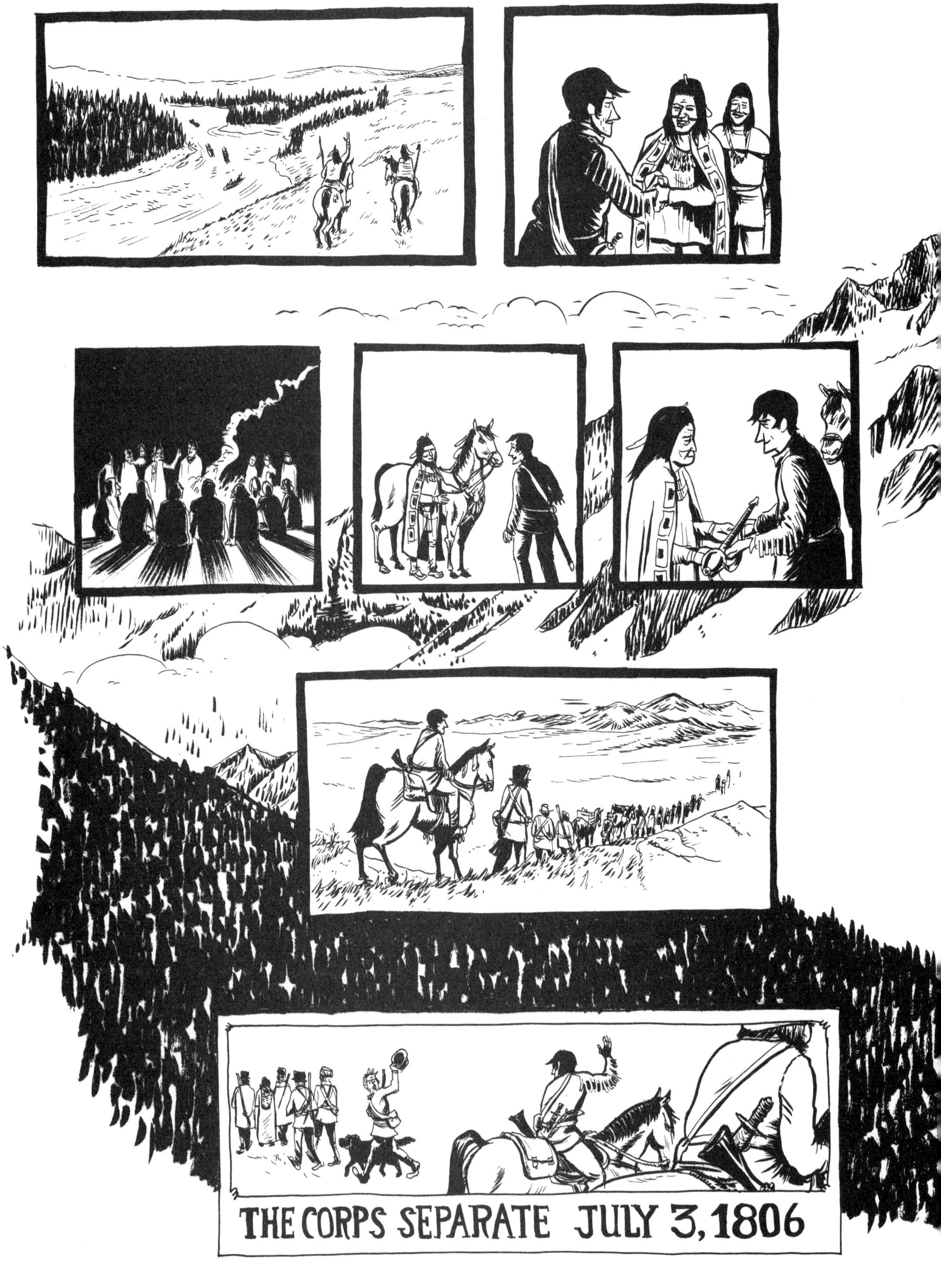
THE CORPS SEPARATE JULY 3, 1806

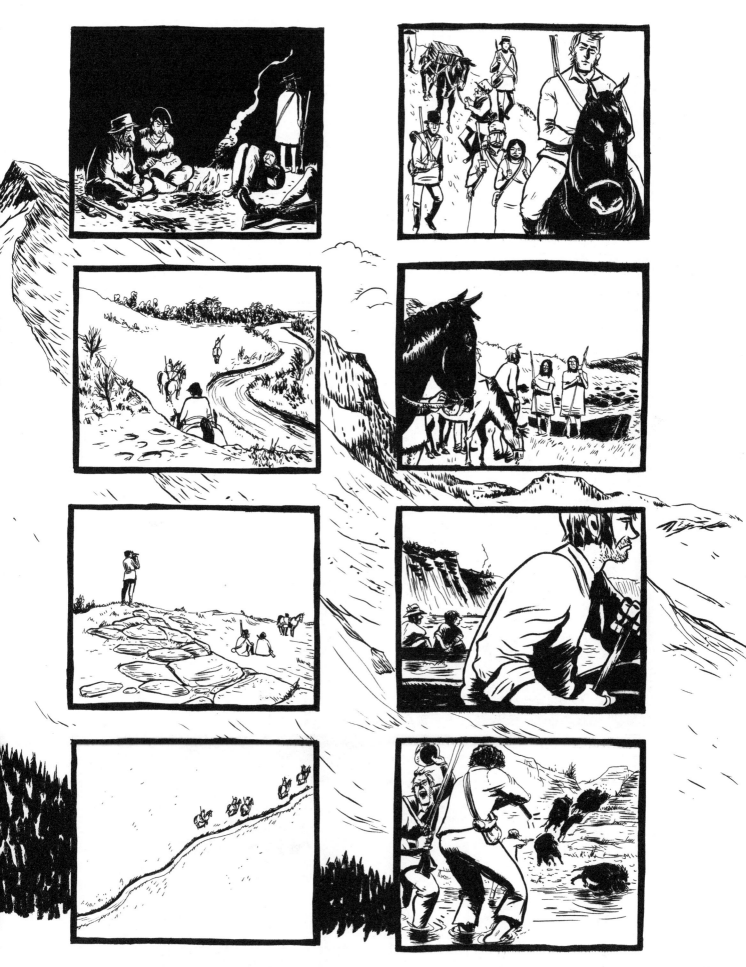

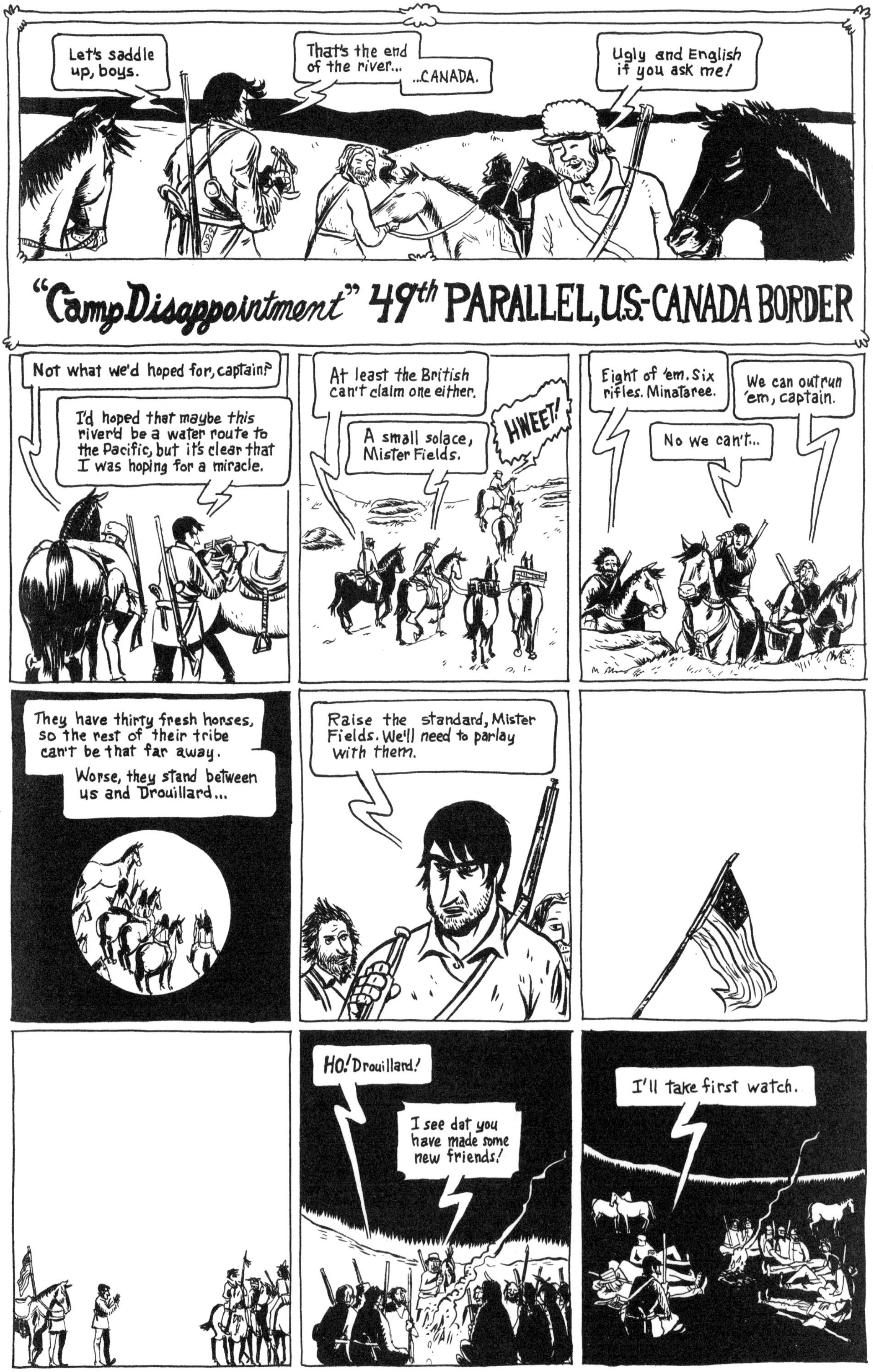

Let's saddle up, boys.
That's the end of the river...
...CANADA.
Ugly and English if you ask me!
"Camp Disappointment" 49th PARALLEL, U.S.-CANADA BORDER
Not what we'd hoped for, captain?
I'd hoped that maybe this river'd be a water route to the Pacific, but it's clear that I was hoping for a miracle.
At least the British can't claim one either.
A small solace, Mister Fields.
HWEET!
Eight of 'em. Six rifles. Minataree.
We can outrun 'em, captain.
No we can't...
They have thirty fresh horses, so the rest of their tribe can't be that far away.
Worse, they stand between us and Drouillard...
Raise the standard, Mister Fields. We'll need to parlay with them.
HO! Drouillard!
I see dat you have made some new friends!
I'll take first watch.

CREAK
HEY!

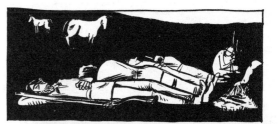

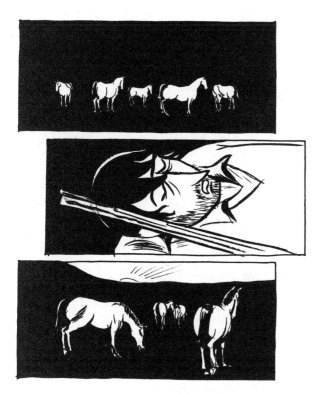

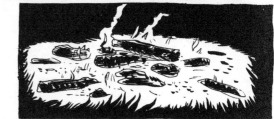

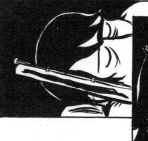

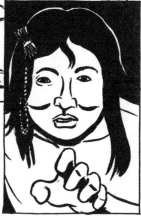

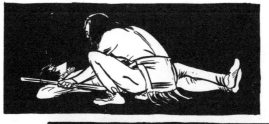

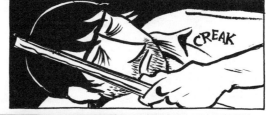

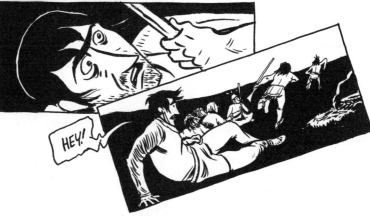

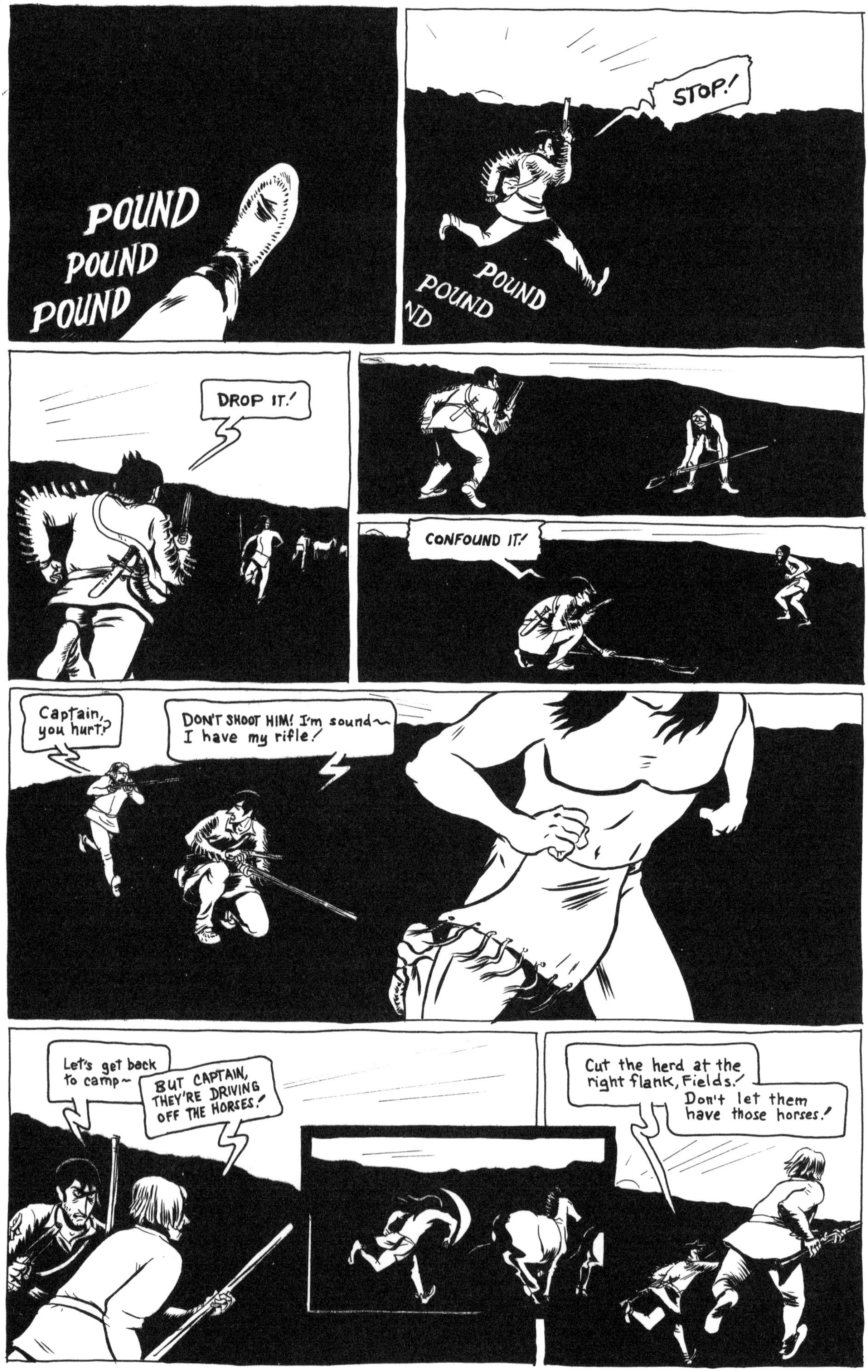
POUND
POUND
POUND
STOP!
POUND
POUND
DROP IT!
CONFOUND IT!
Captain, you hurt?
DON'T SHOOT HIM! I'm sound~ I have my rifle!
Let's get back to camp~
BUT CAPTAIN, THEY'RE DRIVING OFF THE HORSES!
Cut the herd at the right flank, Fields!
Don't let them have those horses!

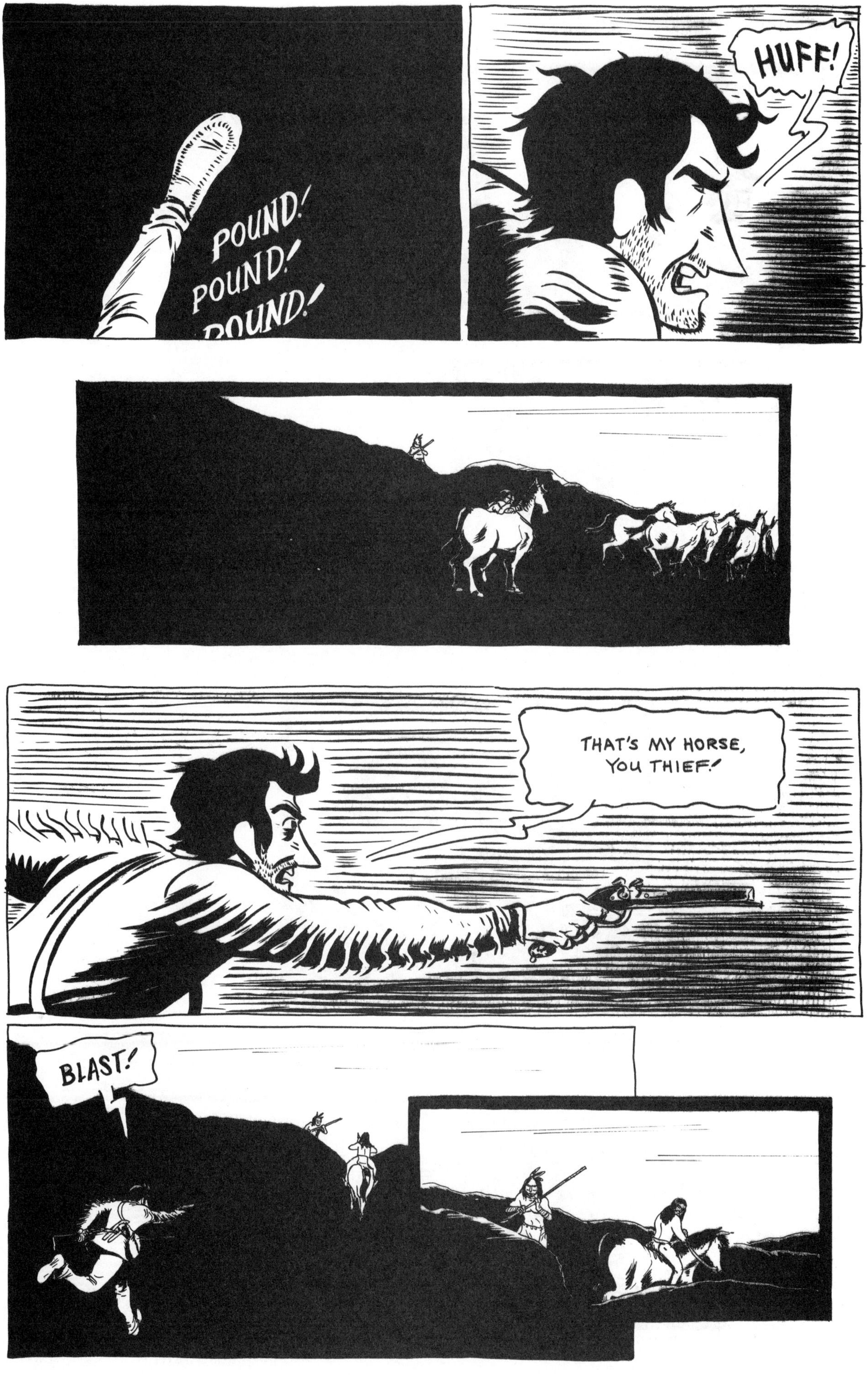
POUND!
POUND!
POUND!
HUFF!
THAT'S MY HORSE, YOU THIEF!
BLAST!

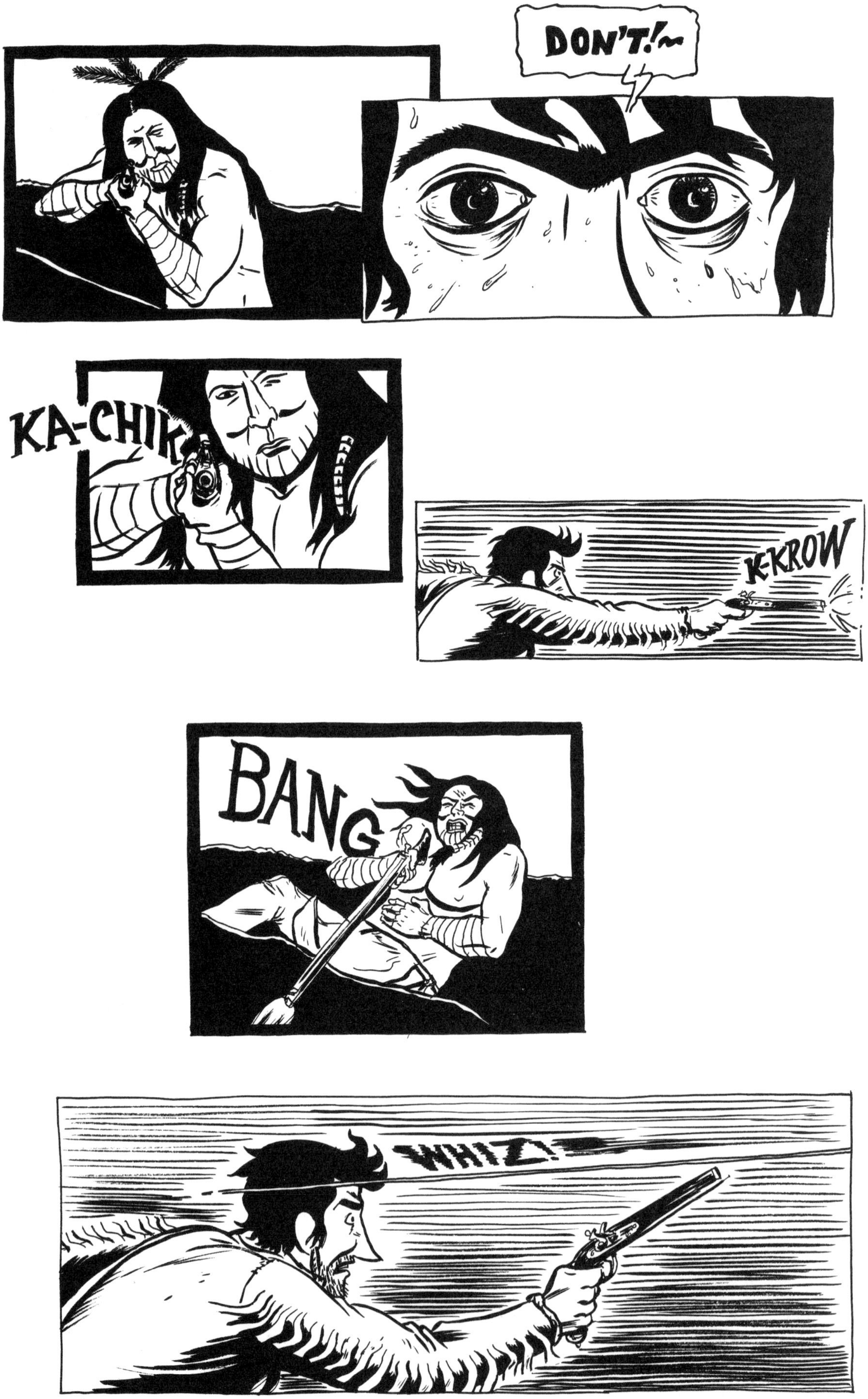
DON'T!~
KA-CHIK
K-KROW
BANG
WHIZ!

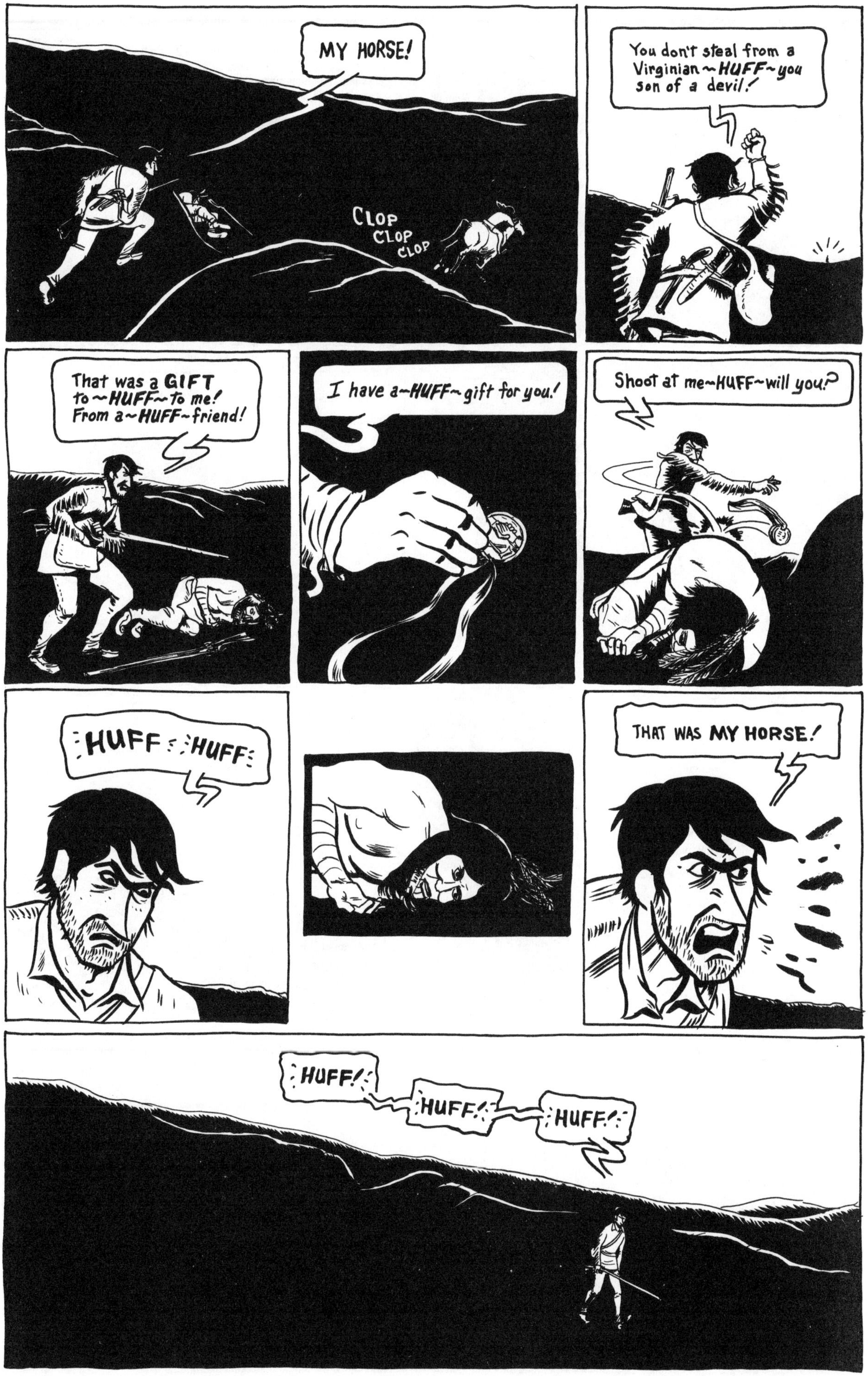
MY HORSE!
CLOP CLOP CLOP
You don't steal from a Virginian ~HUFF~ you son of a devil!
That was a GIFT to ~HUFF~ to me! From a ~HUFF~ friend!
I have a ~HUFF~ gift for you!
Shoot at me ~HUFF~ will you?
HUFF HUFF
THAT WAS MY HORSE!
HUFF!
HUFF!
HUFF!

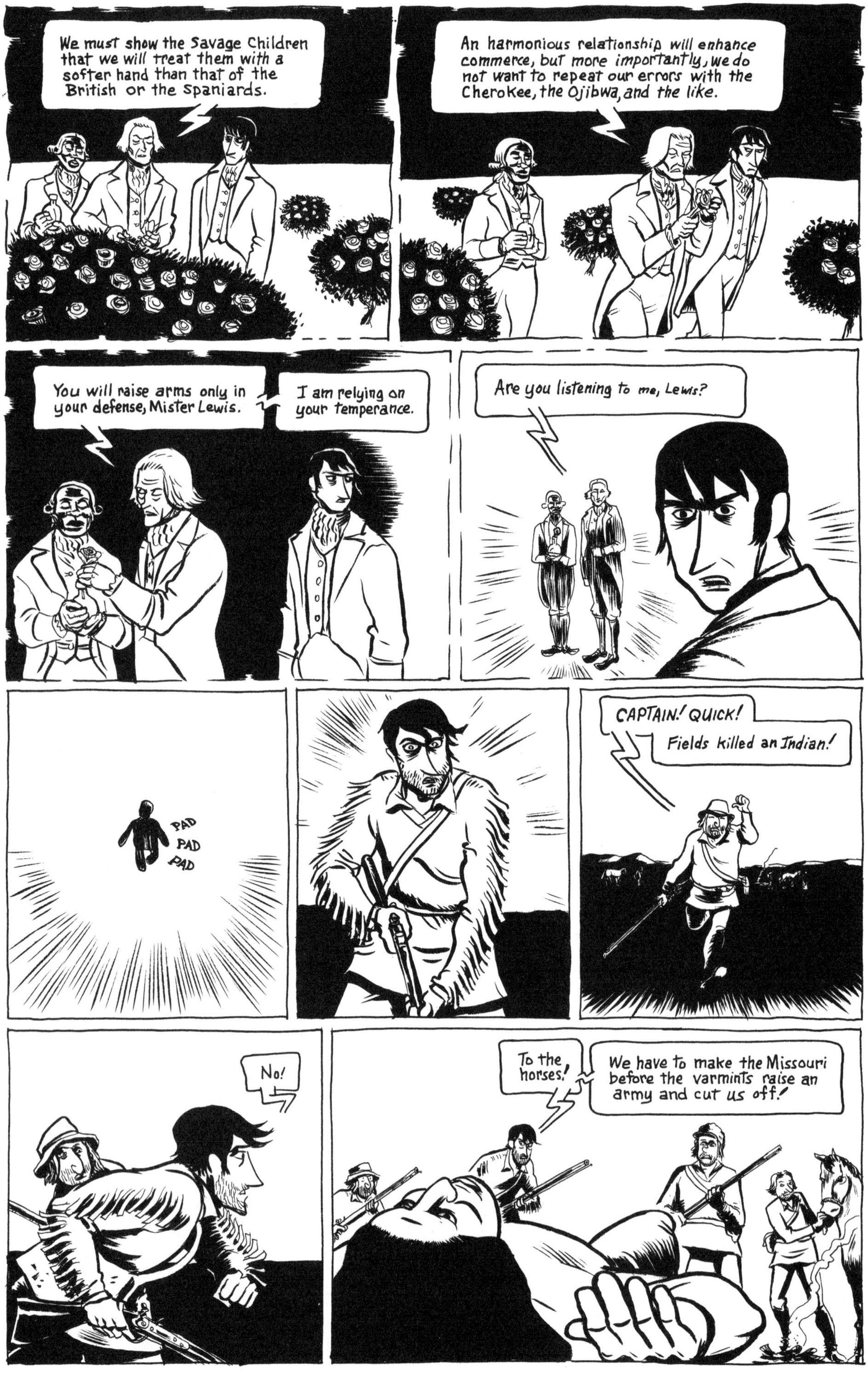
We must show the Savage Children that we will treat them with a softer hand than that of the British or the Spaniards.
An harmonious relationship will enhance commerce, but more importantly, we do not want to repeat our errors with the Cherokee, the Ojibwa, and the like.
You will raise arms only in your defense, Mister Lewis.
I am relying on your temperance.
Are you listening to me, Lewis?
PAD
PAD
PAD
CAPTAIN! QUICK!
Fields killed an Indian!
No!
To the horses!
We have to make the Missouri before the varmints raise an army and cut us off!

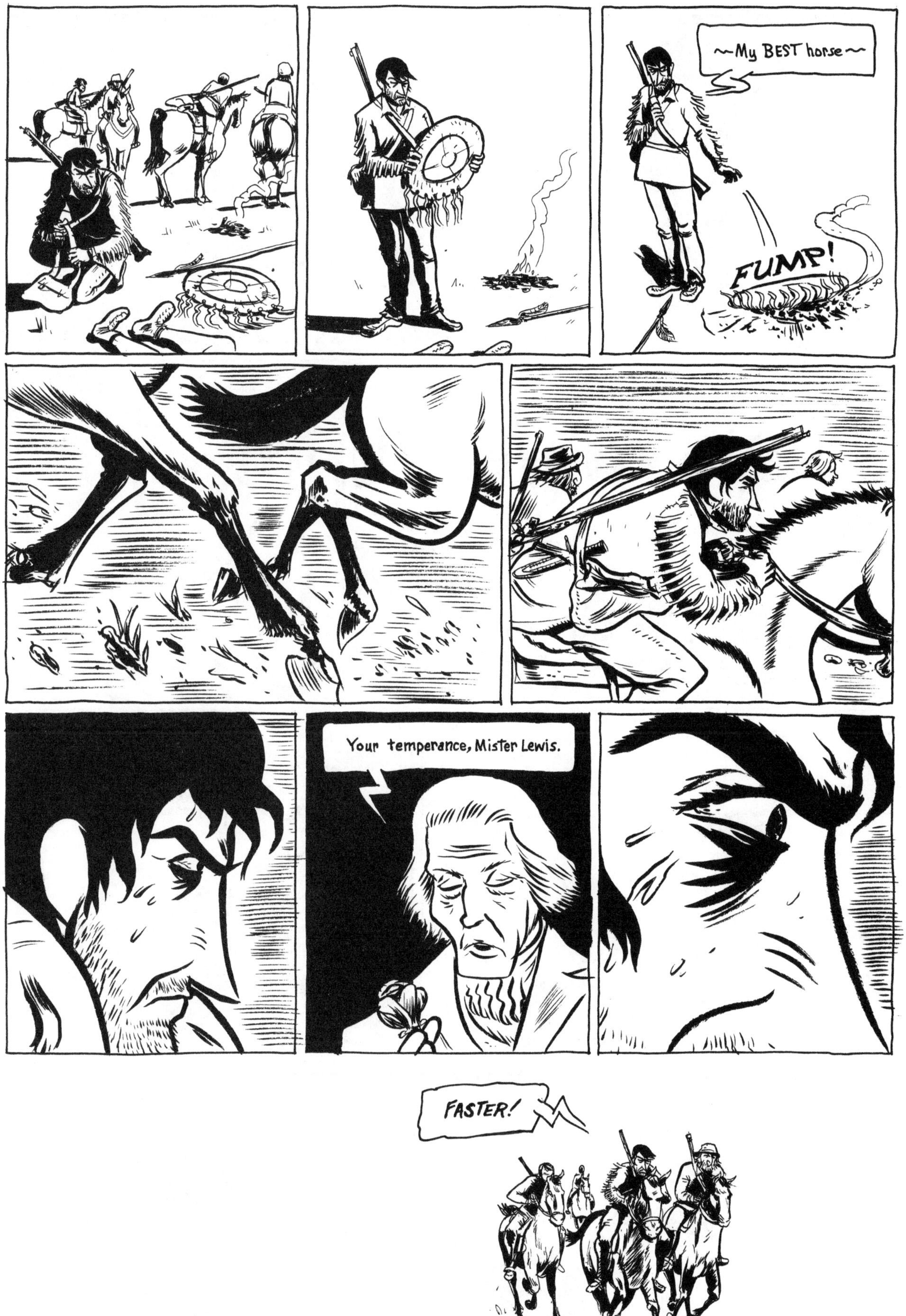
~My BEST horse~
FUMP!
Your temperance, Mister Lewis.
FASTER!

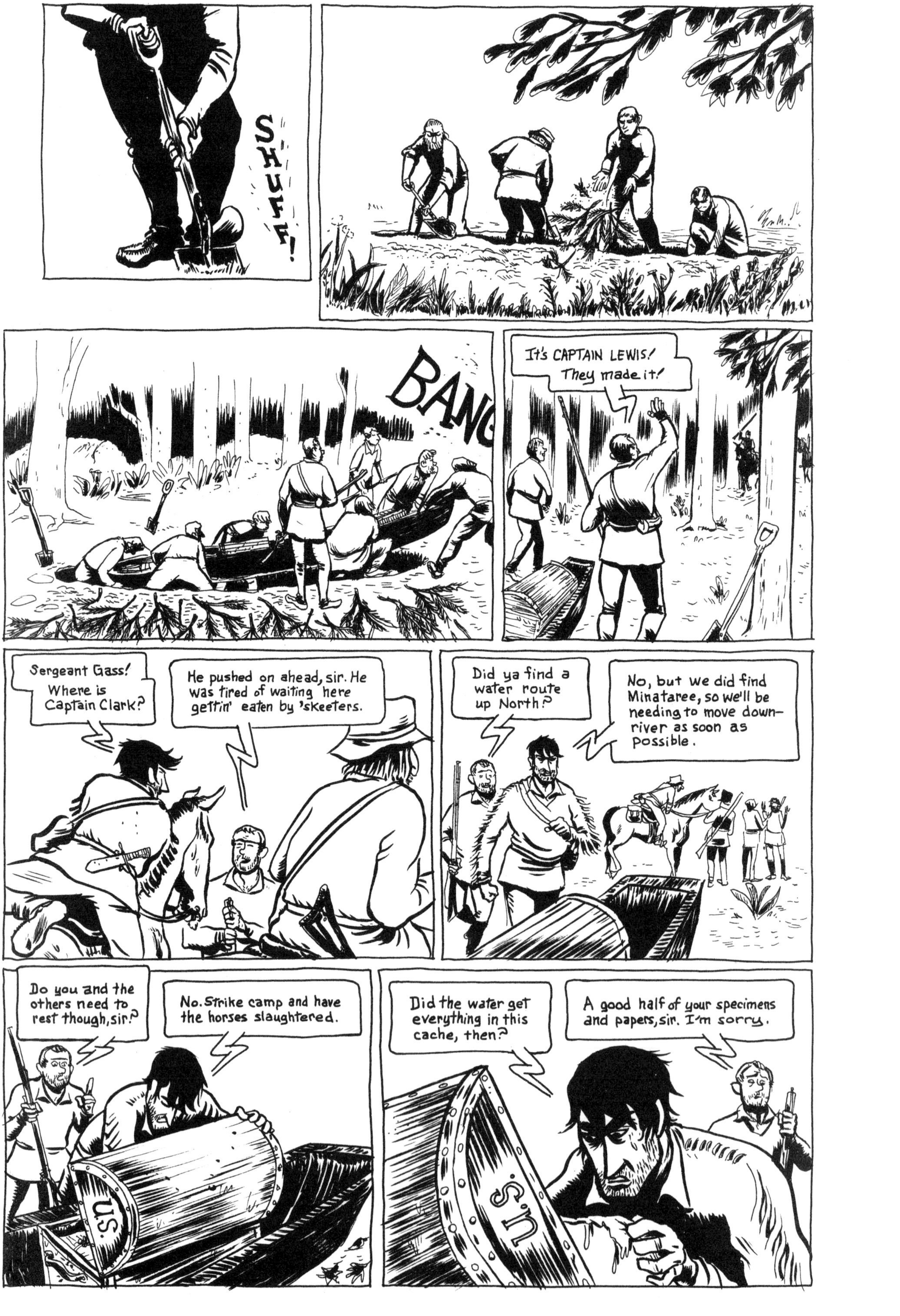
SHUFF!
BANG
It's CAPTAIN LEWIS! They made it!
Sergeant Gass! Where is Captain Clark?
He pushed on ahead, sir. He was tired of waiting here gettin' eaten by 'skeeters.
Did ya find a water route up North?
No, but we did find Minataree, so we'll be needing to move downriver as soon as possible.
Do you and the others need to rest though, sir?
No. Strike camp and have the horses slaughtered.
U.S.
Did the water get everything in this cache, then?
A good half of your specimens and papers, sir. I'm sorry.
U.S.

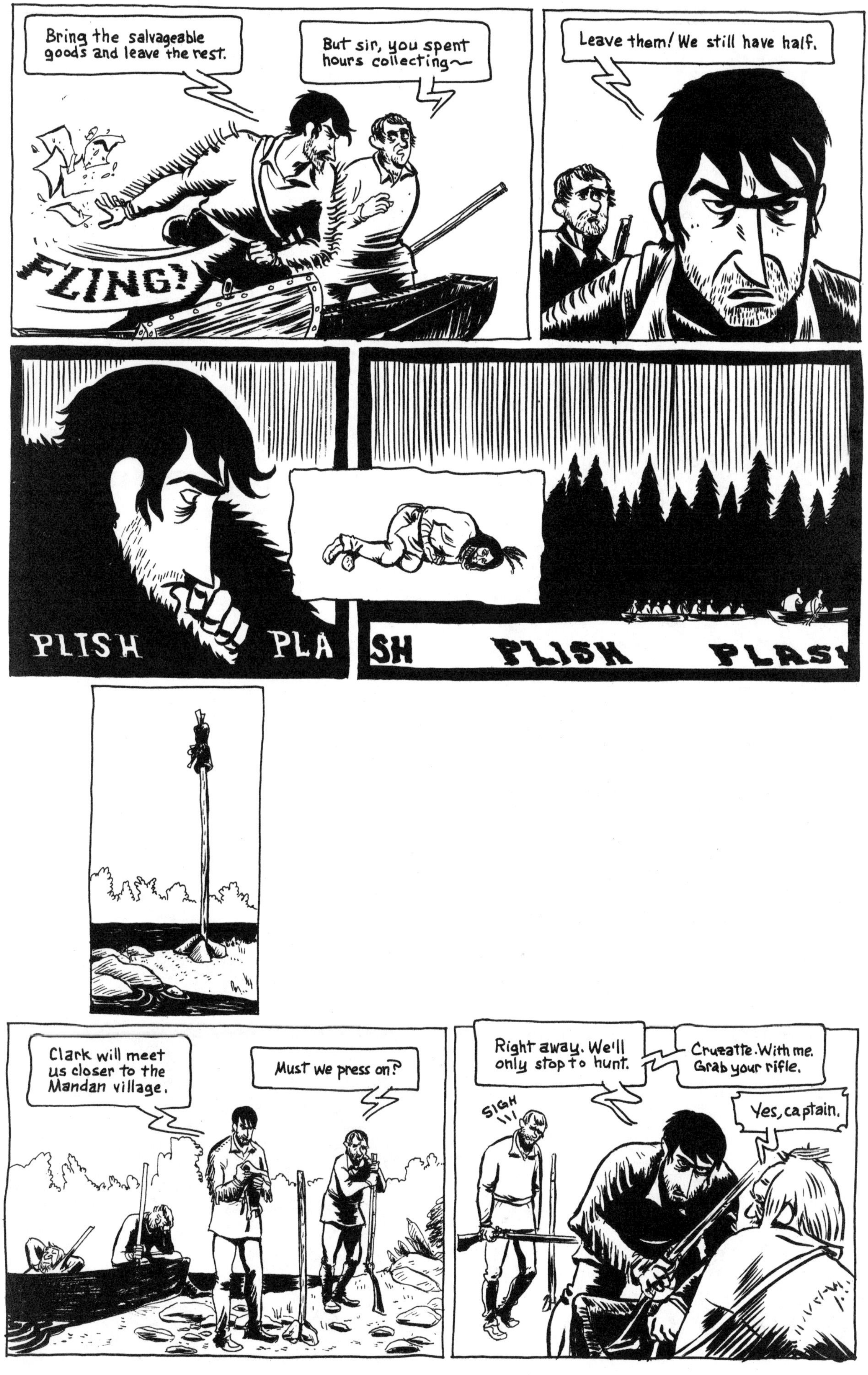
Bring the salvageable goods and leave the rest.
But sir, you spent hours collecting~
FLING!
Leave them! We still have half.
PLISH PLA
SH PLISH PLAS
Clark will meet us closer to the Mandan village.
Must we press on?
Right away. We'll only stop to hunt.
Cruzatte. With me. Grab your rifle.
SIGH
Yes, captain.

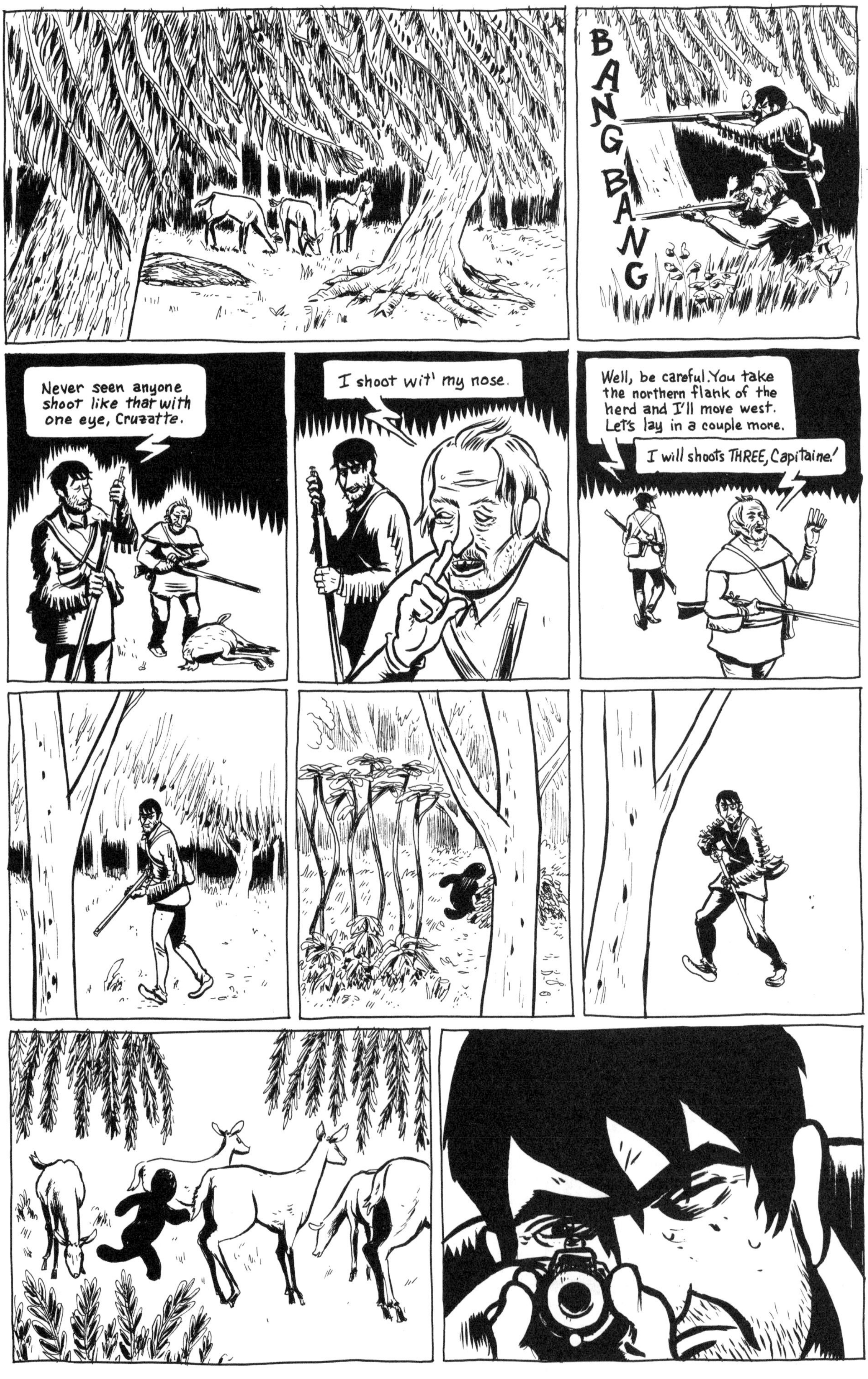

BANG BANG
Never seen anyone shoot like that with one eye, Cruzatte.
I shoot wit' my nose.
Well, be careful. You take the northern flank of the herd and I'll move west. Let's lay in a couple more.
I will shoots THREE, Capitaine!

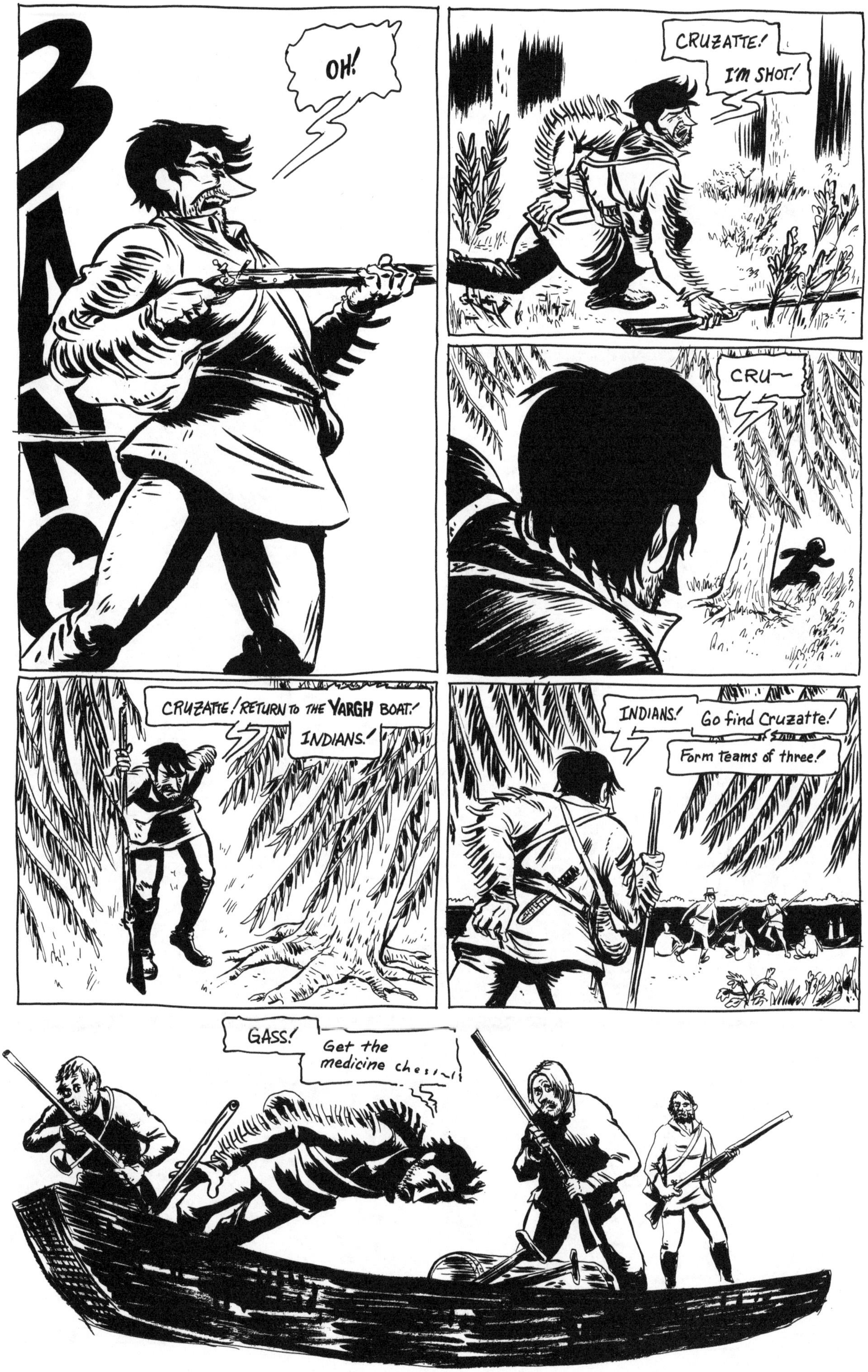
BANG
OH!
CRUZATTE!
I'M SHOT!
CRU~
CRUZATTE! RETURN TO THE YARGH BOAT!
INDIANS!
INDIANS!
Go find Cruzatte!
Form teams of three!
GASS!
Get the medicine ches~

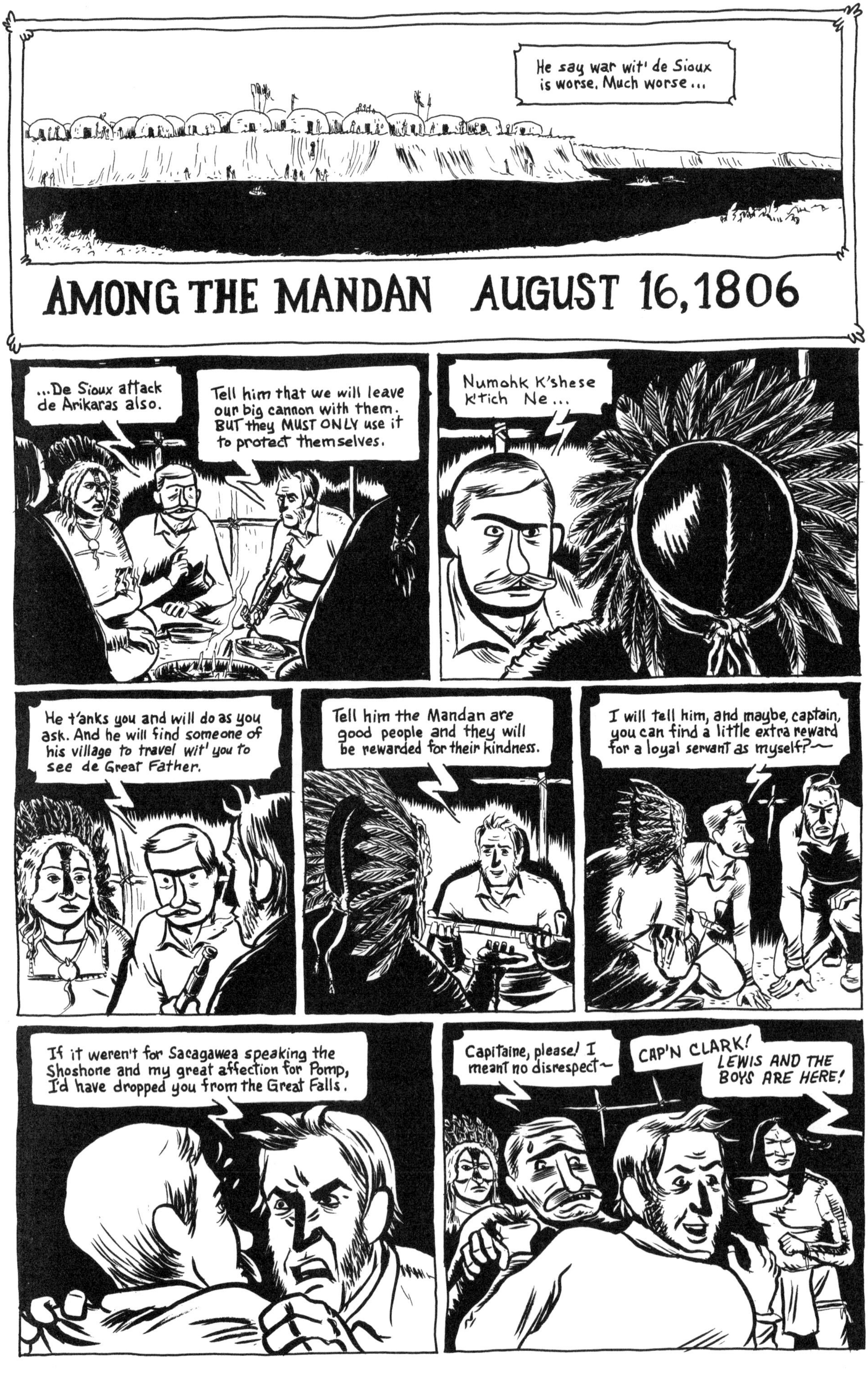
He say war wit' de Sioux is worse. Much worse...
AMONG THE MANDAN AUGUST 16, 1806
...De Sioux attack de Arikaras also.
Tell him that we will leave our big cannon with them. BUT they MUST ONLY use it to protect themselves.
Numohk K'shese K'tich Ne...
He t'anks you and will do as you ask. And he will find someone of his village to travel wit' you to see de Great Father.
Tell him the Mandan are good people and they will be rewarded for their kindness.
I will tell him, and maybe, captain, you can find a little extra reward for a loyal servant as myself?~
If it weren't for Sacagawea speaking the Shoshone and my great affection for Pomp, I'd have dropped you from the Great Falls.
Capitaine, please! I meant no disrespect~
CAP'N CLARK! LEWIS AND THE BOYS ARE HERE!

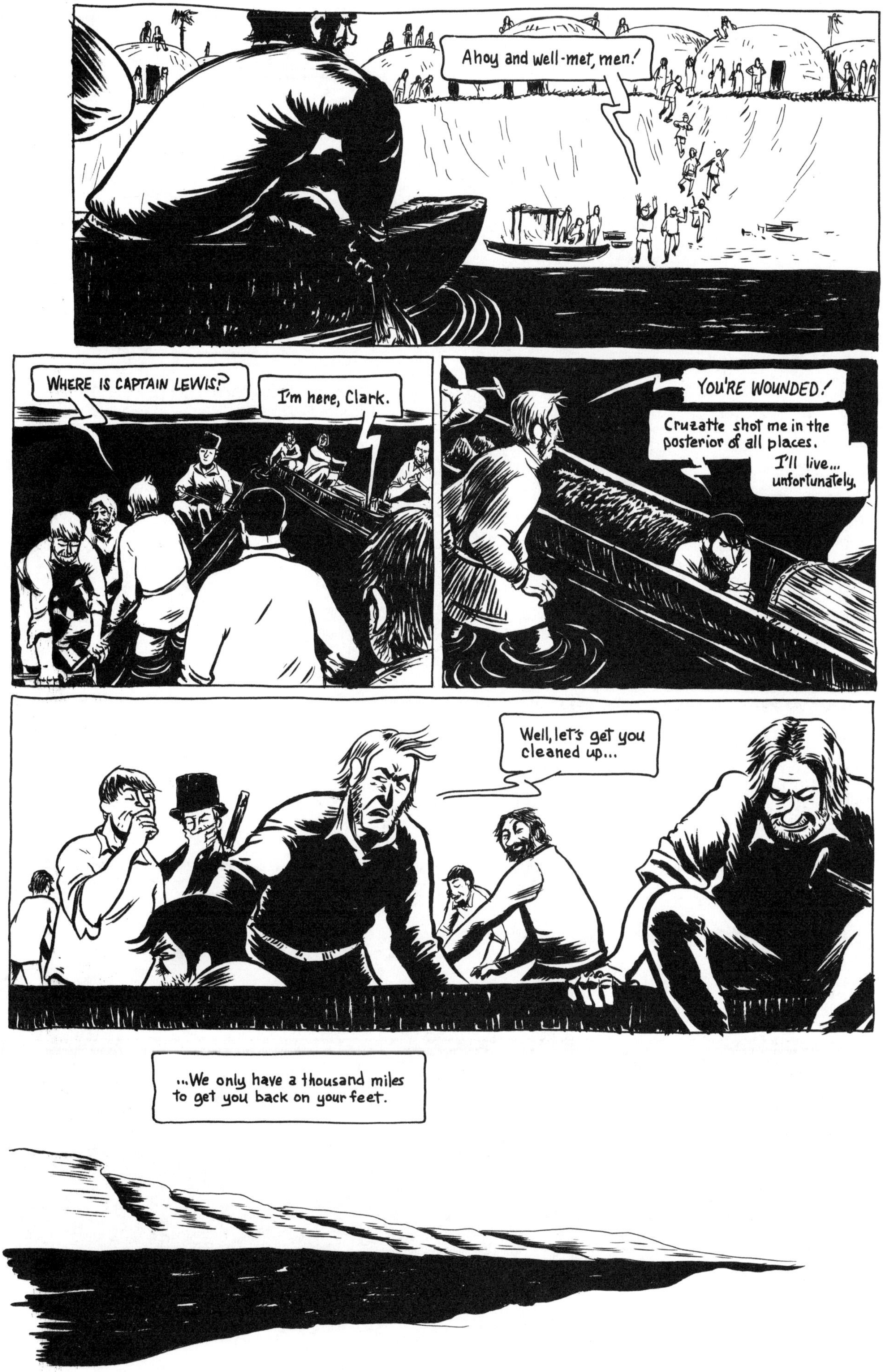

Ahoy and well-met, men!
WHERE IS CAPTAIN LEWIS?
I'm here, Clark.
YOU'RE WOUNDED!
Cruzatte shot me in the posterior of all places.
I'll live... unfortunately.
Well, let's get you cleaned up...
...We only have a thousand miles to get you back on your feet.

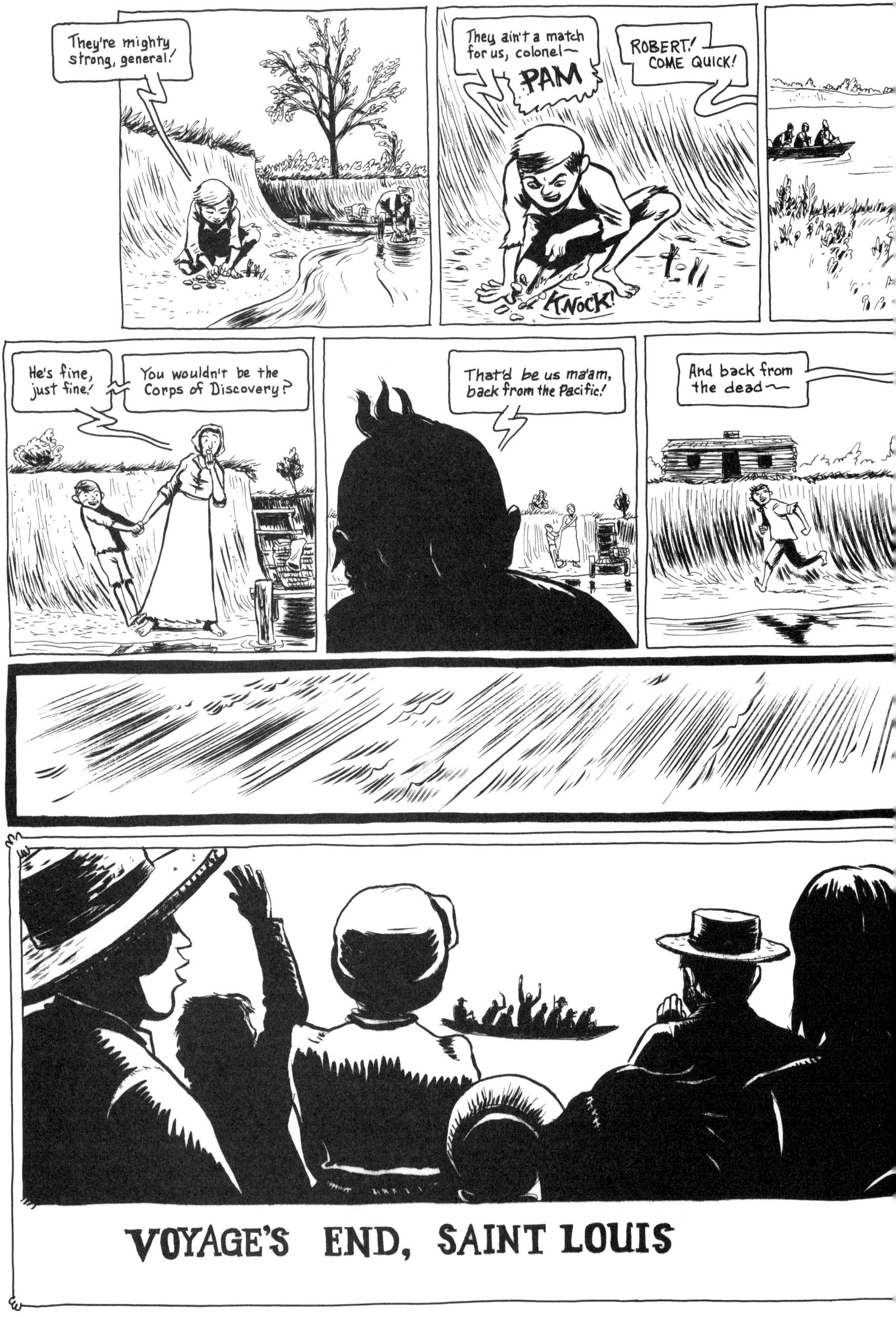

They're mighty strong, general!
They ain't a match for us, colonel—
PAM
ROBERT! COME QUICK!
KNOCK!
He's fine, just fine!
You wouldn't be the Corps of Discovery?
That'd be us ma'am, back from the Pacific!
And back from the dead—
VOYAGE'S END, SAINT LOUIS

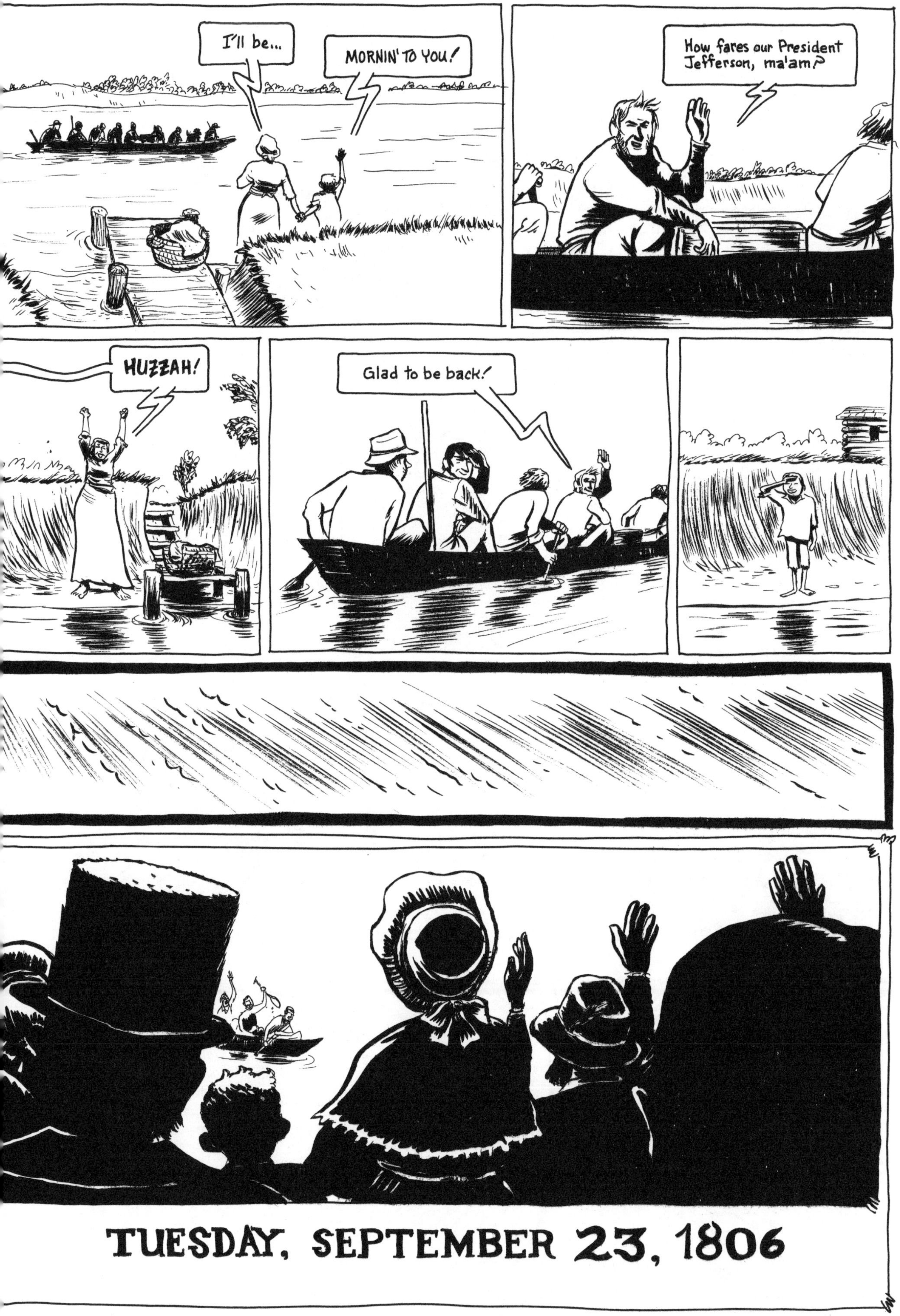
I'll be...
MORNIN' TO YOU!
How fares our President Jefferson, ma'am?
HUZZAH!
Glad to be back!
TUESDAY, SEPTEMBER 23, 1806

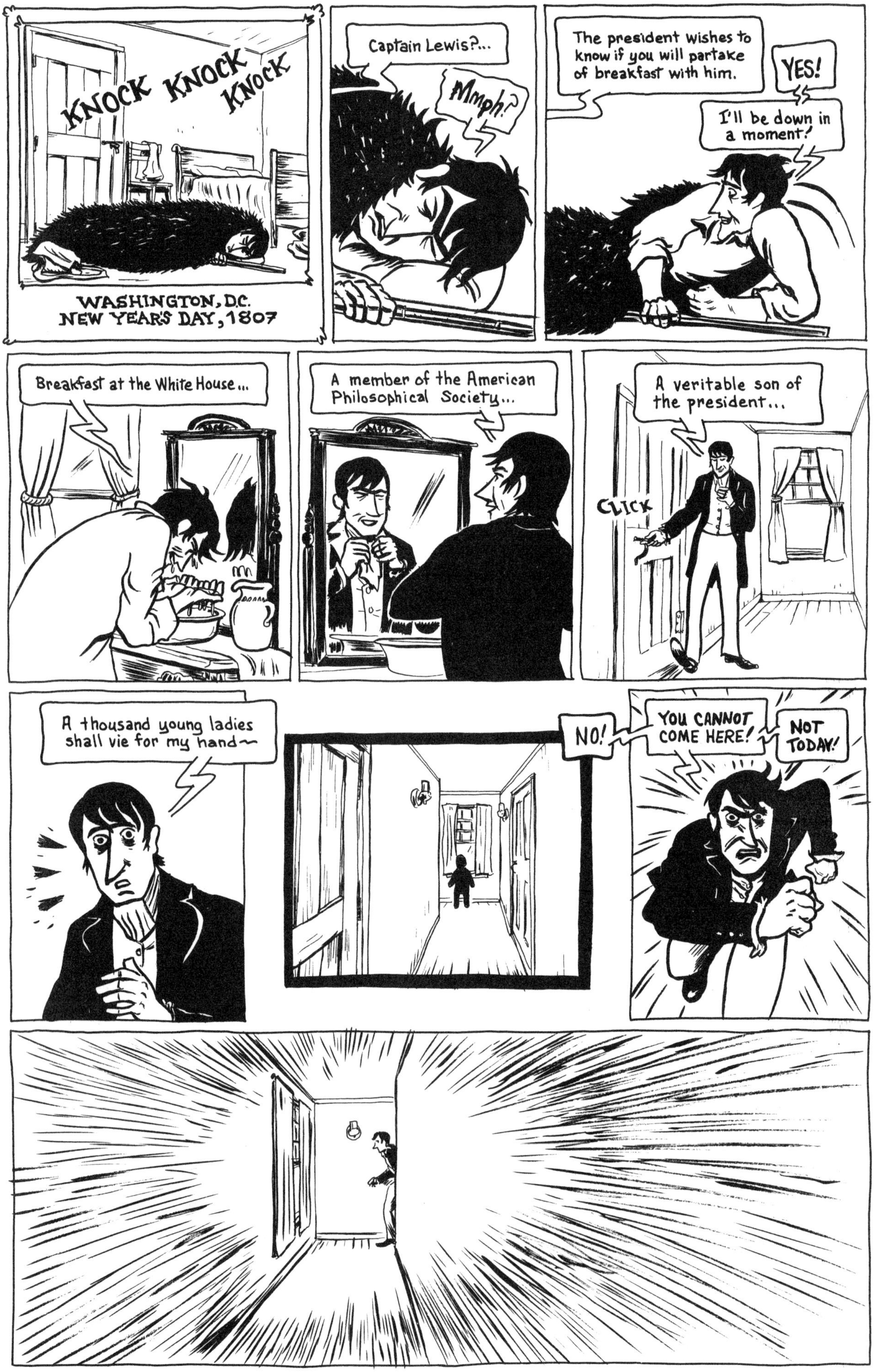
KNOCK KNOCK KNOCK
WASHINGTON, D.C.
NEW YEAR'S DAY, 1807
Captain Lewis?...
Mmph?
The president wishes to know if you will partake of breakfast with him.
YES!
I'll be down in a moment!
Breakfast at the White House...
A member of the American Philosophical Society...
A veritable son of the president...
CLICK
A thousand young ladies shall vie for my hand~
NO!
YOU CANNOT COME HERE!
NOT TODAY!

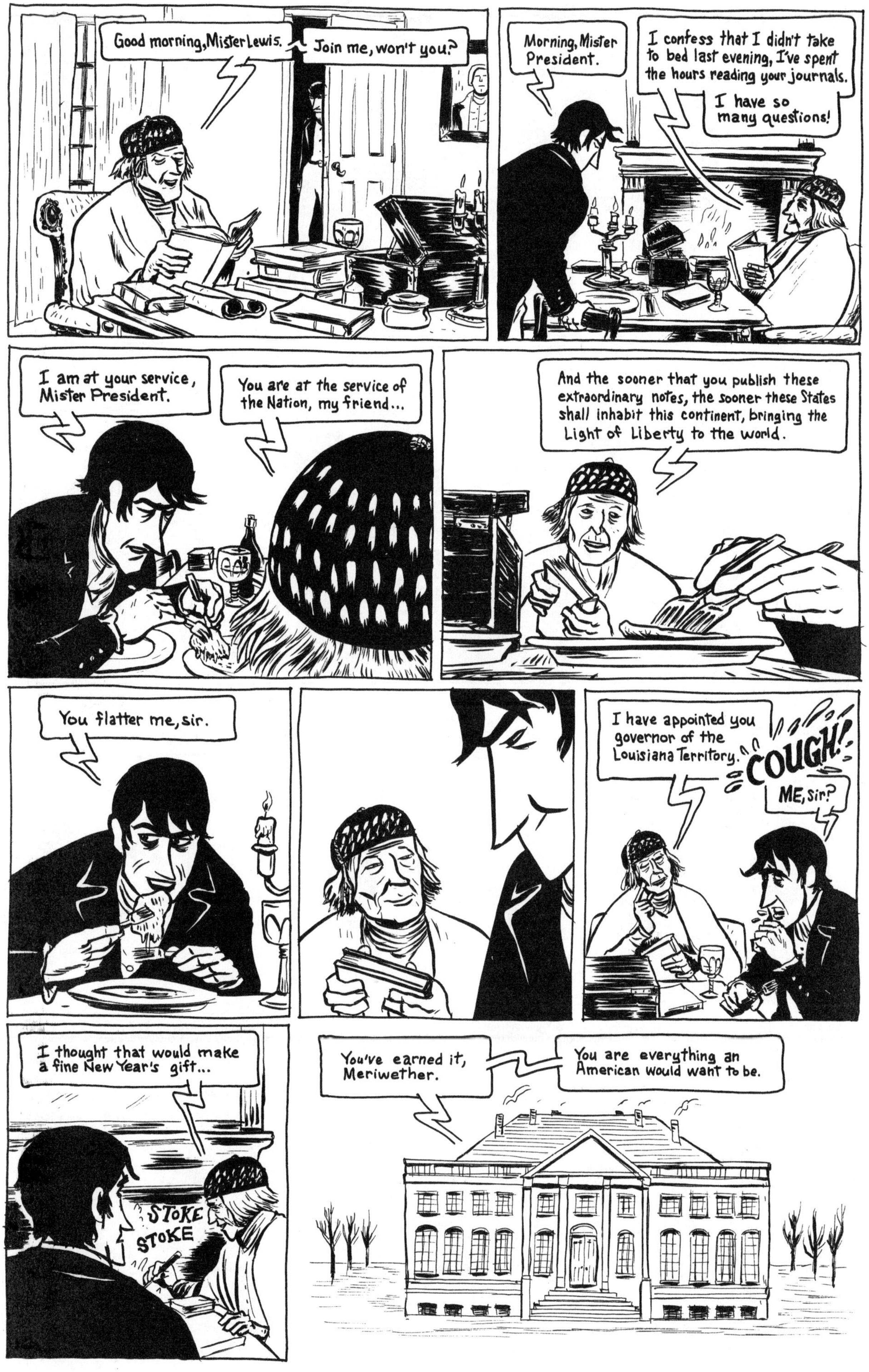
Good morning, Mister Lewis.
Join me, won't you?
Morning, Mister President.
I confess that I didn't take to bed last evening, I've spent the hours reading your journals.
I have so many questions!
I am at your service, Mister President.
You are at the service of the Nation, my friend...
And the sooner that you publish these extraordinary notes, the sooner these States shall inhabit this continent, bringing the Light of Liberty to the world.
You flatter me, sir.
I have appointed you governor of the Louisiana Territory.
COUGH!
ME, sir?
I thought that would make a fine New Year's gift...
STOKE
STOKE
You've earned it, Meriwether.
You are everything an American would want to be.

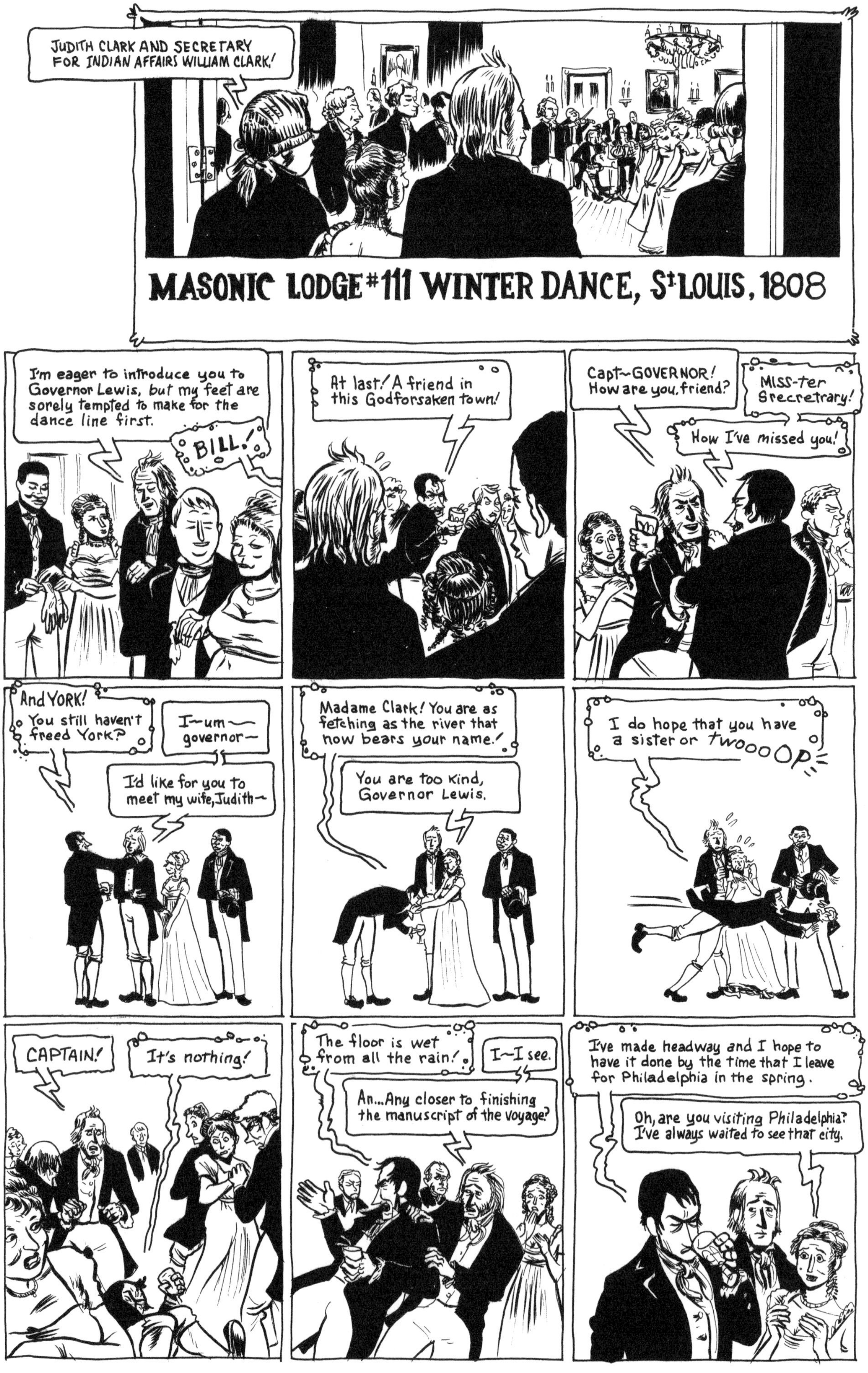

JUDITH CLARK AND SECRETARY FOR INDIAN AFFAIRS WILLIAM CLARK!
MASONIC LODGE #111 WINTER DANCE, St LOUIS, 1808
I'm eager to introduce you to Governor Lewis, but my feet are sorely tempted to make for the dance line first.
BILL!
At last! A friend in this Godforsaken town!
Capt~GOVERNOR! How are you, friend?
MISS-ter Srecretrary!
How I've missed you!
And YORK! You still haven't freed York?
I~um~ governor~
I'd like for you to meet my wife, Judith~
Madame Clark! You are as fetching as the river that now bears your name!
You are too kind, Governor Lewis.
I do hope that you have a sister or twoooOP!
CAPTAIN!
It's nothing!
The floor is wet from all the rain!
I~I see.
An...Any closer to finishing the manuscript of the voyage?
I've made headway and I hope to have it done by the time that I leave for Philadelphia in the spring.
Oh, are you visiting Philadelphia? I've always waited to see that city.

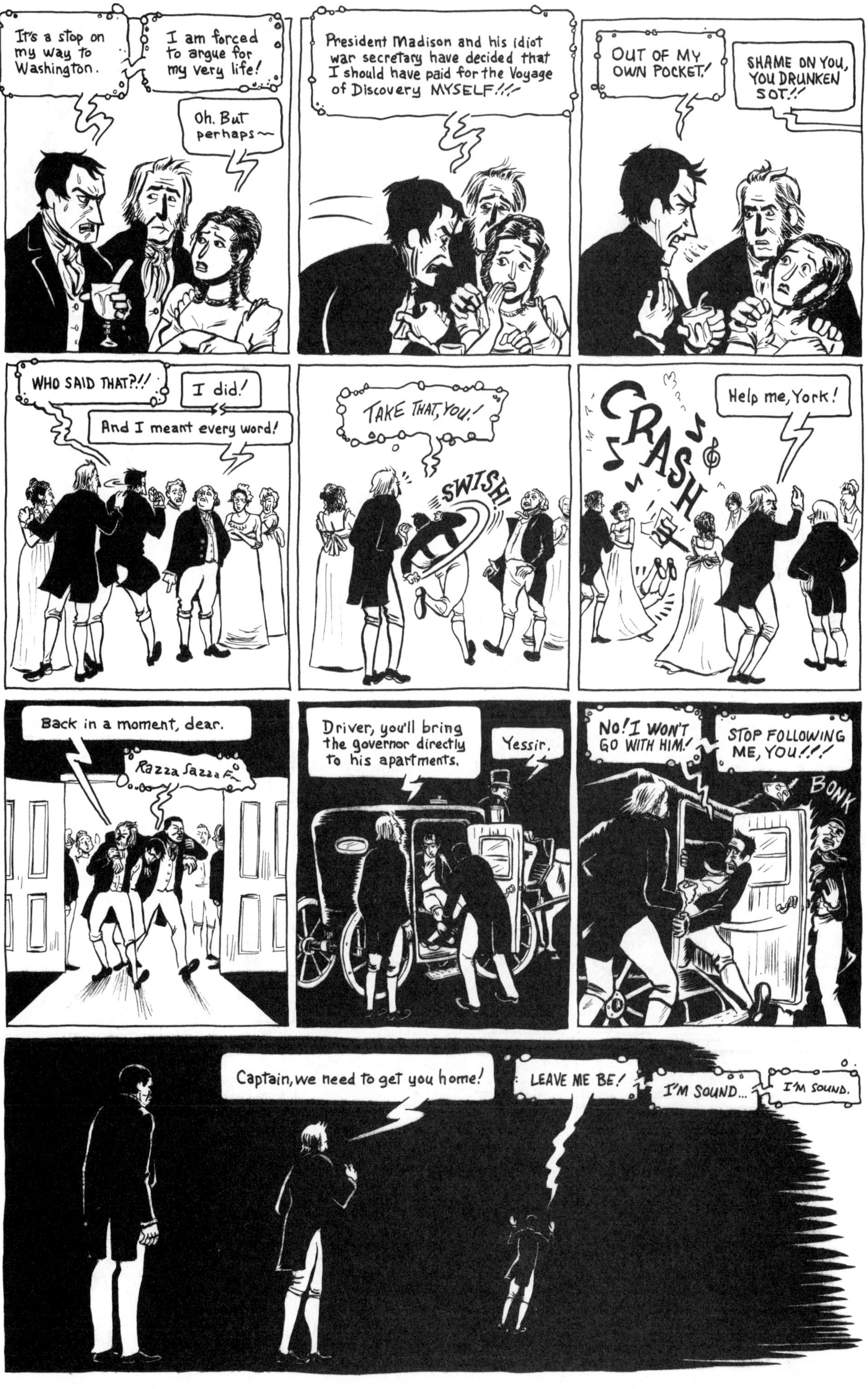

It's a stop on my way to Washington.
I am forced to argue for my very life!
Oh. But perhaps~
President Madison and his idiot war secretary have decided that I should have paid for the Voyage of Discovery MYSELF!!!
OUT OF MY OWN POCKET!
SHAME ON YOU, YOU DRUNKEN SOT!!
WHO SAID THAT?!!
I did!
And I meant every word!
TAKE THAT, YOU!
SWISH!
CRASH
Help me, York!
Back in a moment, dear.
Razza Sazza F...
Driver, you'll bring the governor directly to his apartments.
Yessir.
NO! I WON'T GO WITH HIM!
STOP FOLLOWING ME, YOU!!!
BONK
Captain, we need to get you home!
LEAVE ME BE!
I'M SOUND...
I'M SOUND.

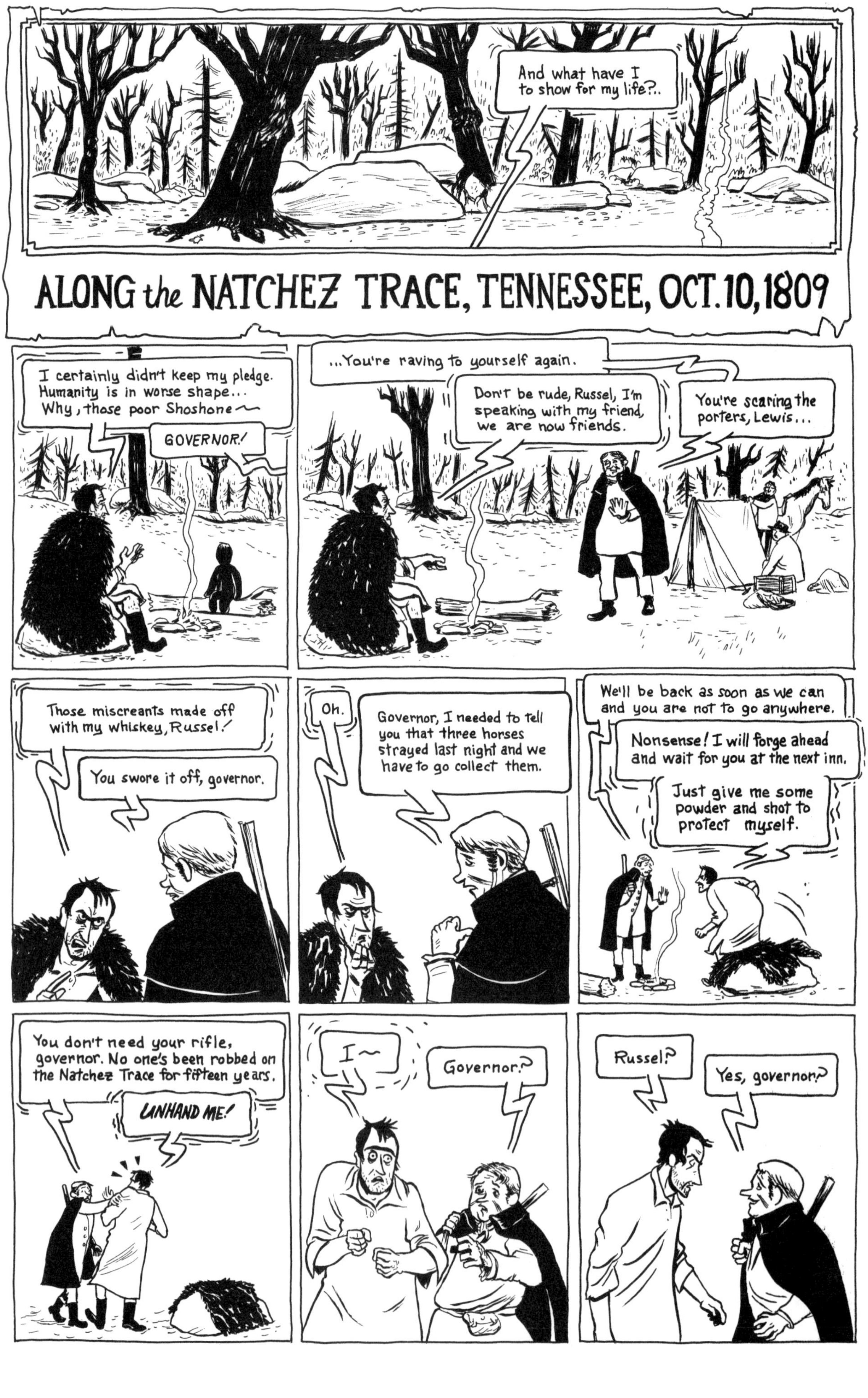
And what have I to show for my life?..
ALONG the NATCHEZ TRACE, TENNESSEE, OCT. 10, 1809
I certainly didn't keep my pledge. Humanity is in worse shape... Why, those poor Shoshone~
GOVERNOR!
...You're raving to yourself again.
Don't be rude, Russel, I'm speaking with my friend, we are now friends.
You're scaring the porters, Lewis...
Those miscreants made off with my whiskey, Russel!
You swore it off, governor.
Oh.
Governor, I needed to tell you that three horses strayed last night and we have to go collect them.
We'll be back as soon as we can and you are not to go anywhere.
Nonsense! I will forge ahead and wait for you at the next inn.
Just give me some powder and shot to protect myself.
You don't need your rifle, governor. No one's been robbed on the Natchez Trace for fifteen years.
UNHAND ME!
I~
Governor?
Russel?
Yes, governor?

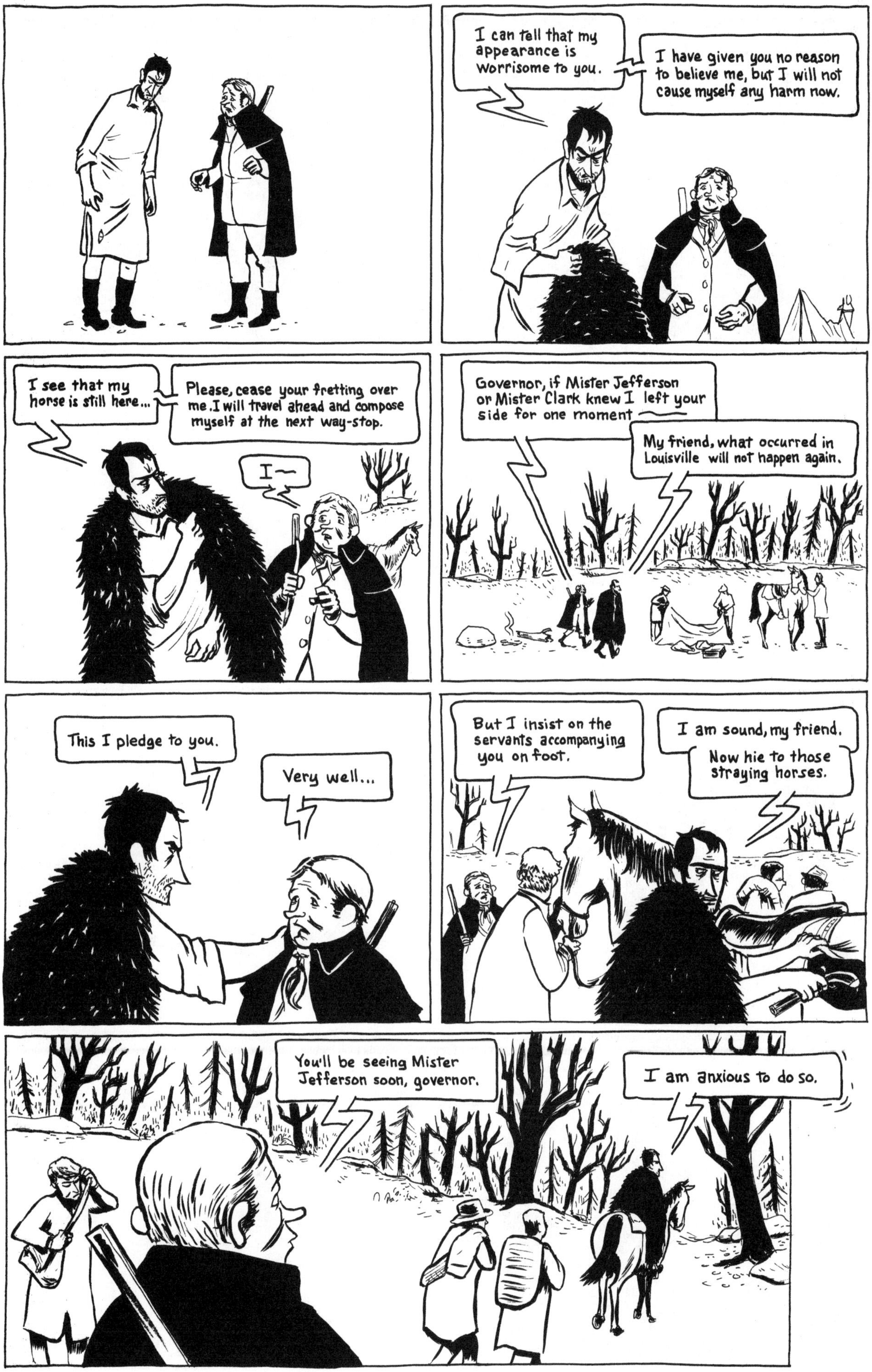
I can tell that my appearance is worrisome to you.
I have given you no reason to believe me, but I will not cause myself any harm now.
I see that my horse is still here...
Please, cease your fretting over me. I will travel ahead and compose myself at the next way-stop.
I~
Governor, if Mister Jefferson or Mister Clark knew I left your side for one moment ~
My friend, what occurred in Louisville will not happen again.
This I pledge to you.
Very well...
But I insist on the servants accompanying you on foot.
I am sound, my friend. Now hie to those straying horses.
You'll be seeing Mister Jefferson soon, governor.
I am anxious to do so.

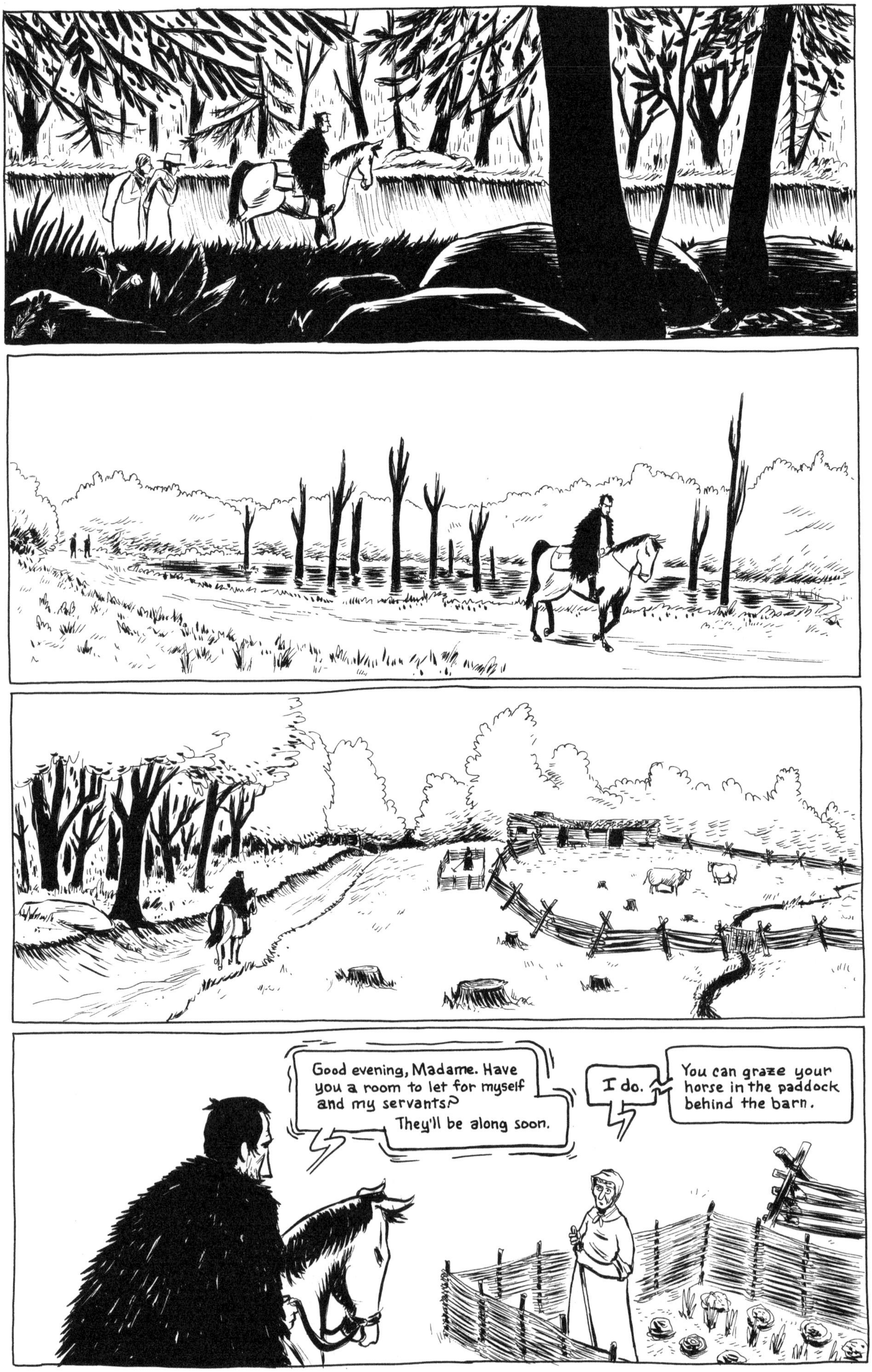
Good evening, Madame. Have you a room to let for myself and my servants?
They'll be along soon.
I do.
You can graze your horse in the paddock behind the barn.

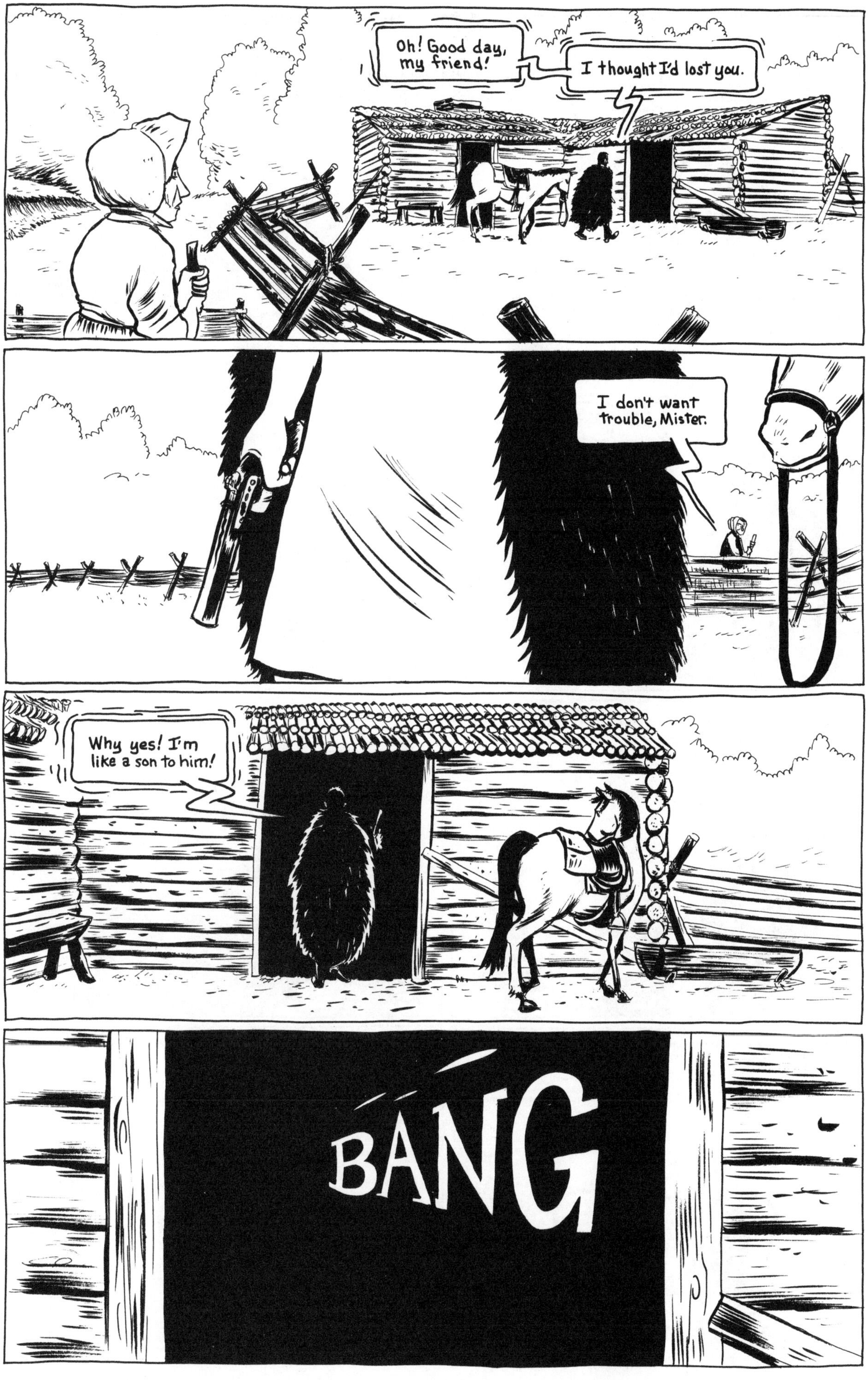
Oh! Good day, my friend!
I thought I'd lost you.
I don't want trouble, Mister.
Why yes! I'm like a son to him!
BANG

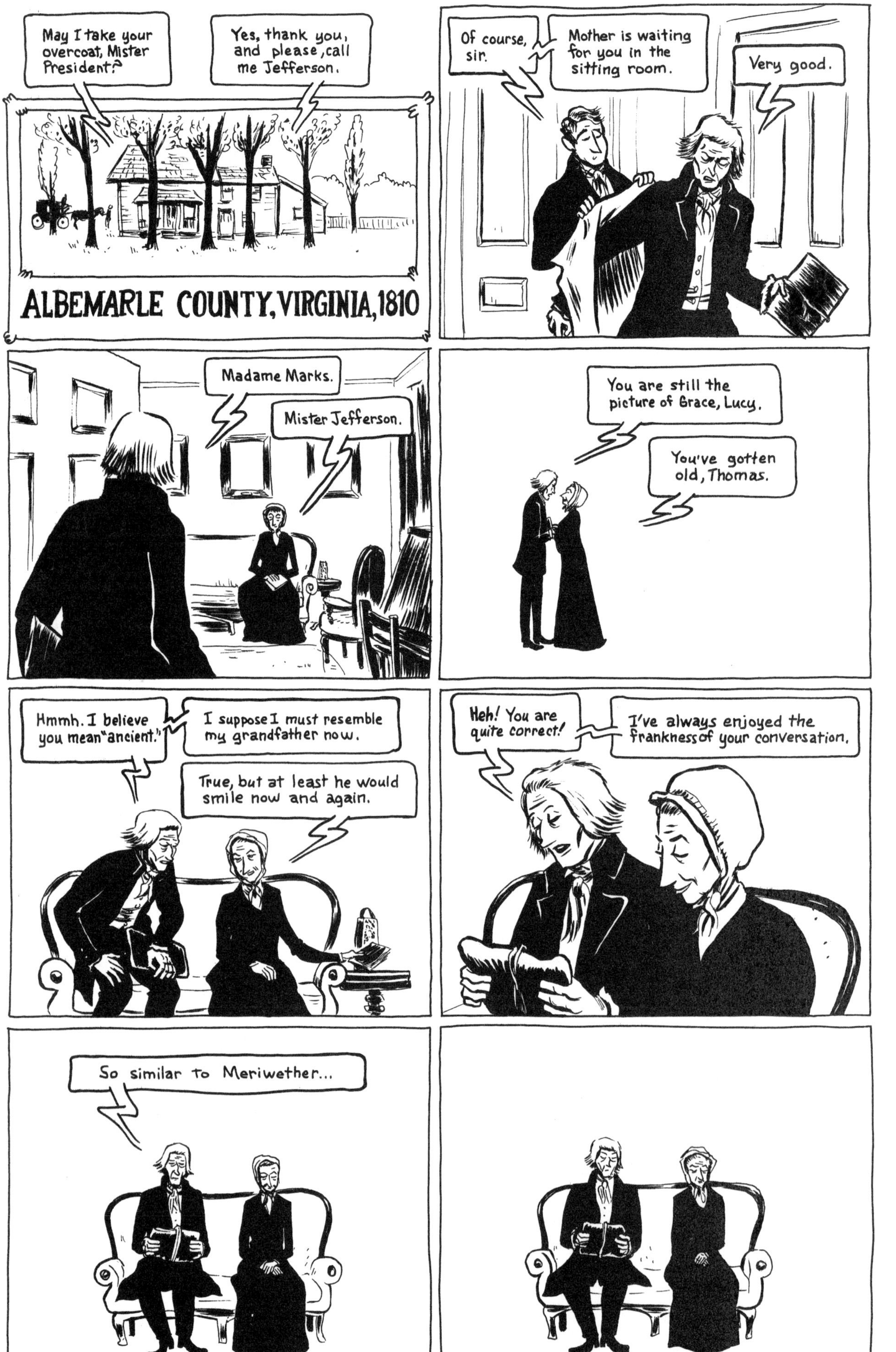
May I take your overcoat, Mister President?
Yes, thank you, and please, call me Jefferson.
ALBEMARLE COUNTY, VIRGINIA, 1810
Of course, sir.
Mother is waiting for you in the sitting room.
Very good.
Madame Marks.
Mister Jefferson.
You are still the picture of Grace, Lucy.
You've gotten old, Thomas.
Hmmh. I believe you mean "ancient."
I suppose I must resemble my grandfather now.
True, but at least he would smile now and again.
Heh! You are quite correct!
I've always enjoyed the frankness of your conversation.
So similar to Meriwether...

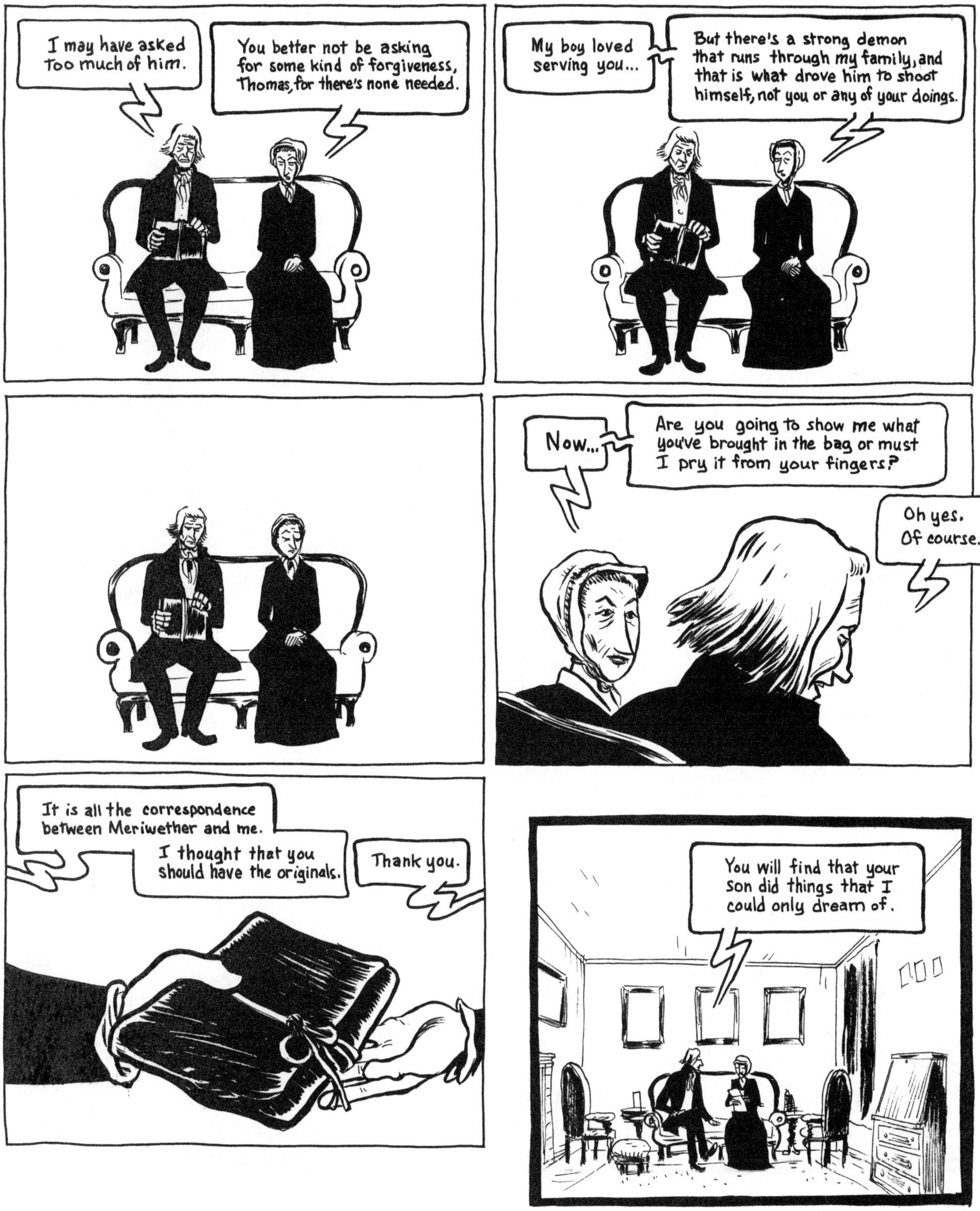
I may have asked too much of him.
You better not be asking for some kind of forgiveness, Thomas, for there's none needed.
My boy loved serving you...
But there's a strong demon that runs through my family, and that is what drove him to shoot himself, not you or any of your doings.
Now...
Are you going to show me what you've brought in the bag or must I pry it from your fingers?
Oh yes. Of course.
It is all the correspondence between Meriwether and me.
I thought that you should have the originals.
Thank you.
You will find that your son did things that I could only dream of.

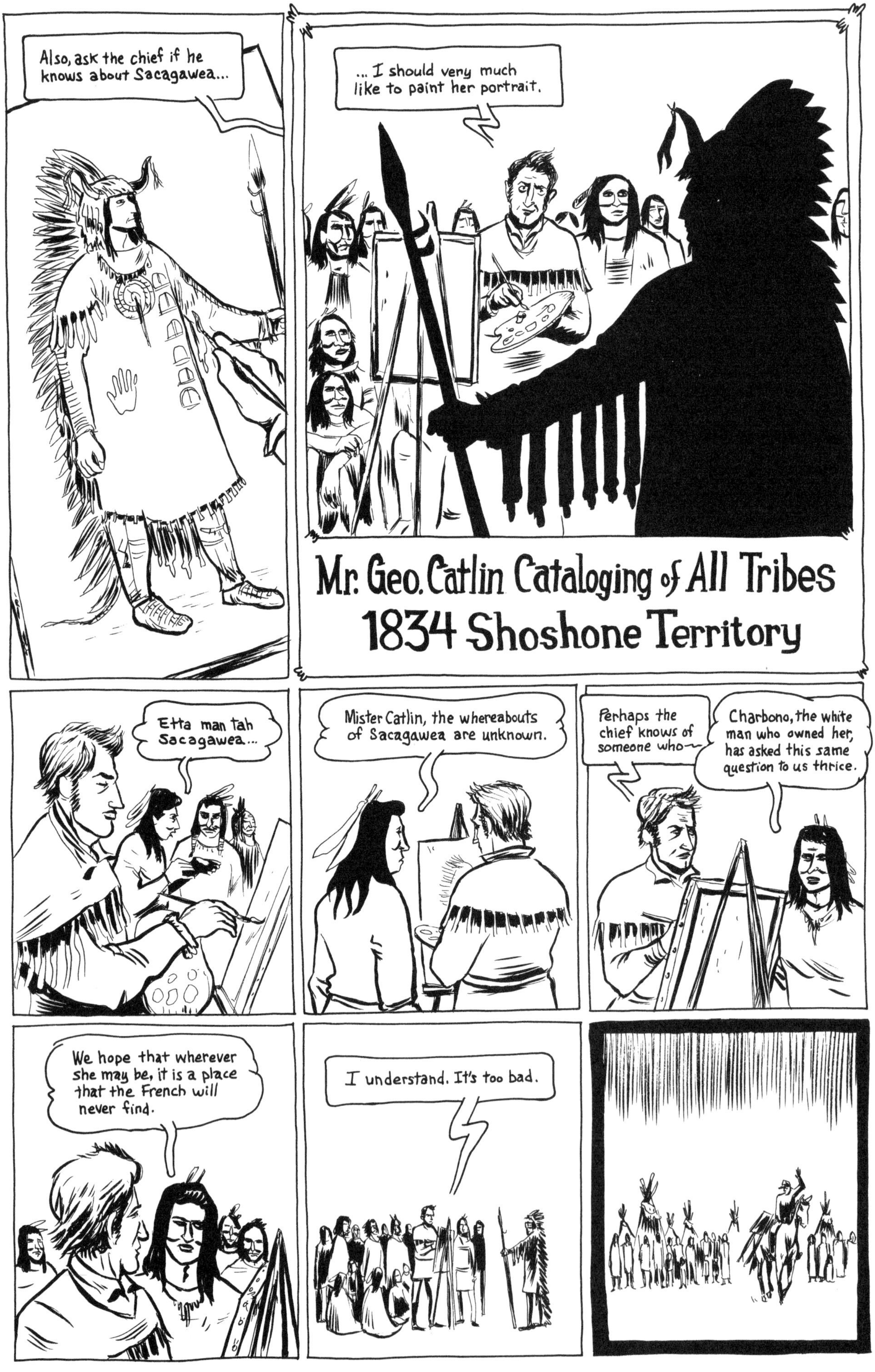
Also, ask the chief if he knows about Sacagawea...
... I should very much like to paint her portrait.
Mr. Geo. Catlin Cataloging of All Tribes
1834 Shoshone Territory
Etta man tah Sacagawea...
Mister Catlin, the whereabouts of Sacagawea are unknown.
Perhaps the chief knows of someone who—
Charbono, the white man who owned her, has asked this same question to us thrice.
We hope that wherever she may be, it is a place that the French will never find.
I understand. It's too bad.

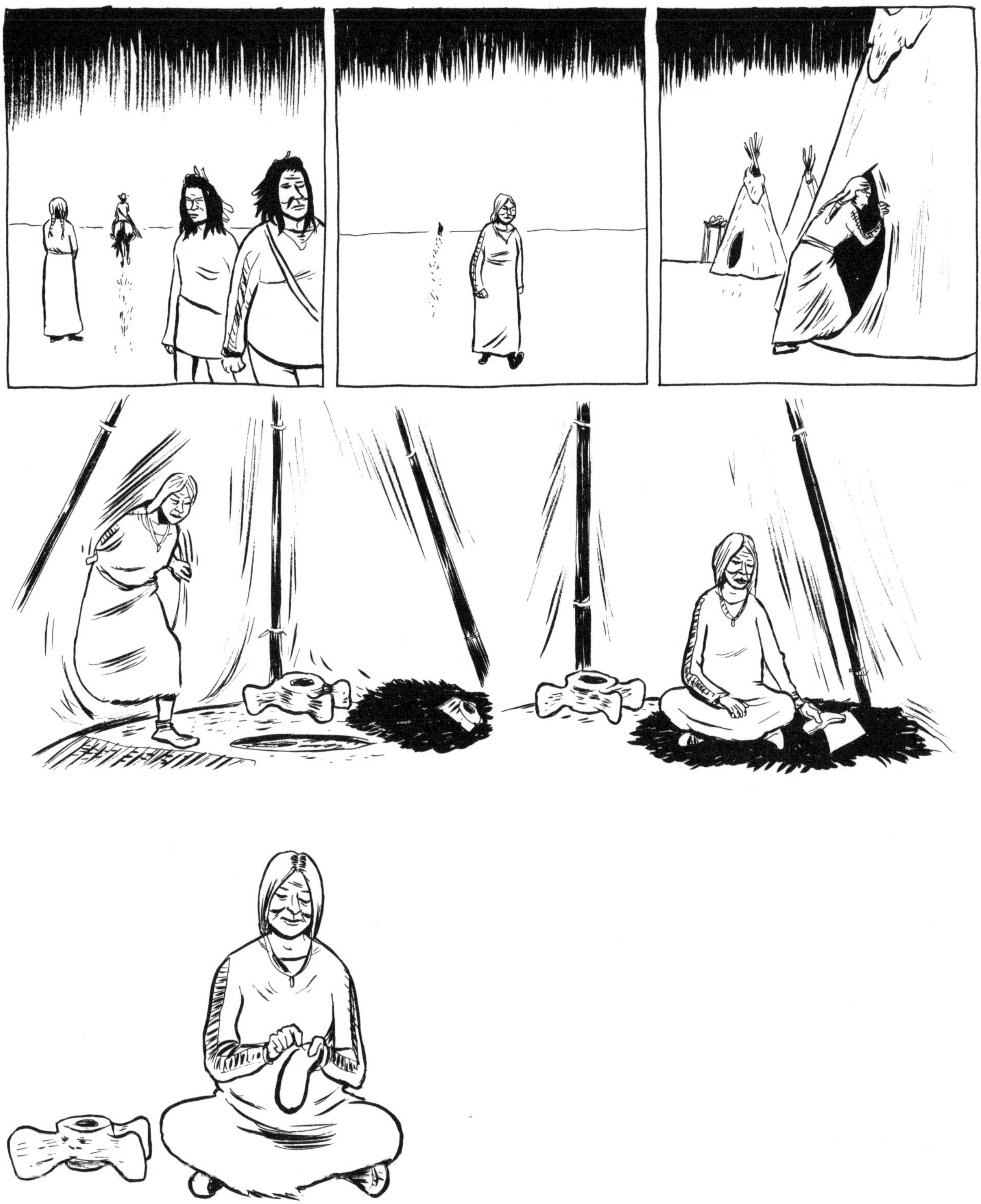

THE END

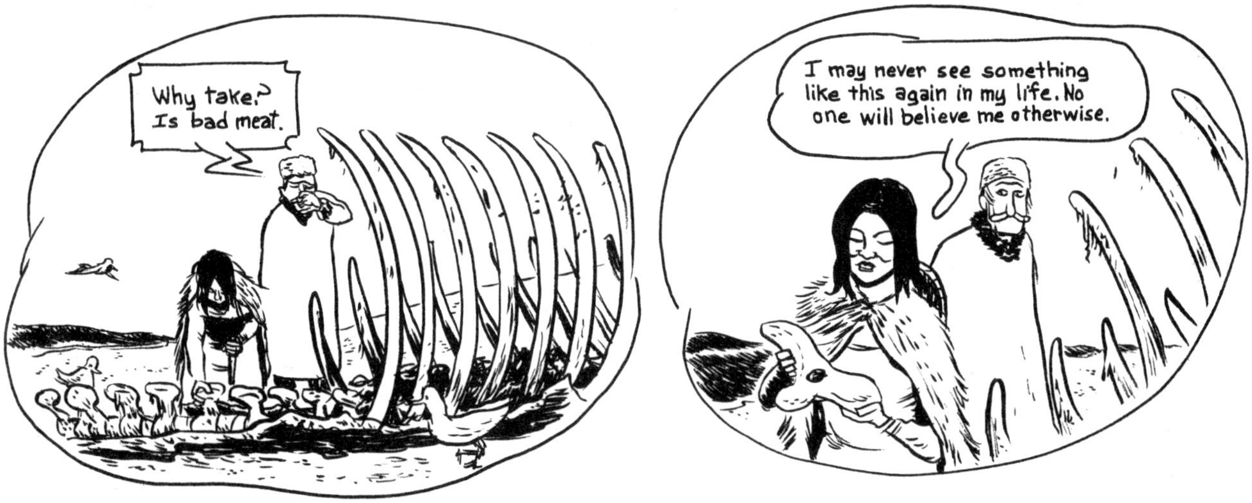
Why take? Is bad meat.
I may never see something like this again in my life. No one will believe me otherwise.

SELECTED BIBLIOGRAPHY

Ambrose, Stephen, *Undaunted Courage: Meriwether Lewis, Thomas Jefferson, and the Opening of the American West*. New York: Simon and Schuster, 1996.

DeVoto, Bernard, Ed. *The Journals of Lewis and Clark*. Boston and New York: Mariner Books, 1953.

Duncan, Dayton, and Burns, Ken. *Lewis and Clark: The Journey of the Corps of Discovery*. New York: Knopf, 1998.

Gilman, Carolyn. *Lewis and Clark: Across the Divide*. Washington: Smithsonian Press, 2003.

Gilbert, Bil, and the Editors of Time-Life Books. *The Trailblazers*. Alexandria, VA: Time-Life Books, 1973.

Mooney, Michael M., Ed. *George Catlin: Letters and Notes on the North American Indians*. Avenel, NJ: Gramercy, 1975.

Ritter, Sharon Anelia. Moscow: University of Idaho Press, 2002.

Viola, Herman J. *Exploring the West*. Washington, D.C., and New York: Smithsonian Books and Abrams, 1987.